Successful College Teaching

Related Titles

Faculty Work and Public Trust: Restoring the Value of Teaching and Public Service in American Academic Life, James S. Fairweather
ISBN: 0-205-17948-7

College Teaching Abroad: A Handbook of Strategies for Successful Cross-Cultural Exchanges, Pamela Gale George
ISBN: 0-205-15767-X

Emblems of Quality in Higher Education: Developing and Sustaining High-Quality Programs, Jennifer Grant Haworth and Clifton F. Conrad
ISBN: 0-205-19546-6

The Art of Writing for Publication, Kenneth T. Henson
ISBN: 0-205-15769-6

Revitalizing General Education in a Time of Scarcity: A Navigational Chart for Administrators and Faculty, Sandra L. Kanter, Zelda F. Gamson, and Howard B. London
ISBN: 0-205-26257-0

Multicultural Course Transformation in Higher Education: A Broader Truth, Ann Intili Morey and Margie K. Kitano (Editors)
ISBN: 0-205-16068-9

Sexual Harassment on Campus: A Guide for Administrators, Faculty, and Students, Bernice R. Sandler and Robert J. Shoop
ISBN: 0-205-16712-8

Leadership in Continuing and Distance Education in Higher Education, Cynthia C. Jones Shoemaker
ISBN: 0-205-26823-4

Shaping the College Curriculum: Academic Plans in Action, Joan S. Stark and Lisa R. Lattuca
ISBN: 0-205-16706-3

For more information or to purchase a book, please call 1-800-278-3525.

Successful College Teaching

Problem-Solving Strategies of Distinguished Professors

Sharon A. Baiocco
Jacksonville University

Jamie N. DeWaters
D'Youville College

Allyn and Bacon
Boston • London • Toronto • Sydney • Tokyo • Singapore

Dedicated to all those professors who influence others daily by their wisdom, their selfless acts, and their devotion to teaching and learning

---

Executive Editor: Stephen D. Dragin
Series Editorial Assistant: Elizabeth McGuire
Manufacturing Buyer: David Suspanic

Copyright © 1998 by Allyn & Bacon
A Viacom Company
160 Gould Street
Needham Heights, MA 02194

Internet: www.abacon.com
America Online: keyword: College Online

Library of Congress Cataloging-in-Publication Data

Baiocco, Sharon Ann.
    Successful college teaching : problem-solving strategies of
distinguished professors / Sharon A. Baiocco, Jamie N. DeWaters.
        p.   cm.
    Includes bibliographical references and index.
    ISBN 0-205-26654-1
    1. College teaching—United States.   2. College teachers—Training
of—United States.   I. DeWaters, Jamie N.   II. Title.
    LB2331.B35   1998
    378.1'2—dc21   97-37760
                                                                    CIP

Printed in the United States of America
10 9 8 7 6 5 4 3 2 1   02 01 00 99 98

Contents

Foreword

This is a book about change in higher education. Specifically, it is about whether professors can view sweeping changes in higher education as opportunities rather than as problems. In sum, professors, depending on their viewpoint, will be either the victims or the agents of change in higher education.

Viewing change as an opportunity rather than a problem is a key theme throughout history. Arnold Toynbee, the British historian, spoke of cultures and individuals responding at critical moments to difficult challenges. Creative visions and a new consciousness flow only from those who can recognize problems as opportunities, then can respond powerfully. This book is an invitation to professors to become the agents of educational change.

There is an ancient tale about a man plowing his field. When his plow encounters an obstacle, he digs down to see what it is. He discovers a large ring that is attached to the trapdoor of a dark cave. He opens the trapdoor and enters the cave. Inside the cave is a treasure chest filled with jewels. And so it is with us in academe. After years of plowing the same field, our plow gets stuck. We can ignore this opportunity and keep plowing. Or we can dig into the problem and potentially discover a treasure.

In the darkest places we often find our greatest rewards. Unless we stop the plow, dig down deep enough to find the ring and open the cave, we will never realize our full potential. The jewels are there waiting. The opportunity is now.

James L. Ragonnet
Professor of English
Springfield College

Preface

In the 1950s, we educators were like Lucy and Ethel in one classic episode of the TV series *I Love Lucy*, trying to keep up with the increasing speed of a conveyor belt. Although we view that relatively slower rate and simpler time nostalgically, our situation today might be considered equally comical if the implications of not keeping pace with the changes around us were not so serious. Ready or not, we are being forced to leap onto the information superhighway where distance learning and electronic networks are replacing the campus, and classrooms and libraries exist in a "virtual reality" called cyberspace. And instead of the prominence nearly fifty years ago of young, white faces in television sit-coms like *Leave It to Beaver* and *Father Knows Best*, our classrooms today resemble Disney's "A Small World," and the new "nontraditionals" are replacing the young, white faces.

Yet despite these seismic changes, we in academe continue to cling to our traditional system of preparing and developing faculty. As teaching assistants, future college faculty are offered immersion orientations in pedagogy and a system akin to medieval apprenticeships as they progress toward their doctoral degrees. When they graduate, they often face years of second-class academic citizenship, picking up courses as part-time adjuncts at multiple sites before they land full-time university positions. Increasingly, new hires are offered term contracts rather than tenure-line positions. Either way, as junior faculty, they will be expected to develop their teaching skills (though they will not be rewarded for them) even as they are required to publish prolifically. Senior faculty, who used to be immune from review after they enjoyed tenure, are now required to demonstrate their productivity by submitting to post-tenure evaluations as well as the ubiquitous student evaluations.

To support professional development, some campuses offer workshops and teaching effectiveness programs, others pair faculty as mentors, but most offer only travel to conferences and sabbaticals to individuals who seek professional growth. All faculty, even those at schools whose missions emphasize undergraduate teaching, have succumbed to the need to "publish or perish." This system has remained basically the same since the landmark 1940 *Statement of Principles on Academic Freedom and Tenure,* drafted by the Association of American Colleges and the American Association of University Professors and later approved by over 135 additional learned societies.

We believe that this system will change because of a confluence of current social, economic, and political conditions that are creating the most serious re-evaluation of the role of higher education in society since the 1940 *Statement.* We also see this emergency as an opportunity to reform those aspects in the professional development of faculty that have not kept pace with social changes or with the best in educational research.

In Chapter 1, we provide a broad overview of the challenges confronting us and argue for faculty leadership in addressing these challenges, particularly as they affect teaching. Chapters 2 and 3 expand our discussion of the agents for change and institutional inertia, as well as provide an historical evaluation of faculty development and argue for the need to reform our traditional system of developing teaching effectiveness.

We propose a new and invigorated system of faculty development centering around excellence in teaching. The heart of our book, Chapters 4 through 8, explores character, a hallmark of teaching excellence, from the perspective of emotional intelligence. It also profiles the presentation styles, scholarship of teaching, and problem-solving strategies of award-winning college teachers.

Based on our study, we propose and illustrate a theory of teaching in Chapter 9 and suggest how it might be applied to identify those with potential for becoming excellent teachers, as well as to develop teaching effectiveness. Chapter 10 provides a summary of the current options for aiding teaching assistants in the development of their teaching, and then shows one application of our theory, how exemplary college teachers address common problems mentioned by such inexperienced faculty. In Chapter 11, we propose another application of a theory of teaching and a new solution to improve college teaching. We believe a national force of distinguished teaching faculty should be marshaled as leaders of learning communities, focusing on instructional problem solving and techniques of self-evaluation.

Acknowledgments

We are deeply indebted to the following individuals who offered their counsel and encouragement:

Patricia Abbott, Assistant Professor of Psychology, D'Youville College; James DeHaven, Associate Professor of Chemistry/Physics, D'Youville College; Robert A. DiSibio, Dean of the School of Arts, Sciences, and Professional Studies, D'Youville College; Edward Hart, Chairperson, Math/Natural Sciences, D'Youville College; Robert L. Nielsen, Associate Professor of Philosophy, D'Youville College; James L. Ragonnet, Professor of English, Springfield College; Sr. Denise Roche, GNSH, President, D'Youville College; Donald F. Sabo, Professor of Sociology, D'Youville College; Leon D. Shkolnik, Reference Librarian, D'Youville College; and Richard Wiesen, former Senior Vice President, D'Youville College.

In addition, we acknowledge Jon Travis, Texas A&M University–Commerce, who reviewed the manuscript for Allyn and Bacon.

About the Authors

Sharon A. Baiocco, Ph.D., Assistant Dean, College of Arts and Sciences, Jacksonville University, and Jamie N. DeWaters, professor at D'Youville College in Buffalo, New York, contributed equally to this manuscript. DeWaters' research has been in teacher training and in pedagogy in higher education; Baiocco's has been in the teaching and learning of problem-solving strategies in writing. They have presented some of the findings in this book at the Lilly Conferences on Excellence in College and University Teaching.

Sharon A. Baiocco, Ph.D., professor of English, holds a doctorate from the Department of Learning and Instruction and an Ed.M. in English Education from the State University of New York at Buffalo. Baiocco is a 1995 recipient of the higher education New York State Educator of Excellence Award, a 1992 winner of a Sears & Roebuck Foundation Teaching Excellence and Campus Leadership Award, and was named 1990 Faculty of the Year by students. She has served as chairperson of the Department of Liberal Arts, president of the D'Youville Chapter of the American Association of University Professors, and chair of the college Faculty Development Committee. She has taught technical writing, journalism, public relations writing, and a variety of literature courses. In 1992, she won a fellowship from the Ministry of Education of the Republic of Russia to participate in a cultural exchange and education program in Moscow and St. Petersburg.

Jamie N. DeWaters, Ph.D., holds a doctorate in Educational Research and Evaluation from the State University of New York at Buffalo. As a teacher trainer with bachelor's and master's degrees in speech pathology/communication disorders, her main area of interest is the assessment and development of trainers and professors. She has served as chairperson of the Division of Education and Social Work, president of the faculty government, officer of the D'Youville Chapter of the American Association of University Professors (AAUP), and as a long-term member of the college-wide personnel committee. DeWaters has twice been the recipient of the Division of Education faculty award for teaching excellence. She currently serves as consultant on teaching effectiveness to various agencies, school districts, and universities.

1

The Need to Improve Teaching Now

Introduction and Overview

On the rehearsal stage sits a young and eager cellist. Years of study and disciplined practice have led to this moment. Other aspiring musicians are seated in the auditorium, and among them is the maestro Yo Yo Ma. One by one, three students have their moment to play a piece, having won this honor to learn from the maestro at a summer music institute. As they play, he listens with rapt attention, hears their unique interpretations of the music, and then applauds their skills. Ever so kindly, he suggests how they might approach the pieces differently and demonstrates on their instruments. Once again they perform and the difference is remarkable, even to the untrained ear. It is a transcendent moment, one to which each of us who commits a lifetime to teaching aspires.

Yet the differences between this master class and our own college classes could not be more striking. Even though there are students like this on our campuses, professors are more frequently reporting difficulties in their encounters with students. Today many of our students are neither young nor eager nor well-prepared. Occasionally, they bring attitudes and behaviors that appear disrespectful, such as tardiness, talking, or sleeping during class, or they may interrupt lectures with personal (and sometimes inappropriate) questions. Nearly every professor we know reports having been asked the impertinent question, "Did we do anything important?" from a student who has missed a class. And unlike those in Yo Yo Ma's class, most of our students upon graduation yearn to make money, not to make music. Their first responses to our instruction may be dissonant, tentative, or confused. Many of our students expect to be allowed to sit and passively receive knowledge rather than to be active performers in the classroom, and when we attempt to engage them, instead of expressing gratitude they may become intimidated, resistant, or hostile.

Such behaviors bewilder professors-in-training (the teaching assistants); distress the junior faculty, who know that low student ratings may put their careers in jeopardy; and puzzle the previously successful tenured professors whose student "evals" tell them to make their lectures "less boring." We predict that, as we approach the millennium, college and university classrooms across the United States will increasingly become the setting for culture clashes such as these. We view these differences as the natural result of a nation beginning to realize the full potential of democracy through the higher education of its citizens.

Dramatic changes in our society—wrought not only by our "New Age" students but by many external forces—are coming to U.S. higher education, and we professors cannot afford to be complacent. Social, technological, and economic changes have turned the spotlight on our classrooms, where the drama of our evolving cultural identity is being enacted. At the same moment, the U.S. public is exerting pressure on educators to be more accessible to students and more accountable. Together these forces will revolutionize how we teach.

In this chapter we will provide a broad overview of the challenges confronting us and argue for faculty leadership in addressing these challenges, particularly as they impact our teaching. This discussion is not intended to be comprehensive, but only broadly suggestive of the current external climate that necessitates changes in the way we teach.

The first and most significant force affecting higher education instruction is the entry of the latest wave of the "new Americans" into our classrooms. During the late 1980s and early 1990s, the economy forced many adults to return to college in order to survive ("The Landscape," 1995; Upcraft, 1996). In response to the declining number of traditional-age students, colleges and universities changed their marketing strategies (McPherson & Schapiro, 1995). Both of these trends resulted in higher education opening its doors to a wider population (Upcraft, 1996).

This wider and more diverse student body is having an impact on higher education equally as dramatic as the flood of GIs after World War II and the entry of large numbers of women and ethnic minority students into the academy after 1950 (Lucas, 1994). This trend is the latest in periodic expansions of opportunities to those who have historically been denied access to American higher education. While we agree with those who believe that admission of students from a broader range of backgrounds is exciting (Berliner & Biddle, 1995), it has also accentuated our inadequacies in the classroom as never before. What we are coming to understand is that this new student population does not simply look different, but it presents an entirely new set of instructional challenges. Many of these students are academically, behaviorally, linguistically, or socially underprepared for college, and they often bring attitudes about themselves and education that are foreign to a professoriate schooled in a different time (Upcraft, 1996).

Three Forces for Change

We have identified three forces that have the potential to change the character of higher education.

Different Students

Today's professors are faced with the challenge of instructing 18-year-olds who may not share their values or their work ethic; who cannot read, write, speak, or do math proficiently, or who do not know how to behave appropriately. In the same classroom are non-traditional-age students who come to class with different agendas than typical 18- or 19-year-olds. Some are women who have raised their children and are ready to resume a postponed career. Others are single parents who see education as a means of creating better lives for their families. Yet others are middle-aged and older men who have been forced into or have chosen a career change. Many of these adults are unsure of themselves as students but are not afraid to question and challenge. They are investing hard-earned or borrowed dollars in their education and demand a return for their money.

The Computer

A second major force for change in higher education today is the omnipresence of computers and other technological innovations with extraordinary power to enhance learning and instruction. Today the mainframe computer has become nearly extinct. Ready or not, even small colleges and universities are being compelled to leap onto the information superhighway where distance learning and electronic networks have become alternatives to the campus, and where classrooms and libraries exist in a virtual reality called cyberspace ("The Landscape," 1995). But many faculty are woefully unprepared to use the new technology (Baiocco & DeWaters, 1995) and require major institutional support for training.

Government and Business Pressures

Together, government and business are exerting a third major force for change. The mid-1990s have witnessed a seesaw of support for higher education by government officials at the state and national levels, depending on the success of political conservatives in advancing their economic and social agendas (Berliner & Biddle, 1995). This unstable support has required public institutions in particular to seek cost-cutting measures—to do more with less. Meanwhile, business leaders have also made relentless demands on the educational delivery system to produce students who are literate, technically skilled, and flexible (Buchbinder & Newson, 1992). As more business leaders have joined boards of trustees, colleges and universities have been pressured to adopt more rigorous performance measures.

The *Chronicle of Higher Education Almanac's* report "The Nation" aptly described the state of affairs in 1995:

> The American academy, never known for its fast pace, is catching its breath after a tumultuous year. Rarely have its members seen anything like the changes unfolding these days in Congress, in the courts, on the campuses, and in the worlds of technology and science—changes that could profoundly alter higher education. (p. 5)

In that same publication (hereafter referred to as the *CHE Almanac*), Gerhard Casper, president of Stanford University whose career in education has spanned 30 years, cited political and economic conditions as "leading to the most significant re-examination of higher education *from the inside*" (1995, p. 5). Brown University President Vartan Gregorian agreed: "We have just been stunned, with everything happening at once" (p. 5). The "everything happening at once" was translated into the following litany of issues presented by the "The Nation":

- A Congress focused on cutting science budgets, Fulbrights, and student loans [but more recently offering tuition income tax breaks]
- A phasing out of the National Endowment of the Arts and National Endowment of the Humanities
- A climate of fiscal conservatism at the state level that leads colleges and universities to compete with prisons and health care for money
- Losses due to investment scandals, for example, the Common Fund fiasco
- Attempts by donors to influence academic programs
- Attempts to negotiate or do away with tenure
- The growing use of part-time instructors, thus increasing the competition for tenure track jobs
- A severe scaling back of affirmative action nationwide (1995, p. 5)

Traditional Academic Culture

Whether these forces will prove to be effective agents for change in higher education is not yet clear. David Breneman, dean of the Curry School of Education at the University of Virginia in 1995, made these observations:

After four decades of largely unbroken growth in resources and enrollment, higher education is several years into a new era, which severely challenges those whose careers have been built on the assumption of unending prosperity.... Higher education can hardly expect to be immune from such pressure [to expand access], and yet its culture is particularly resistant to change. (1995, pp. B1–2)

Some introspection may be necessary if we are to make a realistic assessment of the probability of effective change. What explains the paradox that colleges and universities exist to foster the progress of knowledge and yet are so resistant to change? Why are individual faculty, whose lifetime work is dedicated to the advancement of new thought, so apparently unwilling to take risks? (Wilshire, 1995). A look at the history of higher education affords one explanation. Steeped in medieval tradition, the culture of academe only allows change to occur glacially because of a philosophy of inquiry that continually challenges reform and demands justification. Modern educators continue to revere Descartes' method of reasoning about the universe: "My first rule was to accept nothing as true which I did not clearly recognize to be so; to accept nothing more than what was presented to my mind so clearly and distinctly that I could have no occasion to doubt it" (1960, pp. 220–221). Shaped by this tradition, which demands proof but not necessarily numbers, today's faculty are in a tug of war with forces that insist upon measurable (quantifiable) outcomes as the criteria for decisions.

We agree that the academic culture can be viewed as resistant to change; however, we contend that what appears to be, and is often labeled as, resistance on the part of the faculty is actually our traditionally cautious response to unfamiliar conditions. Regardless, at every turn the diverse forces we have outlined are confronting today's faculty who believe they are fighting to maintain the integrity of a college education. It is clear we are in the midst of a revolution encompassing many aspects of American life, and we faculty have no choice but to respond. The spotlight is on us. What are we going to do? Who is best suited to reform higher education? We are.

Faculty Development—The Key

We will argue that faculty development is the key to reform. We faculty are the infantry, attacking the problems on the front lines within our colleges and universities. In our professional role, higher education faculty are responsible for analyzing, synthesizing, evaluating, and communicating the changes that are occurring not only in our disciplines, but also in society. Our teaching is central to the success of our institutions as well as American society. Therefore, meaningful reforms must begin with the faculty.

Chapters 2 and 3 will expand our discussion of the forces for change and institutional inertia, as well as provide an historical evaluation of faculty development and argue for the need to reform our traditional system of developing teaching effectiveness. The lack of preparation for college teaching has been cause for concern since 1900 (Blackburn & Lawrence, 1995; Lucas, 1994; Nyquist, Abbott, & Wulff, 1989) and has received increasing attention in this decade (Angelo, 1994; Boice, 1992; Jarvis, 1991; Menges, Weimer, & Associates, 1996; Mooney, 1992; Nyquist & Wulff, 1996; Seldin & Associates, 1990; Solomon & Solomon, 1993; Sykes, 1988).

While programs for developing college teaching are evolving on some campuses, few institutions have designed comprehensive approaches (Baiocco & DeWaters, 1995; Jarvis, 1991). Many future college faculty are offered immersion orientations in pedagogy and a system akin to medieval apprenticeships as they progress toward their doctoral degrees. When they graduate, they often face years of second-class academic citizenship, picking up courses as part-time adjuncts at multiple sites before landing full-time university positions (Horwitz, 1994). New hires are expected to develop their teaching skills (though they will not be rewarded for them) even as they are required to publish prolifically (Jarvis, 1991). Senior faculty, who used to be immune from review after they enjoyed tenure, are now required to demonstrate their "productivity" by submitting to post-tenure evaluations as well as ubiquitous student rating surveys. (See data from the Carnegie Foundation International Survey of Attitudes and Characteristics of Faculty Members reported in the *CHE Almanac*, 1995, p. 33.)

To support professional development, some campuses offer workshops and teaching effectiveness programs, others pair faculty as mentors (Blackburn & Lawrence, 1995; Luna & Cullen, 1995; Wunsch, 1994), but most offer only travel to conferences plus sabbaticals to individuals who seek professional growth (Baiocco & DeWaters, 1995). All faculty—even those at schools whose missions emphasize undergraduate teaching—are affected by the "publish or perish" mindset as they strive to advance their careers (Blackburn & Lawrence, 1995; Boyer, 1990; Fairweather, 1993a, b; Leatherman, 1990; Lewis, 1996; Mooney, 1990, 1991, 1992; Schwartz, 1992;

Soderberg, 1985; Solomon & Solomon, 1993; Sykes, 1988; Tuckman, 1979).

Invigorated Approach to Faculty Development

We propose a new and invigorated system of faculty development centering around excellence in teaching. The heart of our book, Chapters 4 through 8, profiles the presentation styles, scholarship of teaching, and problem-solving strategies of award-winning college teachers. Based on our study, we present and illustrate a theory of teaching excellence in Chapter 9 and suggest how it might be applied to identify those with potential for becoming excellent teachers, as well as to develop teaching effectiveness.

We believe that, whether we like it or not, the current system for developing faculty will change because of the current confluence of social, economic, and political conditions that are creating a serious re-evaluation of the role of higher education in society. On the positive side, these conditions also offer an opportunity for college faculty to reform those aspects of their professional development that have not kept pace with technology, social change, or with the best in educational research.

Society has thrown a challenge at our feet, and we must meet it. Either we change from within, or "they" will make the changes for us. Outsiders are likely to emphasize change within the academy in terms of quantity—increased productivity through larger class sizes or reduced costs by "downsizing" faculty—while we faculty continue to insist that improving the quality of education is paramount. Together the forces we have listed pressure faculty to increase productivity, while we resist in an effort to maintain the integrity of education and the human interaction that have been the core of teaching since Socrates (Johnstone, 1995; Massey & Wilger, 1995). Although we agree that faculty ought to educate more students better, we propose a different approach to solving the productivity problem.

Without a new perspective on our role, the prospects for addressing these needs look dim. Academics are under siege from many constituencies during this time of cultural revolution. Warding off the attacks of political conservatives, we have become the focus of the media as well as targets for the "re-engineering" efforts of public officials (Berliner & Biddle, 1995; Bérubé, 1996). And, as Breneman notes, "Educational leaders view rocking the boat as hazardous to careers" (1995, p. B2). Thus it is likely that nothing much will happen right away. Change is a risky business. Yet we argue that it is imperative that we look *within* for faculty to lead the critical reforms that are necessary to preserve a centuries-old ideal *and* to meet the needs of a changing society.

Rather than accept the way the problem is being defined (and ultimately solved) by administrators or outsiders attempting to respond to pressure groups, we faculty must insist on defining the problem in terms of quality, and exploring and implementing our own creative solutions. The final chapters of this book propose some solutions. Chapter 10 provides a summary of the current options for guiding teaching assistants in the development of their teaching. It then shows one application of our theory, how exemplary college teachers address common problems mentioned by inexperienced faculty. In Chapter 11, we propose other applications of our theory of teaching excellence and a new solution to improve college teaching: a national force of distinguished teaching faculty, marshaled as leaders of learning communities focusing on instructional problem solving and techniques of self-evaluation. In our plan, communities of teacher–scholars would harness the power of campus networks and the Internet to promote mentoring, reflection on teaching and learning, and the exchange of principles of sound practice. While administrators are suggesting that we should crank out more graduates at no additional cost and with little additional support, we are recommending instead an improvement in craftsmanship—the quality of teaching—which we believe will be more productive in the long run.

2

*Forces for
Change versus
Institutional Inertia*

Let us imagine that we are observers in a classroom of the future. Education in the next century is likely to bear little resemblance to our classrooms today:

This is a course in English communications, a typical core course for college freshmen. The class is held at three sites: one in the urban center campus, one at a rural satellite, and one at a local suburban high school, all connected via interactive video. Students at the urban center are largely over age 25; five of them are recent immigrants who have taken basic ESL classes at a local high school but whose knowledge of English is rudimentary. Five others graduated from local city schools where they were not allowed to take textbooks home, so they have read little and written less. Their high schools and their homes are not equipped with computers. Though they are eager to learn, they already feel alienated from the college world, as they have to work full-time, and they are ethnic minorities. Among the 15 others, several are mothers of children under 10, recently divorced, at times on welfare. Others are transfers from local community colleges who expect to perform well, but who are unaware of the higher academic expectations of professors at their new alma mater. One student speaks with an assistive device. The rest are traditional students who live in college residences and expect to have an exciting social life away from their parents.

At the urban setting, an instructional team enters the television studio that is fitted not only with movie cameras, but also with computerized student stations to allow the instructors to observe students' responses to their questions on a computer monitor *as they answer them.* The lead teacher speaks about the structure of the course, which includes interdisciplinary readings on a theme taken from an on-line course pack plus individual and group Internet research projects. The "assisting" teachers at the urban center explain their roles as lecturers and on-line mentors for small groups. Students are provided with access codes to the on-line listserve, discussion area, and cyberspace "knowledge centers" for the class.

Meanwhile all of this is being viewed at the two remote sites, where groups of 10 students are seated in front of interactive video equipment. At each site, a coordinator assists students with the technology and distributes faxes of written handouts when necessary. The high school students have enrolled in this college course for advanced placement credit. They are 18-year-olds from an affluent community, and they expect to reduce college costs as well as to accelerate their education by enrolling in this distance learning option. Their backgrounds have prepared them well for this video setting, as all of them have home computers with modems and their own web pages; however, they are not comfortable sitting passively for long, and they sometimes have stereotypical beliefs or gaps in their knowledge which require instructional intervention.

At the rural satellite 40 miles from campus, students who are enrolled in professional programs at the college arrive at a studio similar to the one at the urban center. Because they live outside the city, they have elected to take this course off campus. Half of these students are working full-time in careers related to their majors, and the absence of commuting time allows them to lead a more comfortably paced life. For them, time is the single most important factor in their learning environments. Others in the class are sampling the college from a distance to see whether they are interested in the college's programs.

Before even considering the many opportunities and problems this instructional environment poses for faculty, we believe that this scenario should serve as a vivid illustration of the possibilities for a

"New Age" higher education. The profound impact of diverse student populations, new technology, and economic pressure to be more productive are all evident in this narrative. What may be startling to many professors is that this future is *now*. We have simply combined all of the current classroom conditions we know to exist into this one scenario. The "New Age" is not 20 years hence, but *now*.

In the rest of this chapter, we will examine in more detail each of the factors in the new instructional equation—the student, the environment, and the economy—and then consider the counterforce of institutional inertia.

The American Student: A Lesson in Diversity

Historically, the American higher education system has contended with waves of discontent about the student culture. In her book *Improving Student Learning Skills,* Martha Maxwell (1979) chronicled admissions criteria and policies from 1852 to the present, showing that professors have long had to address issues of student diversity (whether in student academic preparedness, ethnicity, socioeconomic status, age, or gender). Today's academics are feeling the same challenge to their standards as our predecessors, but this time in combination with significant new demands for increased productivity (Lewis, 1996; Lucas, 1994). To promote learning among members of our new student culture, professors will have to become more creative and draw from a larger repertoire of strategies that show students how to overcome obstacles and meet standards. In this regard, professors have much to learn from the distinguished teachers in our study, who appear to excel at teaching regardless of the instructional environment.

A demographic profile from the *CHE Almanac* (1997) provides a snapshot of the U.S. student today. It reveals that total enrollment has risen almost 16.5% since 1985 (p. 5). This is supported by Berliner and Biddle, who reported that over half of all entering high school students will actually enroll in colleges or universities (1995, p. 274). The *CHE Almanac* (1997) also reports that 39.5% of the student population is 25 and older (p. 18), that there are 11% more women than men enrolled, that almost one-quarter are minorities, and that 43% are attending college part-time (p. 5). (See Table 2-1.)

TABLE 2-1   1995 College* Enrollment Trends
in the United States

Demographics	Percentage
Age	
Less than 18	2.0
18–24	54.5
25–39	30.8
40 and older	11.2
Gender	
Men	44.5
Women	55.5
Proportion of minorities**	25.3
Full-time status	57.0
10-year increase in total enrollment	16.5
SAT Average Scores	1,013

Source: Compiled from the 1997 *The Chronicle of Higher Education: Almanac Issue,* 44(1), 5, 18.

*Two- and four-year public and private institutions, undergraduate and graduate

**Excludes foreign students

    M. Lee Upcraft (1996) provided a useful summary analysis of the trends in demographics in the categories of racial/ethnic diversity, gender, enrollment status (full-time/part-time), age, residence, abledness, sexual orientation, and international status. Significant increases in non-white enrollments have already taken place and this trend is expected to continue (Lucas, 1994, p. 312). Upcraft also noted that women have outnumbered men in higher education since about 1980 and that the increase in part-time enrollment has resulted in a longer time required to complete the degree. Although the adult student population is significant, it has leveled off over the past five years (1996, pp. 23–24). Nevertheless, today's students are more likely to have family responsibilities such as childrearing and other family obligations (Roberts & Associates, 1994, p. 21).

    Hodgkinson reported that by 1985 only one in six students was termed a "traditional" student aged 18 to 24, studying full-time and living in a residence hall. Evans and Levine's 1990 study indicated that gay students found the university a hostile environment (as cited in Upcraft, 1996, pp. 24–25). College and university campuses have witnessed a large increase in international students as well, with the percentage rising 30.1% from 1980 to 1990 (*CHE Almanac*, 1992).

In addition to the changing profile of students in the United States, there is now a distinct mind-set about schooling. When listing reasons why they go to college, students reported that they "want to be able to get a better job" (76.7%), "want to be able to make more money" (72.4%), and "want to gain a general education and appreciation of ideas" (62.1%). When asked what objectives they considered essential or very important, 74.1% reported that "being very well off financially" was a priority. More than 39% felt that "it was important to influence social values," but only 17.7% felt that "influencing the political structure was essential." The percentage of students who said that they would "get a job to help pay college expenses" has risen to 44.1% (*CHE Almanac*, 1997, p. 20). Part of the reason for this increase may be that students are more likely to need financial aid, since the average federal student aid grant or loan is worth less than it was 10 years ago (Roberts & Associates, 1994).

Other significant social changes are occurring in students' values, their family dynamics, their health, their high school preparation, and their financial status (Upcraft, 1996, p. 26). The divorce rate, domestic violence, addictions, and a variety of psychosocial problems (as well as a substantial increase in psychological disturbance) often accompany students into the classroom (Witchel, 1991). According to Upcraft, "Students bring all manner of unwanted and counterproductive forces into those chambers of learning [classrooms]" (1996, p. 36).

Some authors believe that the current mismatch between student and professorial expectations is the result of widespread cultural changes that begin in the home and continue through secondary school. Sacks called this gap between "Generation X" and the professoriate—about half of all full-time professors are over age 50 [Crawley, 1995]—a "cultural divide…a break between the modern and the postmodern worlds" (Sacks, 1996, p. xii). The changes in student culture are reflected in attitudes towards education which range from utter disengagement to rudely answering pagers during class. Many faculty report students who reject responsibility because they have been raised in an educational system that pampered them. They are a generation for whom grades were the sole motivator, or who felt entitled to be entertained and rewarded. Award-winning high school teacher John Gatto (1992) identified this mindset among his students and placed the blame either on parents who structure every minute of their children's time outside of school, excessive television viewing that promotes a passive and puerile worldview, or an educational system that rewards docility.

Although we do not agree that the situation is as dire as Sacks and Gatto found, we do believe that today's college teachers will need to change their teaching methods significantly in order to improve this generation's learning. They can no longer assume that students share their values. They will have to incorporate new affective goals into their planning or they simply will not reach many young people.

The problem of students' underpreparedness for college is not just one of attitude, however. Clearly, many students today have not learned the foundation information, concepts, and skills formerly expected of college-bound high school graduates. Gifford (1992) cited a national survey of 250 higher education institutions showing that 84% offered remedial courses and that 15% of all freshmen were enrolled in one or more remedial English or math classes (p. 21), a fact that is related to increased admission of those with lower SATs and less rigorous high school preparation. Indeed, in a Carnegie Foundation survey, only 20% of faculty thought that undergraduate students were adequately prepared in written and oral communication skills, and a smaller number, 15%, thought students were adequately prepared in mathematics and quantitative reasoning skills (*CHE Almanac,* 1995, p. 33). Underprepared students are at greater risk for dropping out, as are those from lower socioeconomic classes, ethnic minorities (with the exception of Asian Americans), females, students with disabilities, those who work more than half-time and live off-campus, those who have mental or physical health problems, those who lack family stability and support, or those who attend college part-time (Pascarella & Terenzini, 1991).

Upcraft explained the dilemma that classes with larger numbers of underprepared students present to faculty:

> In today's classes, the [normal] curve has flattened, or at worst become bimodal. At best, we end up with about the same number

of underprepared, prepared, and gifted students; at worst, we have a class with no mass middle at all. If we persist in teaching to the middle of the preparedness curve, we may not be teaching to anyone. In classes with great diversity of preparation, there must be greater diversity of instruction. (1996, p. 34)

Yet despite this catalog of dramatic changes in the kinds of students in our classrooms, we professors have been expected to carry on and produce the same results—an educated graduate. We agree with Upcraft and Sacks that faculty must be better prepared to address these significant differences in the new students' background, culture, behavior, time and energy constraints, goals, and attitudes. No longer can we fail to recognize the importance of our students' diverse backgrounds and attitudes toward learning as we design instruction. Moreover, if we do not update and improve our instructional methods to meet the needs of these students, which includes recognizing their lack of confidence in their ability to learn, we will most certainly see higher rates of failure and dropping out. We *must* improve "productivity" in terms of reaching a larger number of students, and we can do this without compromising the integrity of their education.

The stakes are very high, but we believe that there are enormous benefits for our students and society—and also for us—if we make the effort. Anyone who has ever guided a student from rookie to scholar knows the inherent personal rewards. As Upcraft said, for this next generation of Americans in higher education, "the college experience can be a life-altering one. We have the opportunity to better meet the serious and significant needs of an increasingly complex and diverse society. It is a time when our work in higher education can really and truly make a difference" (1996, p. 39).

The Consumer Mentality

One particular attitude held by many students today, the "consumer mentality," is so pervasive and so destructive to teaching and learning as to warrant specific examination. "From 1973 to 1988, college costs rose more than 200 percent, a pace well ahead of inflation rates for that same period" (*Parade*, 1989, p. 17). This extraordinary increase has continued in the 1990s and has placed increased financial stress on students and their families, forcing them to change their source of financing through increased student loans (Upcraft, 1996, p. 29). In an attempt to keep pace with tuition costs that have risen faster than family incomes, students and their families are borrowing furiously. But direct lending to students from the federal government has decreased through 1996 and future growth is questionable, despite the fact that "for today's undergraduates, loans, however costly, are what the GI Bill subsidies were to an earlier generation: the key that opens the door to higher education" (Tooley, 1995, p. 84).

These data spotlight the complexities faced by today's faculty who are responsible for educating a population of students for whom a college education may be a huge financial sacrifice and whose primary motivation is to "get a better job" and "make money," not necessarily to earn a well-rounded education in the liberal tradition. We are hearing education being referred to as a product and our students as the paying customers (Pratt, 1994, p. 39). Ironically, these "customers" are being charged more when they take more than four years to finish their programs.

Recent statistics show that students who finish in four years are becoming the exception. Reasons for this include the need for full- or part-time employment—which may result in a lower course load and can be complicated by the difficulty of scheduling the necessary courses around the work schedule—and the fact that many students are unprepared for college-level work. Commencement speeches nostalgically and humorously acknowledge the *five* years spent on campus, and those five-year students are jokingly referred to in the college student vernacular as "super seniors." As we have discussed, diversity among students is in fact much more complex than the single issue of multiculturalism. Nevertheless, faculty are often left to fend for themselves in learning to meet their students' diverse needs. Not only are the students more diverse in the ways we have described, but they also have a new attitude, which we have chosen to highlight because it is so pervasive—a consumer mentality.

Given the increasing costs associated with attending college, students and parents are adopting an educational consumer mentality: Students are becoming "vigilante consumers," manipulating marketers and the marketplace through "pressure, protest, and politics" (Popcorn, 1991). *St. Lawrence University Magazine* highlighted this sense of entitlement by citing student language that is becoming familiar to faculty:

Fill In The Blank:
"I paid $25,000 to come here and I deserve _____"
  • an A on this paper
  • no problems with my roommate
  • a job after graduation, etc. ("Consumerism," 1995, p. 17)

This mentality is also reflected in reports of "grade inflation" at many colleges:

At the very moment that student underpreparedness is at a new high, grades in colleges and universities are higher than ever before. There may be more than one explanation for the paradox. But surely a key factor is the bartering of commodities: my generosity [in grading] in exchange for yours [evaluating me]! Professional survival is, after all, a strong motivation, and when the stakes are high, integrity cannot help but suffer. (Cholakian, 1994, pp. 24–25)

Or, as Kurt Wiesenfeld reported, "If they don't like their grade, they go to the 'return' counter to trade it in for something better" (1996, p. 16). A market model of higher education has resulted in what Sacks calls "A-Mart" colleges where *everyone* is "above average" (1996, p. x). If students are consumers and education is a commodity they buy, then students are entitled to negotiate for a better product at lower cost in terms of effort.

This attitude has historical roots both in the American egalitarian ideal—we aim to educate everybody—and also in the campus turmoil of the 1970s when,

in an era when authority was suspect, when all standards and constraints were under attack, and everything traditional was assailed as undemocratic and elitist, academic administrators and faculty were anxious to sidestep confrontations of angry students. In the face of unrelenting pressure to relax requirements, professors ultimately capitulated. (Lucas, 1994, p. 291)

One professor puts it this way: "Having been raised on gold stars for effort and smiley faces for self-esteem, they've [students] learned that they can get by without hard work and real talent if they can talk the professor into giving them a break" (Wiesenfeld, 1996, p. 16).

To some extent, we have formed an unintentional alliance with business in a knee-jerk response to the change in campus demographics. We have sold the nation the belief that higher education is necessary for economic success, and people have bought it. As reported earlier, most students want training, not the more traditional "liberating experience" promoted by academe. One cause of the current crisis in American education is a mismatch between this drive for economic success by today's underprepared students and the more traditional expectations of faculty. Faculty continue to assume that they are offering an education, not merely a diploma. Author Robert Hughes suggests that

> if America did not place such unreal emphasis on college degrees, this problem [of lowered admission standards, student underpreparedness and grade inflation] might not vanish, but it might at least deflate. A college degree is not necessary for most jobs that people do in the world.... The main effect of American degree-fetishism has been to make skilled pragmatic work seem second rate. (1993, pp. 68–69)

Technological Trends: Academics in Cyberspace

In addition to demographic and cultural pressures, technology has become a power that no one could ever have dreamed of even a decade ago. Technological advances have eliminated many barriers so that access to a degree is available to students who may have been excluded in the past. The new technology supports alternative means of delivering education, such as assistive devices and distance learning, while it also has changed the methods for responding, through innovations such as word processing, multimedia, and hypertext. These options pose new opportunities for professors, but also new problems for those who are not willing or prepared to use the new technology.

Technology has so affected the speed and volume of information and communication today that it boggles the minds of faculty, administrators, and students alike. Faculty who have been used to the lag time and the material reality of print media find it hard to adjust to this immediate access to information and the transient quality of electronic images. At their fingertips, professors and students have information from all over the world *as it is created*. Instant and interactive technological options are swamping us with data, while powerful software allows us to create, design, publish, and edit in the comfort of our offices or homes. The Internet has become a global Wild West, lacking a clear presence of "the law" to govern an unruly electronic community. Electronic communications circumvent traditional publishing processes formerly controlled by the gatekeepers of knowledge—journal editors and other print authorities—and we are often in the dark about issues of on-line confidentiality, documentation, copyright, censorship, or other publishing concerns. In fact, the *Publication Manual of the American Psychological Association* reported that a standard for citing on-line information has not yet emerged (1994, p. 218). With documents online, the rigor of academic review is gone, replaced by a free-for-all where all knowledge is created equal. Some educators are also concerned that electronic media will redefine the very nature of how people think and learn. (Online subscribers to the Learning and Technology list sponsored by the American Association of Higher Education (AAHESGIT), for example, regularly discuss such issues.) Gifford wrote that computer technology would provide new learning systems that would radically change research methods, the kinds of questions we pose, and access to information. The response needed from educators, he said, is a "learning explosion." He predicted that "as we revolutionize knowledge management in higher education, we will also need to transform teaching" (1992, p. 18).

Struggling with budget cuts, institutions are hard pressed to keep up with the demand for faster and more powerful hardware, not to mention software and on-line subscriptions. The competitive world that students are being educated to enter is placing further economic pressure on higher education's already limited resources. And, though 65% of the general American population does not have home computers, and only 12% of those who do, have modems (Gurnett, 1995), students entering the university system arrive with at least minimal exposure to this technology. They likewise expect their professors to be computer literate and their institutions to be technologically equipped.

Economic Trends: The Interface between Government, Business, and Higher Education

Among the forces for change are those exerted by government and business. Although at first glance they appear to be remote and have little bearing on what happens in our classrooms, they can be the most devastating in the long run. Economic conditions mandate that we understand as never before that politics are personal. A policy change at the state or federal level, such as allowing tuition costs to be tax deductible, can have a major impact on every classroom, including those in private institutions whose students rely heavily on national student loans. And shifts in the corporate world, such as downsizing or the consolidation of health care providers, affect the career choices of our students. To ignore the power of economics on higher education is patently foolish.

Higher education today is being put in a tenuous position by national and state governments, while liberals and conservatives jockey for position in their attempts to balance budgets and win votes. Public universities alternately face encouraging support from legislators or consolidations, layoffs, campus closings, tuition increases, sabbatical cutbacks, and so on, while private colleges and universities fall in and out of favor with the current political power, keeping the status of financial support unpredictable.

"Real World Troubles," an article in the *U.S. News & World Report: America's Best Colleges 1996 Annual Guide,* reports that California (along with other states with large public university systems) is experiencing major financial difficulty supporting public higher education (Sanoff, 1995, 125–128). With funds having shrunk for over a decade, formerly low-tuition states are competing for state and federal dollars, resulting in some universities doubling their tuition (pp. 125–128). Consider these data:

- From 1989 to 1994 tuition rose:
  —124.9% at the University of California (Breneman, 1995, p. B2)
  —89.5% at California State University (p. B2)
  —290% at community colleges (p. B2)

- Average 1994–1995 tuition was $2,689 (an increase of 5.7% over the previous year) at 605 public four-year institutions in the United States (*CHE Almanac,* 1996, p. 3).
- Average tuition was $11,522 (an increase of 4.8% in one year) at 1,610 private four-year institutions in the United States (p. 3).

The increase in tuition in 1995–96 was even more drastic. As a result of tuition hikes, many colleges and universities, formerly known as good educational buys, encountered drops in student enrollment (Streisand, 1995):

> As costs have gone up [in California], enrollment has plummeted, dropping by about 200,000 since 1991, to 1.8 million. And besides the money woes and falling enrollment, there is a brain drain. Roughly 2,000 University of California professors have opted for early retirement since 1991, reducing the ranks of the most experienced teachers and the number of classes offered. (p. 125)

A review of economic policy changes in state institutions reveals that the financial woes of California are not isolated instances of a sad song, but a chorus being sung across the nation. Even though political leaders acknowledge the importance of higher education to strong economic growth and development, Breneman thinks that "several years of shrill public criticism of higher education's performance, particularly in undergraduate education" are responsible for this lack of support (1995, p. B1).

Consequently, many students within the state systems facing financial difficulties are again looking to private institutions, where their tuition dollars may become more valuable because they are guaranteed personal attention and access to needed courses. According to *U.S. News & World Report: America's Best Colleges 1996 Annual Guide,* the dismal economic situation of higher education in California will not improve in the near future because allocations have shifted from higher education to tax reductions and police enforcement. Higher education experts suggest that because undergraduate programs draw the most students, graduate programs especially will face cutbacks, as will the provision of remedial services at four-year schools (Sanoff, 1995, p. 128). Yale University's goal of gradually reducing the size of its Graduate School of Arts and Sciences by 10% (Paul, 1996, p. 57) exemplifies this trend.

As we suggested earlier, another jab at higher education has come from the business world. University board members are urging administrators to apply a technological/managerial template to academe. Performance technology (the conviction that there are training procedures that can guarantee learning) has been applied from business and government to higher education with references to "effective instructional design and delivery" (Leap & Crino, 1993). Many faculty are feeling marginalized by the use of an inappropriate commercial model. We believe that colleges are not factories that we are not in the business of mass-producing widgets:

> Proposals to standardize curriculum, develop a single system of accreditation, streamline, utilize total quality management, people administrative positions with managers rather than academics,…threaten to limit diversity in favor of, guess what, elevating, supporting and rewarding the "same old, same old" tried but not so true, methods of narrowing our vision. (Slack, 1994, p. 41)

Thus, as we examine this increasing interface between economic policy and education, we think that dramatic change is imminent.

Smiling Ted Says, "Come On Down! We've Got the School for You!"

In an increasingly competitive milieu, academe itself has taken on some of the marketing tactics of corporate America, and these practices again impact the expectations students bring into our classrooms. Each year in the month of September, families begin the search for "the right school," and leading news magazines lure information-hungry readers to shop and critically compare colleges and universities. Yet "school shopping" has taken on a new meaning as families screen potential alma maters with a new sense of entitlement.

In an attempt to attract students (Sanoff, 1995), college and university recruitment efforts have been expanded to include marketing schemes and econometric models. Some institutions are now hiring consultants to show them how to "maximize net tuition revenue" (p. 121) and increase retention through "enrollment management." In other words, the focus of this advice is on meeting enrollment targets, attracting the most academically prepared students, and gaining the maximum in tuition dollars, while not spending any more on financial aid than necessary. In addition, there is a disturbing "Robin Hood" tactic of charging certain families from higher socioeconomic groups more for their child to attend a particular college:

> Schools are charging a much higher rate, in some cases the full or "sticker" price, to applicants they deem less desirable who have the wherewithal, or the inclination, to pay. The reason: Research has shown that the weaker students are academically, the more likely they will be willing to pay whatever is necessary to attend a school they feel suits their ability. (p. 121)

In "A New Face for the Profession," Linda Ray Pratt, former president of the American Association of University Professors, described how faculty are being asked to respond to this marketing mentality. She said that the professoriate must deal with uniform standards, performance-based assessment, vocationally oriented programs, tenure limitations, heavier workloads, and more part-time and temporary employment for faculty. She referred to this "new face" as the "market-driven debasement of higher education," which undermines attempts to provide a curriculum that "reflects the diversity of our world and meets the needs of an increasingly varied student body" (1994, p. 39). To top it off, faculty at some colleges that are scrambling for students are asked to supplement the sales pitch by writing recruitment materials and participating in phonathons to recruit prospective students.

Public Assault on Academe

Accompanying this economic assault on higher education is a public cynicism about the institution, frequently referred to as the "ivory tower." In 1995, Hugh Petrie, dean of the Graduate School of Education at the State University of New York at Buffalo, described the "glory days" when faculty would "think great thoughts, write great books and papers, and reproduce themselves with some minor attention to preparing professional leadership for this field.... It was a heady period" (1995, p. 1). However, those days are gone, if in fact, they ever existed (Lucas, 1994). In 1994 the vast majority of faculty at U.S. colleges and universities believed that academic professionals were no longer among the most influential opinion leaders in the country (*CHE Almanac*, 1995, p. 33).

Professor and former Chancellor of the State University of New York system Bruce Johnstone suggested in 1995 that because of the public's need for U.S. higher education to increase productivity it had to become more responsive to the undergraduate. He noted that increased accessibility came at a time of great expectations:

> Society seems to expect more than ever before from its colleges and universities: from the engine of economic growth, to the enhancement of socio-economic mobility, to the preservation of a cultural canon, and to the historic Western university role as society's principal bastion of objectivity and critical inquiry. (p. 1)

Our reality check shows that, in an effort to save the financial viability of the institution, administrators are dancing a tango with consultants who have little concern for the traditions of academe. Whether we professors like it or not, our pedagogical ideals are being tested and challenged at every turn. At the height of conservatism in Congress in 1995, prompted by a pro-higher education editorial by Mortimer B. Zuckerman in *U.S. News & World Report*, one professor wrote,

> Their [radical Republicans'] assaults on the nation's colleges and universities are, in reality, attacks on working, middle class people everywhere. Without our system of higher education, the power that accrues through knowledge would be controlled by a wealthy, corporate elite, who would also be its only beneficiaries. The radical Republican agenda, if left unchecked, will trigger inevitable class warfare and put this nation at great risk. (Clausen, 1995, p. 8)

Later that year the situation had only intensified. For example, James Perley, 1995 president of the American Association of University Professors, reported:

> Senator Kassebaum of Kansas, chair of the Committee on Labor and Human Resources of the Senate, proposed cutting spending on Federal Student Loan programs by $10.1 billion, in large

part to be accomplished by adding a 2% charge to colleges and universities on all federal loans their students received. (1995, p. 4)

Though in 1997 higher education received promises of a financial reprieve, political fluctuations have continued to keep institutions off balance, forcing administrators to keep their sights on increased enrollments as their only stable source of revenue.

Institutional Inertia: Power, Status, and the Medieval University

Thus far, the academic world has inadequately responded to the forces for change and society's demands for reform. When faced with the need for change, organizations have three factors to consider: personnel, facilities, and budgets. The current dramatic reduction in financial resources available to colleges and universities is forcing administrators to look to faculty to improve productivity. Although leaders in higher education institutions are alarmed about the challenges ahead, few view the development of the faculty as a key to reform. More importantly, we faculty have not made the connection between the need for reform in higher education and our own performance in the classroom. This book will explore that vital connection through an analysis of the characteristics and strategies of distinguished professors and a proposal for the cultivation of teaching excellence.

What explains the paradox that colleges and universities exist to foster the progress of knowledge, and yet are so resistant to change? (Blackburn & Lawrence, 1995). Why are individual faculty, whose lifetime work is dedicated to the advancement of new thought, so unwilling to take risks when it comes to reforming the processes by which they and others become full-fledged members of academe? (Angelo, 1994; Roberts & Associates, 1994).

A closer look at the history of higher education affords an explanation. Steeped in medieval tradition, the culture of academe allows change to occur glacially because of a philosophy of inquiry which continually challenges reform and demands justification. Modern educators continue to revere Descartes' method of reasoning about the universe: "My first rule was to accept nothing as true which I did not clearly recognize to be so; to accept nothing more than what was presented to my mind so clearly and distinctly that I could have no occasion to doubt it" (1960, pp. 220–221). Formed by this tradition, which demands proof but not necessarily numbers, today's faculty are in a tug-of-war with forces that insist upon measurable (quantifiable) outcomes as the criterion for truth.

The early historical roots of the university as a place for theologians to prepare scholar–masters can still be observed today in the preparation of college faculty. The Ph.D., the doctorate in philosophy, is the symbol of a scholar's having mastered the theory in a particular field and used it to advance knowledge. As far back as the twelfth century, extraordinary teachers attracted students from all over Europe to their centers of learning. The renown such communities of scholars achieved soon attracted the attention of the powerful in the church and the state, but scholars resisted outside control by playing one group against the other (Lucas, 1994). Thus began the university's tradition of independence. A similar "push-me pull-you" between conservative social forces and liberal intellectual forces continues today, but now many administrators as well as faculty at U.S. colleges and universities are in league with political and economic leaders (Kanter, Gamson, & London, 1997).

In this country without a titled elite, a degree from a school with status continues to be the key to economic success. Elite institutions retain their status by continuing "rich" traditions: They act as conservators of society by passing on the knowledge, behaviors, and rites of previous generations, and they also act as shapers of the future through their graduates, who soon occupy positions of power and influence (Lucas, 1994). This dual role has created institutions whose pace of change is evolutionary rather than revolutionary.

In U.S. society, challenges to this cultural dominance have always come from those who have egalitarian concerns: the working class, the poor, minorities, and immigrants (Lucas, 1994). Public university systems, open enrollment policies, and increasing numbers of college graduates have threatened the power monopoly of the elite schools, forcing them to scramble to hang on to their prominence. One of the ways elite schools do this is by flaunting the achievements of their faculty. Publications that "rate" colleges identify the numbers of faculty who hold terminal degrees or publish regularly in their field; in admissions materials, colleges boast like proud mothers about faculty scholarship.

Some faculty, motivated by the same drive to demonstrate their success, are pushed into competing for positions at prestigious colleges and universities. Others fight for contract renewal, promotion, tenure, and merit increases. Publication has become the dominant means for faculty to prove their value to their institutions, with externally reviewed books, articles, and monographs used to document scholarliness because they increase the fame of the institution. This has even been carried to the extent of counting citations through a "citation index" (Centra, 1979; Seldin, 1990).

Teaching excellence, on the other hand, has rarely boosted any faculty member's reputation outside the institution (Lewis, 1996). Since the 1960s it has held only secondary importance for the U.S. colleges and universities that must compete for status, students, and funding. During the same period, higher education expanded tremendously, and traditional liberal arts colleges saw the opportunity to emulate the research universities by hiring graduates from those institutions as faculty. Many of these new faculty brought with them an attitude that producing knowledge (research) was more valuable than cultivating it in others (teaching), a model that may have been borrowed by universities in the U.S. from the German university model at the turn of the century (Kanter, Gamson, & London, 1997). In other cases, the institutions began to hire instructors with doctorates to give the impression that they were also of high caliber. Thus began the current imbalanced system of faculty rewards that undermines a basic mission of at least the colleges and, to a lesser extent, the universities—learning and instruction—and that frequently rewards vacuous writing in inconsequential journals (Soderberg, 1985). But there are a few hopeful signs. Faculty have overwhelmingly recognized the need for a better way to evaluate their teaching (*CHE Almanac*, 1995, p. 33). And for the first time, in 1995, *U. S. News & World Report: America's Best Colleges 1996 Annual Guide* rated colleges on their "unusually strong commitment to undergraduate teaching" (Sanoff, 1995, p. 140).

Faculty Resistance to Reform: Holding On to the Comfort Zone

As with colleges and universities, individual faculty frequently find comfort in maintaining the status quo and by foregoing their own professional development. Change, after all, requires time and effort, and is often resisted unless the benefits can be clearly shown. A look at how faculty have adopted computer technology is a good illustration. A faculty development coordinator at a recent conference classified faculty into four groups, based on their computer literacy: (1) the "clueless," the colleagues who brag that they still prefer "the quill"; (2) those who use the computer only for word processing; (3) those who also use email and the Internet; and (4) "cyberpunks," who "live" inside their computers (Sherer, 1995). This range of skills suggests that, like other groups, faculty include "opinion leaders" who take risks and try new tasks, as well as "laggers" who adopt new skills only when they are forced. Faculty are busy professionals, many working 60-hour weeks during the academic year (see "Faculty Workloads, 1989–90," *CHE Almanac,* 1995, p. 2), and they demand a convincing rationale for donning a new pair of shoes and putting their comfortable, "holy/holely" ones in the cellarway.

Massey and Wilger (1995) point out that even in the face of the harsh economic conditions that demand attention, threats to the academy often result in resistance:

> Faculty express grave reservations about current efforts to improve our gross productivity, such as increasing the ratio of students to faculty or increasing faculty teaching loads. They see such changes not as improvements but as diminishing educational quality, undermining research, or both. (p. 12)

Although we acknowledge that faculty do frequently question directives such as these, we also believe that calling such challenges "resistance" is a misinterpretation. Rather, we believe faculty often see themselves as the preservers of educational integrity. Unfortunately, that may be translated by "bean counters" as rigidity and inflexibility.

But change we must, for if we are too busy or too unproductive to reform our own profession, then it will be done for us. Even though they may be well-intended, movements by administrators and their organizations to reform the profession often have political and economic agendas that undermine their credibility. Many faculty have deep-seated suspicions that higher education leaders are more interested in the ratio of outputs to inputs than in improving the quality of students' education. We believe that we faculty need to reconsider our origins, return to the spirit of a community of scholars, and join together in common cause to preserve the integrity of education through effective faculty development. We feel that faculty development is the key. Agreeing with Boice's reference to faculty as a "neglected resource," we question why preparation for teaching is so much more common for graduate students than for new faculty. Boice postulated that the more prestigious the campus, the more likely that development is deferred to graduate teaching assistants only. He theorized a common belief was that "once graduate students (with or without experience as teaching assistants) join a campus as faculty members, they already know how to teach (or can figure it out on their own)" (1992, p. 52). Earlier in this century, when the American Association of University Professors was founded by John Dewey, we faculty saw the advantages of taking charge of our own destiny. We must do so again.

3

<hr />

We're Talking about a Revolution

The Need for Reform in Faculty Preparation and Development

The greatest investment a college or university makes is in its faculty. In 1991 Jarvis estimated that each faculty member costs his or her university over a million dollars during a 35-year career span (p. vii). But as with automobiles, upkeep and maintenance are essential to faculty longevity and value. The high sticker price of faculty makes it prudent to maintain them. The trouble is, we do not have a manual telling us how to keep them in top condition. Instead we are stuck with an outmoded clunker of a system for preparing and developing faculty.

"The primary impetus for training and development is change," says a maxim from the business world (Leap and Crino, 1993, p. 292). In our introductory chapters, we described the array of forces that are now driving change in higher education. In order to remain competitive, colleges and universities are insisting that faculty meet these demands for change. As with those in the business world, we are being asked to react to the social, technical, and economic upheavals surrounding us, and to change quickly. Academe is experiencing a problem similar to one reported by a corporate training director:

> Since the half-life of a [professional] is about five years, "a twenty-five-year old graduate will have to be reeducated eight times in the course of a forty-year career".... Virtually all workers who draw their expertise from a knowledge base (e.g., physicians, computer technicians) will find it challenging to keep pace with advances in this knowledge base during their careers. (Leap and Crino, 1993, p. 292)

The unfortunate distinction here is that for most college professors, scholarship in teaching is not even part of their initial knowledge base. We agree with Shulman's (1996) definition of scholarship: (a) knowledge of the discipline acquired through advanced study, (b) comprehensive knowledge of the interface of content and student management, (c) knowledge of resources necessary and available for teaching a particular subject, and (d) wisdom to select strategies based on accumulated experiences. Most new professors are initially prepared with only one kind of scholarship—knowledge of the discipline. Compounding this problem are the demand for continual change and the difficulty of defining productivity, a dilemma we share with other "knowledge professions" (Kelley & Caplan, 1993, p. 129).

According to Lee, "In 1991, private sector employers spent an estimated $43.2 billion providing approximately 36.8 million employees (31 percent of the total civilian labor force) with 1.2 billion hours of formal training and development," (cited in Leap & Crino, 1993, pp. 291–292). In the corporate world this huge expenditure is viewed as an investment in human resources. We contend that higher education needs to value faculty in a similar manner, though not necessarily at such great expense. Unlike U.S. businesses, which spend an amount equal to the total budgets of all the colleges and universities in the United States on professional training (Eurich, 1985, p. 6), colleges and universities budget little for faculty development. In 1994, the director of the American Association of Higher Education's Assessment Forum estimated that only one-third of U.S. colleges and universities had some kind of development program (Angelo, 1994, p. 3). We already can hear the skeptics about faculty development out there telling us, "Been there. Done that."

Overcoming Institutional Inertia

One reason for administrators' reluctance to put their faith in faculty development is that, in a climate of budget cuts, it is viewed as a luxury with no direct relationship to productivity. In his book, *Marginal Worth* (1996), Lionel Lewis concluded that productivity in academe cannot be measured by anything that goes on in the classroom. He argued that it is "difficult, if not impossible, to demonstrate effective teaching" (p. 154), so why invest in faculty development?

If we define effective teaching in quantitative terms as numbers of students' taught and graduated or in the "amount of student learning," we would agree with Lewis. However, we assert that it is indeed possible to improve the *quality* of teaching and learning. Moreover, we contend that this improvement in the quality of teaching through better teacher preparation, faculty development, and improved methods of evaluating teaching may in fact increase productivity, if studies in the business sector prove true in the academic setting.

Although we do not subscribe to the corporate model as being analogous to higher education, we find it interesting that studies from the business world suggest that "star performers" are eight times more productive than their counterparts in similar positions (Kelley & Caplan, 1993, p. 129). These "stars" are superior in terms of "taking initiative, networking, self-management, teamwork effectiveness, leadership, followership, perspective, show-and-tell, and organizational savvy" (p. 132). Our observations and interviews with the distinguished teachers who are the subjects of this book suggested to us that they are indeed extraordinarily more efficient in addressing the instructional needs of diverse students and groups than most professors.

While we may agree with Lewis that, based on what we know about curves of retention, students may not remember a great many facts they learned in college, we do believe that they learn *how* to learn, *what* to learn, and the *value* of learning. They may even continue to develop the multiple intelligences that Goleman (1995) defined as "character" through the example of the excellent teachers they encounter. Thus, we reject Lewis' conclusion that teaching is not a particularly productive activity, even though we agree that, until now, its quality has been hard to measure.

Faculty Development Failures

The literature shows that faculty development has not proved particularly effective, even when it is available. We believe that in addition to the claim by some administrators that development programs do not necessarily result in increased productivity, additional reasons why faculty development has not been seen as a key solution are that it has tended to follow educational fads, has lacked cohesion, and has been offered inconsistently.

Formal faculty development programs in academe began in the 1970s as a response to economic pressure for accountability (Total Quality Management, or TQM, and "performance technology"), a time when "institutional excellence" became a rallying cry (Leap & Crino, 1993, p. 256). This was when academic administrators began to "manage, rather than lead" (Blackburn & Lawrence, 1995, p. 241). With this leaning toward the corporate model, where staff development was firmly entrenched, attention turned to creating faculty development programs, especially those focusing on teaching effectiveness; however, they often fell short of expectations.

Our national survey of faculty development highlighted the spotty record of success of traditional faculty development programs (Baiocco & DeWaters, 1995). Unfortunately, the academy has had a history of "innovative" offerings that are, in our estimation, mere repackagings or recycled versions of basic effective teaching concepts. In fact, we fear that our problem-solving theory and strategies for excellent teaching may share the same fate and be reduced to jargon and gimmicks. The reason for this may be that academics have been looking for a quick fix, rather than long-term solutions, to a very complex set of problems.

Consider this scenario as an example: Organizing for their 10-year accreditation review, a faculty committee at a small college with limited development funds is looking over what the college has done in the past. In the files they find a relevant "white paper" nearly 15 years old. They also discover records of travel funding for faculty to attend conferences, a pot that has increased substantially. Let's see: here's a series of writing across the curriculum workshops in the early 1980s. Has that continued? No evidence. Aha! A teaching effectiveness program with good participation was offered for two years, but then disappeared in the mid-1980s. Here is a proposal for a faculty mentor system that was never funded. Nothing for three years, then an off-campus development day with an outside speaker five years ago. What about sabbaticals? Few to none during the 1980s, lean years for student enrollment—but there has been some improvement—now there are *eight* (for 100 faculty) a year!

Our research suggests that our faculty committee review presents a typical record of faculty development offerings on small college campuses (Baiocco & DeWaters, 1995). Faculty development in general has consisted of incidental, sporadic workshop presentations (Boice, 1992; Eble & McKeachie, 1985), occasional offerings of teaching effectiveness programs, travel and research funding, and sabbaticals (Baiocco & DeWaters, 1995; Boice, 1992). In fact, until Jarvis' book in 1991, no one had presented a comprehensive and systematic program of support for junior faculty (Boice, 1992, p. 9).

What about larger, well-funded universities? Surely they can boast about their support for professional development. Although many have teaching centers, newsletters, coordinators, curriculum development grants, and research grants, critics question whether they are reaching those who need the support most. Even those faculty who regularly attend conferences may not benefit over the long term, if research findings are correct. For example, Maryellen Weimer, editor of the journal *The Teaching Professor* and author of *Improving Your Classroom Teaching* (1993), equated the effects on college teaching of faculty attendance at conferences with "conversion" experiences. Admitting that research questions the value of faculty's attending such conferences, she stated that the effects usually wear off after a few months, and that faculty soon return to their "unreformed" classroom practices (Weimer, 1995).

The general consensus among faculty development researchers (and most faculty we know) is that traditional development programs have not resulted in permanent changes. The literature about the effectiveness of training programs in business suggests that this failure of development programs to produce long-term change is not unique to academe: "Typically, effectiveness [of training programs] is greatest on the last day of the program and falls to zero after a year" (Kelley & Caplan, 1993, p. 138).

To assess the faculty perceptions of the current status of faculty development programming nationwide, in the spring of 1994 we conducted our own survey of faculty development trends. (See Appendix A.) For respondents we targeted the presidents of the

American Association of University Professors (AAUP) chapters in 436 colleges and universities across the country. We assumed that as senior tenured faculty, their perceptions about faculty development programs would more closely reflect the views of faculty than those of academic officers. AAUP presidents from 140 schools reported on their institutions' faculty development programming and their perceptions of job satisfaction, training needs, budget allocations, and future priorities. (See Table 3-1 for major findings.)

The respondents reported that the vast majority of institutions in our study (71%) funded *at least three* of the following activities: travel, research, consultant-led workshops, faculty-led workshops, development personnel/mentors, and equipment/office space/supplies. Figure 3-1 presents details relating to development offerings available to individual faculty, as reported by our study respondents.

Only 14% of the respondents said that their institutions allotted office space for faculty development, and fewer than half had someone assigned to coordinate development programs—more often an administrator, not a faculty member. On the vast majority of campuses (83%), there were no formal evaluations of program offerings (Baiocco & DeWaters, 1995). These findings reveal a consistent lack of institutional commitment, and probably a corresponding lack of faculty motivation. As Angelo says, faculty "know well enough not to take short-term, unstructured, inexpert activities seriously" (1994, p. 5).

One of our most disturbing findings was how poorly prepared faculty were for using computer technology. The American univer-

TABLE 3-1   Faculty Development Programming at 140 Schools

	Yes	%	No	%
Is the program comprehensive?	98	71	40	29
Is the program ongoing?	106	77	2	1
Does it have an annual budget?	100	72	8	6
Are there offerings for groups?	56	41	82	59
Are there offerings for individuals?	107	78	31	22
Is office space allocated?	20	14	93	67
Is development staff assigned?	45	33	58	42

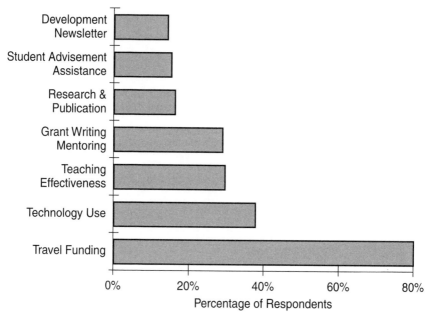

FIGURE 3-1   Development Offerings to Individual Faculty

Source: Reprinted with permission from *Academe: Bulletin of the AAUP, 81*(5), 38–39.

sity system was among the first to embrace computer networks for communication, yet fewer than half of the respondents in our study said that their colleges and universities had a "front seat" on the information superhighway. Only 47% of their institutions provided a campus computer network, though more (66%) reported that faculty had access to an external computer network (if they had their own computers). (See Table 3-2.) A more recent survey of presidents of independent colleges found that 74% of the responding institutions provided faculty with access to campus computer networks, and 92% provided access to connections with the Internet (Fennell, 1997). Even though these figures are encouraging, simply being "connected" does not assure that faculty are prepared to use the full power of the technology.

Other studies of trends in faculty development have reported fluctuations in support for faculty development programs. In fact, "by the early 1980s, almost a third of the faculty development programs operating in 1975-76 had closed, and more than half had

TABLE 3-2   Computer Technology and Faculty Development

	Now	%	Soon	%	Unavail.	%
Access to External Network	90	65	NA	NA	22	16
Campus Computer Network	64	46	NA	NA	48	35
Using Computer Assisted Instruction	66	48	4	3	23	17
Training for Using Computers in the Classroom	61	44	7	5	27	20
Training in Using Computer Networks for Research	50	36	9	7	37	27
Developing Computer Assisted Instruction Aids	30	22	15	11	42	30
Developing Multimedia Teaching Aids	29	21	20	14	35	25

suffered budget cuts" (Toombs, 1983, cited in Kalivoda, Sorrell, & Simpson, 1994, p. 257). Angelo asked why,

> when "many college teachers, especially novice ones, invest great amounts of time, on their own, trying to improve their courses and teaching"…do so few of them choose to become involved in organized campus efforts? And why does faculty development so often fail to achieve measurable success with those faculty? (1995, p. 3)

A coordinator of faculty development for eight years at an eastern state university gave an interesting answer. He reported that during that time, he had received only three faculty requests related to teaching effectiveness, despite his perception of his institution as primarily a teaching institution. A teaching effectiveness mentor program three years earlier that paired new faculty with "old-timers" had been "a miserable failure." He conjectured that faculty do not talk openly about the teaching process because "what it says is that the person doesn't know how to do it.… It takes a good deal of courage [to acknowledge problems with teaching], because of "the nudity that people feel with examining the teaching process." However, he did report some success with an instructional development discussion group that met weekly and was attended by 20 to 30 faculty, usually the same people, and "never those who were research 'superstars'."

To address these weaknesses, Angelo recommended the need for a paradigm shift from a model of faculty development as "additive" to one that is "transformational," from a focus on improving teaching to improving learning, from providing answers to helping define questions, from generic offerings to discipline-specific offerings, from individuals to communities, from extrinsic to intrinsic motivations, from short-term quantity to long-term quality. The old model has an "underlying assumption that by participating in a number of faculty development activities—regardless of their content or coherence—teachers will somehow improve" (1995, pp. 3–4). He added that the focus on the teacher, not the learning process, often leaves faculty feeling threatened when confronted by an outside consultant or expert who is going to "remediate" them (p. 6).

What is the future of faculty development? Our 1994 study identified faculty leaders' perceptions of future priorities for faculty development. Travel funding continued to be the first priority—reflecting, we think, the faculty's preference for discipline-specific development. However, we contend that funding support for faculty travel to conferences, the most common development support, may prove too expensive to survive in an era of budget cuts. In addition, highlighting a nationwide reawakening of interest in the faculty teaching role, faculty leaders in our study listed as the next priorities mentoring for teaching effectiveness, and assistance in using technology and developing materials. Training in the use of computer technology was both a significant current need and a future priority, according to respondents. Awareness of a recent educational thrust toward the faculty as "reflective practitioners" who use the classroom as an experimental laboratory for research on teaching and learning (Schön, 1983) was virtually nonexistent among respondents. A mere 1.5% said faculty teaching effectiveness programs were available to faculty teaching at the graduate level. The drive to publish continued to be alive and well on the campuses of our respondents, for they also cited the need for mentoring in research, publication, and grant writing as priorities for future faculty development (Baiocco & DeWaters, 1995, p. 39).

We have concluded that higher education institutions must increase efforts and offer a radically different faculty development program to ensure that faculty will understand the changing nature of the student population, education, and their respective disciplines. We believe that higher education faculty need major retraining and ongoing support in learning theory, cultural sensitivity, teaching effectiveness, multimedia and technology use, evaluation and assessment, field supervision, and classroom research. Moreover, that support must include administrative backing, which, as Eble and McKeachie reported, is predictive of program success (1985, p. 5)

No longer can colleges and universities be satisfied with periodic offerings of in-service training peripheral to the instructional process. In the current climate of cost cutting and demands on institutions to provide evidence of the value of institutional efforts, such traditional methods of promoting professional growth may prove too expensive and too ineffective to survive. We predict that the dramatic impact that demographics, globalism, cultural pluralism, individualization in instruction, and technology also are having on the learning environment will necessitate a radical reconceptualization and delivery of faculty development (Blackburn & Lawrence, 1995; Boice, 1992; Lucas, 1994; Nyquist, Abbott & Wulff, 1989).

The Apprenticeship: The Lack of Preparation for Teaching in Higher Education

Faculty skepticism about the effectiveness of faculty development initiatives often begins during their graduate years with inadequate programs to prepare them as graduate teaching assistants. Indeed, before the 1960s, the expectation among academics was that doctoral research was the only requirement for college faculty, and that research in one's discipline would naturally result in good teaching; hence, there was no further need for professional development (Kalivoda, Sorrell, & Simpson, 1994, p. 256). We believe this attitude still prevails within circles in higher education. In the remainder of this chapter, we will dramatize the current state of preparation of graduate teaching assistants (TAs) for their teaching role, illustrate the conditions confronting junior and senior faculty, and demonstrate how each of these relates to a flawed academic reward system.

Nyquist, Abbott, and Wulff predicted that half a million new professors will be needed by the year 2014, and that to "ignore the issues of TA preparation that have remained unanswered since 1930 will have serious consequences" (1989, pp. 8–9). Today, the lack of respect for the faculty teaching role begins in graduate schools, where future faculty are trained in content and research, but rarely in teaching methodology (Kalivoda, Sorrell, & Simpson, 1994). In 1989, only 25 percent of the institutions that used teaching assistants offered campuswide training programs, only half of all academic departments trained teaching assistants, and often that training consisted of a day-long or, at best, a week-long orientation. This was true despite the fact that at some institutions, the number of teaching assistants equaled the number of faculty (Seldin & Associates, 1990, pp. 210–211). (See Chapter 10 for an additional discussion of the current offerings for training graduate teaching assistants.)

Yet the teaching assistantship is not a venerable institution. At one point, an aspiring academic left college with a bachelor's degree or graduate school with a master's degree and became an instructor under the guidance of a senior faculty member. That rank of "instructor" is now nearly extinct, and there is no longer any training period at the entry level. Interviews with teaching assistants, faculty, and staff in teaching effectiveness centers reveal a shocking lack of consistent support for inexperienced teachers, as well as the underlying expectation that graduate students will develop teaching skills with minimal guidance (Seldin, 1990).

We suspect that this disdain for pedagogy is a remnant from bygone days when the only programs that prepared students in teaching methods (schools of education) were often perceived as offering "fluff," lacking in substance. We have to agree that to date, much of what is promoted through faculty development is a superficial bag of teaching tips without any underlying theory, even though there is a wealth of excellent research on learning and instruction. But departments in the university have a kind of pecking order of respectability, often based solely on the age of the discipline, and the field of education is a young upstart among them. This lack of credibility for educational research has had a profoundly negative impact on higher education pedagogy, which is, at the least, a decade behind the best practices in primary and secondary education. Whatever the causes of our failure to train graduate students in pedagogy, the effects are evident.

A strike by Yale teaching assistants, which resulted in their being recognized as a legitimate group of employees of the university, is likely to change the economic equation at research universities. The causes of the strike were greater than economic issues, however.

During the summer of 1995, a passionate dialogue was "overheard" on the teaching assistant forum of the electronic bulletin board of the American Association of University Professors (AAUP). Revealing the same consumer mentality as undergraduates, teaching assistants expressed outrage and disappointment at their universities' inadequate resources, space, and training to support their teaching role. Numerous messages highlighted the need for reform. Other more senior graduate students, who had apparently had several years of teaching experience, noted that the isolation of TAs left them without anyone to help them gain a perspective on the normal development of teaching competence. Without guidance, they cannot know that their current problems will often disappear as they mature as teachers.

Not all teaching assistants are provided so little support or are under so much stress. Member institutions in the National Council for Staff, Program, and Organizational Development (NCSPOD), for example, participate in a network that offers conferences, resources, research publications, and newsletters nationwide to teaching assistants and other faculty. Yet many graduate students endure hardships and lack of support because faculty see the assistantship as a rite of passage.

Junior Faculty: Baptism by Fire

As with the medieval apprenticeship system, upon completion of the doctorate, would-be faculty must complete another test of suitability for the profession: the first full-time position. In recent years, they have often become the "migrant workers of academe" (Horwitz, 1994, p. A6), passing several years as literal "journeymen" by accepting temporary positions or part-time posts at a number of colleges. If they do land permanent, tenure track positions, like medieval apprentices they have seven years to prove that they can perform as teachers, scholars, and members of their profession.

During the first six years of their employment, junior faculty undergo a ritual acculturation into academe. Under the best circumstances, the pre-tenure years are taxing; however, today's climate of budget cuts, research demands, diverse and critical students, and overworked colleagues has made matters worse. The fact that in many fields there are large numbers of doctoral replacements waiting for junior faculty to fail adds to this extraordinary recipe for stress. Tony Horwitz, writing for the *Wall Street Journal,* described this situation:

> Now, in hard times, schools must look elsewhere for cuts, usually punishing newcomers. They also are raising teaching loads, largely in response to public pressure. This creates contradictory pressures for young professors, whose advancement depends on published research rather than classroom skill. (1994, p. A1)

Furthermore, graduate students prepared at large, well-endowed universities may discover that their new campuses—with "unsophisticated student bodies, outdated equipment and limited funding for research"—are nothing like their alma maters (Horwitz, 1994, p. A6). Placed against the backdrop of these conditions, the academy's antiquated and negligent system of preparing faculty for their teaching responsibilities looks more than foolish, it looks cruel.

In his 1991 book, Donald Jarvis described the traditional notion of junior faculty development:

> For the most part, [it] has been a matter of institutions raising their standards and the junior professors doing their own developing as best they could. In the clear employers' market of the 1970s and 1980s, American institutions could select the best among many excellent candidates and give them each a full teaching load, a few administrative chores, and three to six years in which to produce significant publications. Most institutions put the burden almost entirely on the junior faculty members, and many schools discouraged cooperation among young recruits by hiring several to compete for each permanent position. If an untenured teacher performed any function inadequately, the responsible thing was simply to fire that person and hire someone else. (p. 2)

Jarvis then outlined the criteria, methods of evaluation, and reward systems for junior faculty development. He included programs for

improving teaching, research, and university service and concluded with a strong argument for changing the current system of
developing junior faculty.

Senior Faculty: Re-Lighting the Fire

We suspect that senior faculty are the most seriously neglected
group when it comes to faculty development. The following is an
example of what typically happens on many campuses when senior
faculty are invited to participate in professional development. A
group of professors was invited to attend a recent faculty development offering, which consisted of a consultant who lectured separately to administration, faculty, and staff. Unfortunately, the
consultant had been hired by college administrators without consultation from faculty as to what their wants or needs were.

During the time in which the consultant presented to the faculty,
they responded in two ways. After listening courteously, some faculty were receptive; many others expressed skepticism about how to
apply the topic based on their view that the proposal was simply another "warmed over" version of a previous trend. Adding to their
skepticism was the belief that the administration would not provide
ongoing funding to support their efforts. An outsider might view
this faculty reaction as "negative and resistant to change," whereas
faculty would contend that their responses were historically
grounded in past faculty development failures. Clearly, any initiative to reach most faculty, especially seniors, who lead busy professional lives and whose need for stimulation and renewal is often
overlooked, will have to overcome this disappointing record.

A Perverted Academic Reward System

As we have alluded to earlier, academe is not immune to external
economic forces. College and university professors in the United
States labor under not only an outmoded system of professional development, but also a warped system of professional rewards. A
1993 faculty survey conducted by the Carnegie Foundation found
that the primary interest of 63% of the professors surveyed was in
teaching, but that 75% felt compelled to conduct research to earn

tenure. In the last four years, the percentage of those who said their primary interest was teaching has dropped 8% (*CHE Almanac*, 1995, p. 33; Leatherman, 1990, p. A16).

Soderberg (1985) described the prevalent myth among faculty that research is more important work than teaching, an attitude into which graduate students are indoctrinated and noted,

> We *get released* from the dulling binds of merely teaching in order that we may marshal our higher resources for the hallowed halls of research.... Carried to its logical extreme, this system of rewards in the university conditions professors to behave as if they believe that the discovery of new knowledge, no matter how trivial, is preferable to the effective disseminating of knowledge, no matter how important. (p. 170)

This attitude not only hurts the faculty who focus their efforts on what the public believes is the central mission of colleges—to educate—but it also hurts students. An editorial in a daily metropolitan newspaper called attention to this problem. The editors noted: "The way to faculty stardom—and, not incidentally, the safety of tenure—may have very little to do with actually teaching anybody anything.... As a consequence, many undergraduates find themselves being taught by graduate students instead of the tenured faculty" ("Can't Professors Teach More?" 1995, p. C2).

The editorial used data from a 1991 survey by the Higher Education Research Institute at the University of California at Los Angeles to document "troubling results": Only 43.8% of undergraduates at public research universities were satisfied with their contact with faculty members. At private research universities, the percentage was higher—64.2%. At private four-year colleges with no big stress on research, 75.4% were satisfied. The editorial concluded, "The principal mission should be to inspire students to learn, to inspire them on a journey to knowledge. A school that can do that has a lot to brag about, whether its faculty publishes any papers or not" ("Can't Professors Teach More?" 1995, C2). But how does that school determine whom to brag about? And how does it spread the word?

That teaching is devalued by the current reward system is widely known (Boyer, 1990; Fairweather, 1993b; Lewis, 1996; Schwartz, 1992; Soderberg, 1985), and our society may suffer just as much from the failure of colleges and universities to honor and reward college, community, and professional service. Mooney reported,

> Institutions that expect their professors to conduct research might weight those three areas—in theory at least—like this: Teaching and scholarship would each count 40% and service would count 20%. In fact, junior professors at research universities are routinely told to forget about service if they want to achieve tenure and to distinguish themselves through scholarship....The time is right to provide better rewards for service activities. Universities and their faculties are increasingly being looked at as resources for helping society deal with lots of external problems. (1990, p. A16)

This is a matter which is getting increased attention nationwide and has been an impetus for "service learning." As with the focus of this book, the improvement of college teaching, rewards for service will certainly warrant further investigation.

Many researchers who have studied the comparative rewards for teaching, scholarship, and service in academe have pointed to several vexing problems. Fairweather, for example, challenged the common belief that teaching and research are mutually supportive:

> Unfortunately, the view...however accurate or inaccurate, has prevented a rational discussion about choices that faculty must make in how they allocate their time. This view also has allowed academic administrators and faculty to gloss over the manner in which faculty rewards emphasize the discreteness, not mutuality, of research and teaching. (1993b, p. 44)

He argued that if full-time faculty are teaching less than one-quarter of all undergraduate courses, the other 75% of the classes are not even exposed to the potential benefit of faculty engaged in exciting research. And, citing a "landmark" study by Ken Feldman (1987), Fairweather also questioned the notion that the best researchers are the best teachers: "Analysis answers the question...: the two are far from synonymous. The more time a faculty member spends on teaching, the less she or he spends on research and vice versa" (1993b, p. 44). Not everyone agrees with Fairweather. In fact, many researchers have found a slight positive correlation between the two (Bok, 1991);

nevertheless, there is a widespread belief that teaching excellence and scholarly publication are incompatible (Massey & Wilger, 1995).

Several studies have shown that outstanding teaching and time spent on teaching are not valued by the academy. In a survey of faculty who had won teaching awards (16% men and 18% women), no monetary reward was reported, and "outstanding teaching was not significantly related to promotion to the full professor level" (Tuckman, 1979, p. 169). Schwartz called teaching awards "exercises in public relations," (1992, p. 33), and Soderberg also suspected that sabbatical leaves, release time, and so on, were increasingly being granted (solely) on the basis of the recipient's intentions to publish (1985, p. 170).

But the shocking disdain reflected by academic institutions for a professor's devotion to teaching has its most serious impact in terms of salaries:

> The more time faculty spend on teaching, including hours in the classroom, the lower the pay. This relationship holds true for all types of institutions except for the percentage of time spent on teaching for faculty in liberal arts colleges. Conversely, the more time spent on research and the greater scholarly productivity, the greater the pay...These results support the view that teaching activity and productivity are at best neutral factors in pay, at worst negative predictors of pay.... If research and scholarship are valued more highly in promotion and tenure, taking time away from research to devote to teaching may adversely affect faculty careers. (Fairweather, 1993b, p. 46)

The following example of this perverted reward system on one campus is symbolic of the problem: One faculty leader whom we interviewed said that on his campus, outstanding scholarship is defined as "putting ink upon the pages of a refereed journal," and is rewarded by selection as a "University Professor," something akin to an endowed chair. The award included a pay raise of 10% added to base salary. Outstanding teaching awards, on the other hand, had been given only twice, and the practice was dropped as "too divisive." Award recipients had their names engraved on a plaque, which had since been lost.

This discrepancy in rewards for publication and teaching eats away at the self-respect of those faculty who commit their lives to students and the scholarship of teaching, and can create an atmosphere of self-loathing or resentment that carries over into the classroom. As head of the National Commission on Educating Undergraduates in the Research University, Ernest Boyer judged that there was a divided culture separating students from faculty, and that faculty success seemed to come only with separation from the students ("Can't Professors Teach More?" 1995, p. C2).

The causes of the perverted academic reward system include the status seeking of colleges and universities, the medieval apprenticeship system of faculty acculturation, and the current processes for evaluating faculty performance. Furthermore, a controversy currently exists as to whether there are effective means to evaluate teaching in higher education, with some researchers asserting that there are effective measures of evaluating teaching (Lowman, 1996; Ramsden, 1992; Seldin & Associates, 1990; Svinicki & Menges, 1996), and others disagreeing (Blackburn & Lawrence, 1995; Boice, 1992).

Most colleges and universities use a combination of peer reviews, administrative reviews, student ratings, self-evaluations, and portfolios to assess faculty performance for the purposes of renewal, promotion, and tenure. Although we acknowledge that current researchers are attempting to identify a means by which we can objectively assess teaching, we believe that (a) a lack of consensus regarding criteria for teaching excellence and (b) the complexity of identifying and controlling for all of the variables that influence student learning, are serious obstacles to valid assessments.

Setting aside the questionable means by which some faculty personnel committees assess scholarliness by counting publications ("indexing") (*CHE Almanac*, 1995; Mooney, 1991; Soderberg, 1985) and their common failure to recognize service other than administrative work, we have chosen to focus our attention on what we believe is the most egregious problem—our inability to define, beyond vague generalities, characteristics and behaviors of excellent teachers.

Problems in Assessing Teaching

The evaluation of teaching is rife with problems: inadequate methods, including over-reliance on student ratings; widespread beliefs that teaching is an art and that creativity cannot be measured; disproportional weighting of publication to the detriment of teaching; and nearly exclusive use of assessment for the purpose of personnel decisions, rather than for improving teaching.

Faculty report that they are regularly evaluated for teaching (97%), research (77%), and service (68%). A look at the kind of teaching evaluations they receive reveals that faculty are most frequently evaluated by students (91%), then by heads of departments (78%), and peers (49%). They are seldom reviewed by members of other departments (16%) and externally (7%) (*CHE Almanac,* 1995, p. 33). Even though teaching performance is the most frequently assessed aspect of the professional role, faculty are very dissatisfied with the current processes: 73% of faculty agreed with the statement that "At this institution, we need better ways to evaluate teaching performance" (*CHE Almanac,* 1995, p. 33). Why are faculty so dissatisfied, and why is teaching effectiveness so difficult to verify in colleges and universities? For answers, we focused on what happens during performance reviews for renewal, promotion, and tenure.

A major problem is that during personnel reviews, often only one source of information—student ratings or opinions—is given any weight in the evaluation of teaching because an extensive literature exists to support the reliability of this rating (*CHE Almanac,* 1995, p. 33; Soderberg, 1985, p. 169). Nevertheless, Sheridan (1990) recounted a catalog of "myths" held by faculty about high student ratings: that they accrue to popular teachers who make their courses easy, that students are incapable of assessing their own learning while it is in progress, and that presentation style has the most impact on ratings. And Cholakian described the reaction of some students when they learned about the effects of their evaluations on faculty: "So little understanding do they have of the impact their judgments might actually have on people's professional careers, that many students are horrified when they learn how it all works" (1994, p. 25). Thus student ratings continue to be controversial sources of evaluative data.

Despite the use of multiple measures during personnel reviews, a comment by the vice president for academic affairs at one university is representative: "We know we value teaching, but how do you measure creativity, and how does that reflect quality teaching?" (Leatherman, 1990, p. 16). Sheridan also described other myths which make faculty question the validity of measures of teaching effectiveness; the widely held view that peer reviews are inconsistent, unreliable, and inefficient; and finally, that teaching is an art and therefore too individualistic to be effectively evaluated (1990, pp. 171–72). We suspect that some of the reasons for faculty dissatisfaction include a distrust of the rigor of peer assessments, which are limited by the reviewers' knowledge that they may still have to work with the person under review after the evaluation.

As we have shown, although institutional mission statements and faculty leaders espouse teaching as their highest priority, reward systems in academe favor instead those who are successful in terms of the most easily documented criterion for faculty performance: scholarship as measured by publication. We believe that the desire for objectivity during performance reviews leads colleagues to seek external verification (for instance, through refereed journals and so on), and to largely avoid making distinctions regarding teaching effectiveness among their peers because of the lack of a model, fear of internal bias, and campus politics. The Carnegie study also found that many faculty agree with the following disturbing attitudes:

- The pressure to publish reduces the quality of teaching at this institution. (42%)
- In my department it is difficult for a person to achieve tenure if he or she does not publish. (75%)
- I frequently feel under pressure to do more research than I actually would like to do. (30%)
- Publications used for promotion decisions are just counted, not qualitatively evaluated. (45%) (*CHE Almanac,* 1995, p. 33)

Part of an explanation for the problem may be that the primary focus of the research activity on teaching and evaluation to date has been on the development of effective measures of teaching performance for the purpose of personnel decisions (summative evaluation). However, according to Gil (1987), these evaluations have had little effect on improving college instruction, which is the aim of our book. And, while significant strides have been made to categorize principles for good teaching practice (Chickering & Gamson, 1991), what appears to be lacking is a comprehensive theory of teaching that allows us to identify attributes of effective teaching and then to set goals and objectives for the improvement of performance. A review of the literature also reveals that there is no widely accepted theory of teaching excellence, although there are many teaching theories based on established cognitive, motivational, and social learning theories (Leatherman, 1990; Menges & Svinicki, 1991; Whitman & Weiss, 1982). In 1995, the dean of the University at Buffalo's Graduate School of Education wrote, "There is, indeed, nothing so practical as a good theory" (Petrie, 1995, p. 4). Indeed.

A Call for Reform

We agree that conditions mandate that we improve the quality of teaching, and though it would be foolish to think that we can do this at no expense, we must do so economically. Proposals to reduce sabbaticals and increase class sizes and teaching loads, as leaders in state governments have recently suggested (Massey & Wilger, 1995), are misguided because they assume that educational quality is not affected by these changes. Instead, we need to increase the effectiveness of instruction. By focusing on developing faculty, we provide "quality assurance." A partnership of administrators and faculty focused on developing faculty, particularly in the area of improving the quality of teaching, as opposed to "dumping" them, is far more proactive and optimistic.

We further agree with Petrie that there is nothing so generative of good theory as real, practical problems (1995, p. 4). It is clear that we have many of those. What seems desperately needed is a theory of teaching which will enable us to make distinctions about performance and a corresponding new system for preparing and developing teaching. This reform will not be easy, as one professor notes: "While a majority of the professors on campus may wish to change the reward system, 'all you need on the campus is a small number of elites in the status system to overcome the majority'" (Leatherman, 1990, p. 16).

It is also apparent that in order to accomplish this reform, teaching must be valued more highly. A report of the Carnegie Foundation for the Advancement of Teaching has called for an expanded definition of faculty scholarship that would include teaching and other activities. The report proposes that scholarship be defined as having four components: The discovery of new knowledge, the integration of knowledge, the application of knowledge, and teaching (Boyer, 1990).

Leatherman was cautiously optimistic about the possibility of implementing reforms, pointing out that professors create the faculty reward system, but that they are also "very responsive to act to what they perceive the will of the administrators to be" (1990, p. 17). Similarly, the public may take some hope from the creation of The National Commission on Educating Undergraduates in the Research University, which has "no power to impose anything on anybody, but should be valuable in highlighting issues and proposing answers" ("Can't Professors Teach More?" 1995, p. C2).

We believe that the current call for a return to teaching as the top priority in higher education cannot be answered without a theory of teaching excellence that is experience-based. Ideally, it would derive from research on the characteristics, scholarship, and practices of exemplary college teachers. This book is our answer to that call. Through interviews and observations, we will identify who they are, what they know, and what they do. Our analysis will include an examination of their character and their scholarship of teaching, and then test our hypothesis that teaching involves a complex set of problem-solving processes. Our goal is to demystify those creative processes and identify markers of excellent practice. The book will also propose a theory of teaching and a paradigm for developing new faculty and rejuvenating experienced faculty. The final chapters will point the direction to a new system for enhancing college teaching, an on-line mentoring program, the Collegiate Development Network, centered around a problem-based curriculum for college teaching.

4

Studies in Excellence

What better way to begin examining distinguished teaching than by observing the masters? To capture their distinctive traits and behaviors, we sought to locate professors in a variety of disciplines who had been identified by faculty leaders on their campuses as having received and, in their perception, *truly earned* an award for teaching excellence. Because we believed that the criterion of having won a teaching excellence award was insufficient by itself to identify distinguished teachers, we also incorporated the perception of a senior colleague who was elected to a leadership position (AAUP chapter president) as a second validity check. After we had identified our participants through a process described below, we interviewed them, collected their teaching philosophies or other statements they had made about teaching, and went to the home institutions of 10 award winners to observe their teaching.

We began our search for exemplary teachers with a related research project in which we interviewed presidents of chapters of the American Association of University Professors (AAUP) about the selection processes and awards for excellence in college teaching at selected New York State colleges and universities. Ultimately, our research included institutions in Delaware and Massachusetts as well. We hoped to: (a) shed light on the sometimes mysterious process of the selection of teaching award winners, (b) obtain the names of truly deserving teacher/scholars on their campuses who had received awards, and (c) collect peer perceptions of award winners. Then, through interviews with the distinguished teachers who were named by the AAUP presidents (see Appendix B for the teaching excellence survey), we began this study of why distinguished teachers are successful. Our research tested a theory of teaching excellence through an examination of the characteristics, the practices, and, in particular, the problem-solving strategies of faculty who had been identified for their distinguished teaching. We hypothesized that distinguished teachers effectively utilize a set of creative problem-solving behaviors that free students to eventually behave as independent learners.

We had selected AAUP presidents as our initial respondents because we knew that they would be tenured senior faculty who had been elected to leadership positions by their peers on each campus. Our experience with the AAUP, which often has a collective bargaining role on campuses, also suggested to us that AAUP presidents would be more likely to be well-informed about campus processes and politics and unafraid to speak to us honestly about their perceptions. Our research findings supported our assumptions, with the presidents having an average number of 21 years of experience in college teaching. We selected the 50 New York State campuses with active AAUP chapters because they reflected a diverse sample of higher education institutions and their geographical proximity made interviews convenient. Conducting our surveys by e-mail, mail, and telephone, we received responses from 30 subjects, for a response rate of 58%. The results of our "Presidents' Survey" are reported in Figures 4-1, 4-2 and 4-3. (See Appendix B for the teaching excellence survey and a list of participating institutions and respondents.)

After analyzing all the data, we took a closer look at the faculty satisfaction with selection of teaching award winners on the campuses we studied. Faculty satisfaction ratings of the existing selection processes were distributed on a normal curve. The most dissatisfied 34%, however, were most vocal. They claimed that campus politics were involved in the process, thus tainting the selection. Among the undesirable influences they cited were campaigning by individuals and chairpersons for the award, deans' paying back social debts to faculty, selections based on support for the president during a no-confidence vote, administrators selecting only those who were "palatable," favoritism, decisions designed to help a faculty member gain promotion, cronyism, and "old boy" networks. On campuses where these perceptions were held, the teaching

Frequency of Awards

- Three-quarters of the faculty presidents (23) surveyed reported that their schools had a teaching excellence award. This percentage was slightly higher than that reported by Menges (1996, p. 3). Surprisingly, nearly all of the research (AAUP Category I) and comprehensive institutions (AAUP Category IIA) reported that their universities offered teaching awards, yet only half of the general baccalaureate colleges (AAUP Category IIB) gave awards, despite their missions' focus on teaching/learning and undergraduate education.
- The odds of receiving an annual teaching award ranged from 1:50 to 1:125.

Cash Prizes

- The AAUP presidents reported that only a little more than half of their institutions awarded cash prizes, which they believed were usually under $1,000, and almost never added to the award-winner's annual salary. (In fact, we found that the presidents underestimated the number of awards that were accompanied by a cash prize, for the award winners told us in a separate survey that 74% had received cash awards for their teaching, but 65% of the awards were under $1,500, and the range was from no money to over $3,500).
- Only 3 of 20 (15%) institutions offered salary additions to base.

Selection Processes

- 63% award recipients were nominated by faculty, 27% by students. Students and faculty were more frequently involved in the nominating process than in the selection process, and faculty and administrators participated about equally in the selection decision. The most common means for selecting a winner was a faculty committee, sometimes with administrative members and/or past award winners.

FIGURE 4-1 **AAUP Presidents' Perceptions of Selection Processes and Awards for Excellence in College Teaching at Thirty Colleges and Universities in New York State, Delaware, and Massachusetts**

award was often described as a battleground for power disputes. We speculate that one of the primary reasons for the dissension is, as Menges found, a "tension between secrecy and openness" in the selection process appears to make it difficult to assess whether the results are valid (Svinicki & Menges, 1996, p. 4).

One faculty at a Category IIA institution said that "All such awards are evil and destructive to faculty morale." Another at a Category I university said that teaching awards should not be given at a research university, where winners are "not the strongest

The most common traits that the AAUP presidents ascribed to their award-winning peers, in order of frequency from most to least, were:

1. Work ethic and commitment (leadership, activity on campus, reputation, quality service, good campus citizenship, omnipresence)
2. Positive affect (enthusiastic, pleasant, personable, nice)
3. Excellent communication skills (listening to students, sensitivity to students)
4. Creativity in the classroom (student involvement in learning, addressing student problems)
5. Concern for students (caring, motherly, maintain open contact)
6. Intellect/knowledge (love of subject, inspiring, scholarship)
7. Demeanor toward students (engaging, maturity, patience)
8. Humanistic values
9. High standards, rigor
10. Positive evaluations (popularity with students)

Award winners' self-descriptions were similar to those their peers ascribed to them, except that they did not cite "work ethic."

FIGURE 4-2   Peer Perceptions of Award Winners' Characteristics on Selected Campuses in New York State, Delaware, and Massachusetts

professors." He noted that he would not consider it an honor to receive a teaching award.

Faculty split evenly in their perceptions of the fairness of the selection process on their campuses. In several cases, faculty were dissatisfied because they perceived the process as unfair in terms of its "closed" system for nominations, especially by excluding student input or self-nomination. Other questions about fairness derived from the appointment, rather than the election, of the faculty selection committee. One professor believed that when the selection is made by general vote of the students, the process is biased toward those who teach large classes. This suspicion of bias toward popular professors was also reported by Menges, who found that awards are especially open to criticism when students have a strong role in the selection process (Svinicki & Menges, 1996, p. 5).

Those who were most satisfied seemed to like the fact that on their campuses, faculty and students both participated in the nomination and selection processes. In summary, then, our findings supported those reported by Menges (1996), and we concur with his recommendation that academics must find better ways than teach-

Demographics of Award Winners

- The 30 award winners were evenly distributed among research universities (I), comprehensive universities (IIA), and general baccalaureate colleges (IIB).
- 60% were professors or distinguished teaching professors.
- The award winners were equally divided by gender.
- 63% were from the liberal arts (humanities and social sciences). Feldman reported a similar preponderance of humanities faculty among award winners (1996, p. 48).
- 20% were from science and technology disciplines.
- 17% were from professional fields.
- Winners were very experienced faculty, with an average of 23.5 years of college teaching.

Numbers of Awards

- Many of these faculty had received multiple awards; 43% had won 2 or more, with the average for the group being 1.9 per faculty.

Elected Campus Offices

- Award winners were elected an average of 3 times each for campus offices, such as Faculty Senate, department chairperson, and so on.
- Nearly 1/3 had been elected president of the Faculty Senate.

Teacher versus "Scholar"

Is it possible to be both an award-winning teacher and an award-winning scholar? (Based on the responses, we acknowledge that the question was too vague. The term "scholarliness" was interpreted in a variety of ways.)

- 92% responded that it was possible for a faculty to be both an award-winning teacher and award-winning scholar, but many of them qualified those responses.

FIGURE 4-3   **Survey of Faculty Teaching Award Winners on Selected Campuses in New York State, Delaware, and Massachusetts**

ing excellence awards to reward collaboration and to motivate faculty to improve their teaching.

Into the Classroom: Case Studies of Ten Award-Winning Teacher–Scholars

The following section presents case study descriptions of 10 award-winning college professors in action. We selected them (a sample of convenience) from among the names provided by the AAUP presidents, and went on-site to interview them and observe their teaching. Their class sizes ranged from laboratory sections of nine students to a lecture hall for 400 students with standing room only. Two of the 10 professors were female. They represented a traditional cross section of arts and sciences disciplines (economics, geography, history, biology, math, philosophy and English) and they taught at diverse kinds of institutions—three large public research universities, one private comprehensive university, and two small liberal arts colleges. Their teaching experience averaged 28 years, nearly five years more than faculty in our larger survey population.

Professor Charles Ebert (Professor E.), Geography
State University of New York–Albany

Professor E., Distinguished Teaching Professor at a large, public university, (AAUP Category I research) has been teaching 43 years. Born in Europe to American parents, he has a melodious voice tinged with a trace of accent. With his white hair, tall carriage, and graceful movements, he looks every bit the kindly professor. Still an active scholar, he has taken sabbaticals in Eastern Europe and Asia, as well as served as dean of undergraduate education and founder and chair of the Department of Geography.

"My main concern is that I am honest and fully devoted to my efforts as a teacher. I wish to be a catalyst in learning, not a mere conveyor of facts," he says. He believes he was selected for the distinguished teaching rank because of his preparedness, his punctuality, clarity of expression, good visual aids, sense of humor, and strict but fair policies. He first learned how to teach in the military and then in graduate school, where he was a teaching assistant and a teaching fellow. He says he has improved by working on his performance after reviewing evaluations. Dr. E. has also analyzed successful teaching for the purpose of teaching a graduate course, "The Art of Teaching."

We observed Dr. E. lecturing to a class of 200 students who were enrolled in a course called "The Ocean World" taking place in a large, tiered lecture hall at a state university one morning. The 50-minute lecture subject was beaches, or "coastal modification," which he had organized into three parts: lecture, film, lecture. Dr. E. arrived 10 minutes early, neatly dressed in sport coat and tie, talking with students as they arrived. Promptly at the start of the hour, he flashed the lights, put his notes/lecture outline on the overhead projector screen, and turned the lights down in the lecture hall and off in the front to signal students that class was about to begin. The students, mostly of traditional age, became attentive as he put on a body microphone and began reviewing the results of the first test. He gave students advice about how to do well on the test: "Read the book carefully, but certainly, attendance [was] the most important factor." He indicated that those who did not attend regularly (missing 35% of classes) had a failure rate of 22% as compared to those who did attend regularly (7% failure rate). He told them that if he did not present the material in a lecture, it would not be on the test. Then Dr. E. began to talk about how to study for the tests, suggesting that students break their study time into half-hour segments, then review. Gently, he said that was his "pearl of wisdom," but the rest was "up to them." Test three, he told them, would be more difficult.

After launching into a preview of the structure of the lecture, Dr. E. began to discuss the construction of breakwaters, using beautiful hand gestures to suggest the movement of the waves. Referring to the notes on the overhead, in the form of a handwritten outline with terms underlined, he proceeded to show a series of slides, using a light to point out key features of the beach photos.

After apparently detecting some talking in the large classroom, he stopped and reminded students that the material would be on their next test. Next Dr. E. showed a 1965 film, "The Beach," while making jokes here and there, such as "This is you on spring break," for a picture of children with a sand castle. Throughout the movie, he stood in front at the right, watching, and the class was quiet and attentive. At one point, he emphasized a distinction made in the film between longshore current and longshore drift, attempting to clear up misconceptions. As he gestured with his right hand, left hand in his pocket, he lectured with a clear, pleasant voice.

After the film, Dr. E. began presenting new material, "Life in the Ocean," warning the class that they must attend and that the material would be on the next test. Giving a variety of examples, he contrasted land and water environments. Using slides and lecturing again in the dark, Professor E. related the new material to a previous lecture, making the point that science and religion are complementary, "as I told you before."

Returning to his lecture outline and the overhead, Dr. E. pointed out that students should be taking notes. For each slide, his descriptions mirrored what was on the screen. For example, for a slide of beached whales he remarked, "They suffocate because they are being squeezed by their own weight." He brought in current discoveries and computer-generated photos of the surfaces of the moon, Mars, Venus, and the Earth.

Making a reference to an article in a local newspaper on the decrease in the amount of forest, Dr. E. cleared up a misconception: "There is *more* forest than before, but it has changed." He defined the terms "monoculture" and contrasted it with "diverse culture." As he lectured, his hands now in his pockets, he drifted comfortably around the front of the auditorium.

Finally, just as the class was about to end, he reminded students to know what the terms meant, not simply memorize a definition, by giving them a humorous example to help them. For the term "omnivore" he said, "Bears eat berries, but can also eat your hunting dog!" Giving students a preview of the next lecture, he twice described photosynthesis as a "miracle" and referred them to a textbook figure on a specific page. Following the class, he remained to answer questions and chat with the students as they filed out.

Overall, Dr. E.'s class was a model of careful organization. His consistent attention to students' learning needs and study guidance mark him as a very experienced teacher who prods students without nagging them or belittling them. He was friendly and approachable, yet every bit in control of the learning environment. His musical voice made his lectures interesting, even in the dark. He reported that he changes his teaching plan on an ongoing basis to eliminate unsuccessful aspects, but stressed that change should be purposeful. To determine whether his teaching is successful, he said that he monitors students' facial expressions, background noise in large classes, student attendance, and students leaving a lecture—"I know when my lecture was not up to my expectations or when it was a hit."

Dr. E. provided us with his version of what "good teaching" is in a thoughtful essay. In it he quoted Ralph Waldo Emerson: "The man who can make hard things easy is an educator." According to him, "To make hard things easier may be a very significant element of good teaching; however, one should immediately ask whether it is possible to learn how to become a good teacher." Professor E. believes that certain aspects of good teaching can be learned, yet many elements of good teaching are "more ethereal and cannot be 'learned,' although they may evolve with experience, maturity, and wisdom."

He disapproves of teachers who "fail to hone their intellectual blade, fail to prepare thoroughly for each class, and who stride into battle with a dull sword!" Dr. E. also explained that preparation extends beyond content to include the careful attention that must be paid to visual and technical aids, tables and graphs. He asked, "How many times have we been frustrated by overly detailed tables which were unreadable beyond the third row of an auditorium?"

Another element of good teaching, and one that Professor E. feels can be acquired is "effective vocal control." Dr. E., who has a distinctive voice, describes the effective voice as being one that should be "directed like a beam of light, aimed at the audience and searching out the attentive listener." In addition, he said, "A controlled amount of pacing, and supporting hand and body motions, will maintain that attention."

The question of what skills can or cannot be acquired is one that Dr. E. again addressed by asking the question, "How can one train an instructor to genuinely like students, to enjoy teaching, to share feelings, and to be sensitive to the moods and reactions of the hundreds of young persons who depend on the total quality of the teaching effort?" He suggested that a good teacher must be fully aware of the "tremendous responsibility he or she accepts when entering the profession."

Professor Clyde Herreid (Professor C.), Biology
State University of New York–Buffalo

Professor C., a Distinguished Teaching Professor at a large research university, has taught 35 years and is also the director of the Office of Teaching Effectiveness and the academic director of the Honors Program at the university. Dr. C. said that his background as a magician and actor in high school provided the model for his theatrical style, which "fits his personality." Learned through observations and analyses of excellent teachers in graduate school, but not through formal instruction, Dr. C. believes that tempo is important. More recently, in the last decade, he has changed his emphasis to group interactions and cooperative work: "think–pair–share." His research in biology has taken him on sabbaticals to Alaska, India, Panama, Africa, New Zealand, Indonesia, and, most recently, Mexico.

On one March morning, Dr. C. greeted and chatted with students briefly before he promptly began his lecture on "The O_2 Revolution" before a class of 400 students in an evolutionary biology course at the state university. He began by asking the students to participate in an experiment. Directing them to stand up and hold their breath as long as they could, then to sit down when they took a breath, he illustrated the main point of the lesson: "We need oxygen to breathe." (This was also a neat way of getting everyone to pay attention and be quiet.) When two males ended up competing in the breath-holding contest, he made a joke about how males typically make this into a contest, then gestured to quiet the students as they laughed.

With a neatly trimmed beard, and professionally dressed in a coat and tie, Professor C. placed his handwritten notes on the overhead and began the lecture with a question: "How did oxygen impact evolution?" Reminding students that he had given them a short version of the answer in a flow chart in the previous lecture, he said he would be reviewing and expanding on what he had given them before. He referred them to a previous handout, and students dutifully retrieved it. Using a chart, which he had updated based on new scientific evidence, he began to describe the theories of the origin of life. Latecomers arrived to find the seats taken in the large hall, so they sat on the steps while he continued. As he lectured, we found ourselves fascinated by the topic, continually attracted to what he was saying and distracted from our observation of his teaching.

As Professor C. moved up the steps into the aisles of the auditorium, he described processes and theories of the oxygen revolution, pointing out areas he was purposely setting aside. He drew on his chart using different colored markers to help students understand the significant material. During the class, he developed a raspy throat, so considerately removed his body mike to clear his throat. As he moved around the front of the auditorium, he used elegant hand gestures and summary statements to sustain attention.

Switching to a new topic, "The Evolution of Protista," he used a visual aid transparency to show the process, covering up all but the information that he was explaining, and gradually revealing new features. Referring to new discoveries within the last few months, he asked a rhetorical question and then explored several solutions, all the time moving up the steps of the auditorium and among the students. Repeating important distinctions and facts, Dr. C. presented two competing hypotheses about the evolution of protista. Questioning the students while he pointed to a slide, Dr. C. led students along a line of reasoning. Using an anecdote of his own student experience, he told a story of how his professor had ridiculed the theory he had just presented, even though he had thought it was interesting. Walking around the front of the hall, he then presented an alternative theory, asking questions of students and concluding, "Is this bizarre, or what?"

Beginning yet another review, Professor C. turned to the question of the evolution of plants, or the development of chloroplasts. Asking rhetorically "What evidence is there for this theory?", he proceeded to use overhead transparencies to begin another line of reasoning. A steady, even pace with no verbal pausing characterized his lecture style. When a student asked a question, he repeated it for all to hear, said it was a good question, and then led the class to the answer by giving them information and asking, "Remember?" Using wonderful, broad hand gestures, he asked students to recall definitions, which they repeated aloud. Again turning to the overhead, he told students what they did not need to know, used the terms and definitions again, and ended with an experiment to show evidence. He underlined the conclusions of the experiment in red marker on the screen.

Beginning his next topic with a rhetorical question, Professor C. moved on, again blocking off part of the screen while he was talking so students focused on him and then the subject as he uncovered the screen. He repeated, "Is this bizarre?" and "Pay attention!" His conclusion of the topic and the entire lecture was to lead students to understand that the first theory, which had formerly been ridiculed, was now widely accepted. After class, 10 students waited in line to speak with him. When they asked him for clarification, he leaned forward, focusing attention directly on specific students.

A two-hour class in lab instruction for 20 teaching assistants for the "Evolutionary Biology" lab sections provided our second observation of Dr. C.'s teaching. The class was held in a biology laboratory, with the TAs sitting in rows on lab stools at dissecting tables. They included graduate and talented undergraduate students who worked together in pairs of experienced and inexperienced assistants. The class was loud and chatty before Dr. C. entered. He had loosened his tie and removed his jacket for this afternoon class, setting a more informal tone than in the previous morning lecture.

Distributing handouts for the student teaching assistants and a special one for us on the apprenticeship system we were observing, he began by asking the class to vote on the success of their previous lab session. "How many rate it a B? An A?" For those rating theirs less successful, he asked why. This began a problem-solving session in which the TAs identified problems, shared solutions, or looked to Professor C. for guidance. Some of the problems that were raised were:

1. Not enough content material for the lecture, and the specimens were old and hard to see. Professor C. called on someone else about what to do, and a student gave good advice.
2. Inadequate lab equipment. Dr. C. suggested that the TA bring it to his attention, but that seemed inadequate, so Dr. C. suggested a petition. Nodding, the student replied, "Okay, I'll draft it."
3. Students didn't understand the lecture handout. Another TA offered a solution of writing explanations on the overhead projector.
4. Students were not prepared for their oral presentations. Dr. C. discussed the cause of the problem—fear of public speaking— and gave this advice: "Give students little, safe experiences first."
5. The specimens, hissing beetles, did not always hiss as expected when touched. Professor C. responded, "Oh, well!" (Obviously, there was no solution to that problem.)

Calling TAs by their names and moving around the lab rows, Dr. C. asked for additional negative experiences in the previous lab. Like a maestro, he called on one TA then another, asking them to identify problems and suggest solutions, and explaining. The pace was intense as he explored the litany of problems the students posed. During the discussion, several students in the class mentioned the electronic listserve that had been set up for them to discuss course concerns, and two students who were not yet on-line were razzed. They blushed. Without Professor C.'s having said a word, pressure was exerted on those students to "get with the program"—a very effective use of peer pressure.

Then a TA in the class questioned whether it was wise to offer extra credit options for students. Dr. C. referred the class to an article on teaching that contained an extra credit experiment. His conclusion: "It's worth a try, but you have to be equitable." This was a natural segue into Dr. C.'s description of a model to improve students' discipline and study habits, one in which they turn in their work as they enter the class; while one TA takes the homework at the door, the other checks to see that it is completely done. If it is completely done, the student gets five points each class. If partially done, the student gets nothing: "Nada. Yes, Dr. C. is cruel," he told them. "But this is the way to handle the workload. The assignments must be done in their handwriting to discourage copying. Notes should be fleshed out, not just the outline. Record the grade in your gradebook/spreadsheet. This should take only 30 seconds per student, and you'll get better at it as you gain experience." He said, "The first week, be tolerant, but say, 'Next week, improve.'" He explained the grading system: 700 points in the course, 725 with extra credit, and advised the TAs what to look for in student responses. "There are many ways to cheat," he concluded, "but the value derived is worth the slop in the system." Then he reviewed the whole procedure again. After one TA reported he would have difficulty implementing the procedure because he had no teaching partner, another student volunteered to assist him, which suggested that a real community of learners existed among these lab assistants.

Next the class discussed how to grade oral presentations. One student offered advice: "Do it immediately, but pencil in the grade." Dr. C. suggested providing a peer evaluation and a TA evaluation for each student, then averaging the grades. The subject of grades led Dr. C. to a discussion of how to grade student lab groups. Unhesitatingly, he advised, "10 points for the group grade, 5 points for the peer grade, 10 points for the individual grade."

Again, Dr. C. asked for questions. The logistics of who would be assigned to proctor the next exam were discussed, and then Dr. C. answered the question of how to deal with religious zealots, as the exam was scheduled for Good Friday: He advised his students, "Do not announce this policy, but *say* to anyone who complains, 'No religion prohibits this; there are no make up exams'; and, 'It's been on the syllabus from Day One.' If students in the course still object," he recommended, "tell them to write a letter, stating that they did not take the exam for religious reasons. The grade will not be counted." He advised his lab assistants not to tell students that in advance or they would not study. Before taking a break for five minutes for a pizza party (paid for by Dr. C.) to celebrate birthdays, he asked TAs each to give him one essay question and one short discussion question for the test.

Promptly after the five-minute break, class began again with a TA demonstrating the next lab lecture using overheads and handouts, and making suggestions about timing and pacing. The student distributed aids and transparencies for the other lab assistants, and Dr. C. interjected to explain a point. The student, an undergraduate, had an excellent delivery. He made suggestions about how to group students by fours, saying he had tested that method the week before. Other students suggested pairs, and he concluded with a suggestion on the best choice of equipment for the dissection. The class ended with students chatting and joking as they left.

In our interview with him, Dr. C. reported that his self-image is "vital" to his role as a teacher. For 30 years he has listed his profession as "not professor, not researcher, not college professor—but teacher." He believes that his most distinctive teaching methods are his lecturing skills, along with active learning (cooperative learning and case studies). He reported that in addition to these methods, he "experiments a lot," using small group learning with many variations—group tests, group projects, and presentations—activities that he believes are very unusual in science. His expertise in teaching has made him a frequent presenter at faculty development workshops, and he is the author of many papers and three books in the fields of physiology, ecology, anatomy, behavior, and education.

Professor John S. Pipkin (Professor P.), Geography
State University of New York–Albany

Professor P. is an associate professor of geography and planning at a large state university. In addition to his undergraduate teaching load, he serves as dean of undergraduate studies. He has been teaching at the college level for approximately 20 years.

Dr. P. is the winner of two teaching awards: the university President's Award for Excellence in Teaching, and the statewide Chancellor's Award for Excellence in Teaching. He reports having held several leadership roles on campus such as department chair, as well as several terms in the University Senate. He believes that it is "absolutely" possible to be both an award-winning teacher and scholar.

We observed Dr. P. teach a morning class of approximately 180 undergraduate students. The class was a 100-level course in economics (specifically dealing with trade, manufacturing, and so on) taught in a large lecture hall.

Professor P. arrived 15 minutes early for the class. He was neatly dressed in a suit, but removed his jacket prior to class. He walked about the hall placing neatly prepared handouts at the end of each row. As he did this he stopped and talked casually with students who were early. After distributing the handouts he focused the overhead (which was neatly typed and easy to see from the back of the hall), reviewed his notes, and, finding a mistake, corrected the overhead.

As class began, he clipped on a microphone and announced that exams had been graded and scores posted. He said that he would post an answer key as soon as a few late exams were completed. He also announced that besides regular office hours, he would have additional ones if there was a need. He took time to write on the chalkboard "Yes, It's A. L." A student in the class told us that "A. L." was "Active Learning," something that each student is required to do approximately every other class. They are given 10 minutes at the end of class to submit a short summary of what's been going on in class and in the reading. They can also ask for clarification of a point or comment on a test. If they haven't done this prior to class, they can use the 10 minutes to do so. After reading the summaries, Professor P. reported that he has a better "read" on any problems or misconceptions the students have and addresses them in the next class.

Dr. P.'s method of presenting was primarily lecture. He used prepared overheads, but also supplemented them by writing, highlighting, and drawing pictures on them and the board. He also referred to the text frequently (citing the page number where the information could be found). The day we observed, he placed on the overhead an outline of topics to be covered during the class and returned to it as each new section was introduced. He labeled everything and drew models and pictures to clarify every term or concept covered.

The material he was teaching was incredibly dry, but he did a fine job of keeping a good pace and using personal stories to clarify concepts. Even though students were constantly entering class late (up to 45 minutes late), getting up, leaving or returning, and others were sleeping or talking, Dr. P. maintained a rhythm. He used a very smooth, calm, flowing speech pattern, moved about the front of the class consistently, and made eye contact with the students. He frequently interjected humor to emphasize a point.

Dr. P. was very well-prepared, knowledgeable, and comfortable as a presenter (thus putting others at ease). His sincere interest in making the material as clear as possible for the students was most evident. After class he remarked with humor about the students' energy levels, demonstrating his awareness of their condition on the first day back to class after Thanksgiving break.

Professor James L. Ragonnet (Professor R.), English
Springfield College, Springfield, Massachusetts

Dr. R., a professor of English at a small, private Category IIB college, is the winner of a Sears & Roebuck Teaching Excellence and Campus Leadership Award and a meritorious military service award for teaching and writing. He has been teaching English grammar and usage and various courses in American literature for over 25 years. Prior to teaching here, he taught technical writing to fellow officers in the military. Now he maintains a writing consulting business, teaches learning strategies to elementary school and junior high school students privately, and does creative writing.

Dr. R. was aptly characterized by the student newspaper when they superimposed his head on the photograph of Robin Williams as the teacher in *Dead Poets' Society* following his receipt of the teaching excellence award. He told us that his sole purpose on campus is to teach; this is where he puts all of his energy, talent, and humor. Witty, intense, and articulate, he poses a "boyish" figure and walks the fine line between formality and informality, taking risks to shake students out of complacency. He dresses in a coat and tie, with a military sense of neatness and a classic sense of style. Blonde and youthful, he moves athletically around the room or conducts intimate discussions while seated in his seminar classes.

We observed Dr. R. on two separate occasions teaching four different classes. The classes ranged from an introductory grammar and usage course required of all education majors to a senior seminar on Walt Whitman. Typically, he arrived early and chatted with the students as they arrived. On this first observation, knowing that observers would be present he had instructed the class to warmly welcome us by holding up handmade signs and a chorus of "Welcome!" on cue. Using a questioning technique for review, he sensed that some students were unclear on a few issues covered in a previous class so he dropped the immediate activity and provided review for those who were "signaling."

Dr. R. took away the mystery of the upcoming test by giving a sample test for homework and reviewing it in class. It was very dry material, yet *all* of the students were contributing. At one point each student in the class was providing answers to the quiz. Moving up and down the rows in sequence, Dr. R. accidentally skipped a student, who immediately raised his hand, and said, "Hey, Dr. R., I didn't get to go! You skipped me!"

While Dr. R. was very flexible during the 50-minute class, he had a very definite agenda, which included preparing them for the upcoming test by being sure that they truly understood the material. He drew a set of boxes on the board that he apparently had used in some earlier analogy. Always referring to material covered previously, he was determined that each student demonstrate his or her current level of knowledge by responding in class. He reinforced student responses, whether they were completely accurate or mere approximations, in a positive and redirective manner. If the answer was offbase, he reshaped the response to the correct one by having the student locate the problem in the response and then helping him or her find the solution logically.

Dr. R. used a great deal of humor through stories about himself or mythical cousins, all the while maintaining a respectful manner; he frequently alternated between using students' first names and calling them "Miss" or "Mister" and the last name. Professor R. was enthusiastic when the students had success. Physically emphatic while in front of the class, he did not appear to let ego enter into his teaching. It was apparent to us that the students came first, and they knew it.

A second set of observations took place in three 75-minute classes, the first of which included approximately 50 traditional-age students in a standard classroom. Dr. R. was presenting William Faulkner's story "Barn Burning" to a 200-level American literature class. Initially, he held a monologue, giving background information about the times to set the stage for the story, displaying a wide range of knowledge, giving the comprehensive insight into the story for it to be meaningful to students. Throughout the class he used analogies—for example, to compare and contrast authors' writing styles, or the antebellum South and Bosnia. Primarily lecturing, he told stories about the authors' lives and how their lives were affected by their ancestry, then drew diagrams on the board. When he attempted to draw the students into dialogue, it was clear that many had not read the assignment. It was almost as though they were waiting to be "spoon fed" the material. Undismayed by this lack of enthusiasm, he summarized the story, and when he made specific references to points in the story, the students began to take notes. Dr. R. told us later that a teacher's "fact of life" is that not all classes will rate "five stars."

In contrast, the following 75-minute class of approximately 20 freshmen was active and the students were prepared. The classroom was arranged in a semicircle as they began. The topic was D. H. Lawrence's short story, "The Blind Man." Remaining seated during the entire class, Dr. R. read a passage and then related the story to World War I and trench warfare. He encouraged students to offer insight and reinforced any response with phrases like, "Interesting insight; those points make sense." He often asked one student to expand on an idea presented by another student. Frequently, the students began discussing with one another, and he sat back and let them "take the wheel."

The last class we observed was a senior seminar of approximately 12 students; this also was organized in a semicircle. The topic was Whitman's elegy, "When Lilacs Last in the Dooryard Bloom'd." This class provided evidence of Dr. R.'s awareness of student development. His expectations were that the students would lead the discussion after minimal direction from him. He gave some background about Whitman's deep admiration for Lincoln and how his death affected the poet. He then asked the class to make their own analogy about a death that affected them with the same intensity, prodding them to consider how events can shape one's life and writing.

Dr. R. is so in tune with his teaching that you can almost feel the "radar" probing while he's with a class. From the moment he walks into the class, a focus is evident. Before this class, he told us he had done his homework in preparation (even though he has taught this course for years). He reported that he always reads to find new angles or new bits of information that will offer the students more, and at its conclusion, he evaluates each class to decide if it was a "great class" and why. He knows every student by name and says he feels responsible to each student. Although teaching is very important to Dr. R., when he finds himself taking things too seriously he says he stops and listens. Then he "hears the panpipes in the distance and views the satyrs leering and laughing at [him] from their wild places."

Dr. R. uses the Socratic method when teaching, as he believes that "dialogue is the key." He says that he "brings humor in the front door": "When the ancient Greeks ordained that Dionysius (the god of wine and revelry) and Apollo (the god of reason) share the great temple at Delphi, they knew what they were doing."

Professor R. learned to teach from those who taught him to question: "To be on a quest is to become an asker of questions." He also learned to teach from looking at his own mistakes. He told us the story of how, when learning from his brother to drive, he learned to put the car in reverse and rock back and forth when stuck in the snow. By knowing how to back up (to see the past), he has learned to go forward (to see the future). He said that he asks his students to help him become a better teacher, and he listens.

Another factor that has profoundly shaped Dr. R.'s teaching is his study of Buddhism:

> My students and I are buddhas. *Buddh* in Sanscrit means to wake up, to become awake. You cannot learn unless you're awake! Learning means having "beginner's mind," the opposite of knowing that you're right. If you think you're right, you don't ask questions and you don't listen to what others teach you. I teach my students to question, to withhold judgments, to learn from every situation, to become possibilists—buddhas—questioners.

Professor R. says that his teaching differs from others' in that he doesn't lecture in the traditional sense. He never teaches a specific subject; instead, he teaches "universal wisdom—using a particular subject." Dr. R. told us that he shares his life with his students, doesn't stress answers. He "demands, in the most tender way, more than the students think they can give." He shifts the spotlight in class from himself to the students by redirecting questions back to them and guiding them toward answers.

Professor Marilynn P. Fleckenstein (Professor F.), Philosophy
Niagara University, Niagara Falls, New York

Dr. F., an associate professor of philosophy at a private comprehensive university, teaches both graduate and undergraduate core courses, primarily in the area of ethics. She is innovative in her classroom and also in the university as a whole, where she has had faculty leadership roles and now spends half of her time administering a service learning grant-funded program throughout the university. As a result, she has two campus offices. When she was a full-time faculty member, she taught eight or nine different courses, customarily four per semester (with three different preparations).

Professor F. comes from a family of educators: Her father was a philosophy teacher; her mother is a teacher; her sister, a principal. She majored in biology as an undergraduate, but models her teaching after one of her theology professors, a priest whose teaching style was "charismatic and energetic." She said he had the ability to make contemporary theologians understandable and he inspired her to read texts in the original German. Another role model, a nun, had a calm, methodical style which she greatly admired as well.

Dr. F. defines "scholarliness" in the broad sense of the term, not simply as publication, and she fully believes that one person can be outstanding in both teaching and scholarship. However, Dr. F. reported that her primary focus as a professional has been teaching, a decision that she believes was in part a response to her being the mother of five during most of her 29 years of teaching. When we interviewed her, her youngest child was a senior in high school, so she had been "freed" to pursue more of her scholarly interests. She said that previously she was turned down for a promotion to full professor by the university president just prior to her winning the campus teaching excellence award. Always active in campus life, Dr. F. planned to serve on the negotiating team of her AAUP chapter, which was attempting to include in their contract the process for selecting the distinguished teachers.

Dr. F. described the events that led to her current position as coordinator of service learning at the university. About 10 years earlier, she noticed that her philosophy students were apathetic and were "not asking the right questions" in class. At the same time, she served on a university committee to award scholarships to students who were active in the community. With the additional impetus of the Catholic Worker Movement, she began to believe that service learning, incorporating community service into course requirements, was a solution to student apathy. She first initiated the curriculum component in her MBA classes in business ethics. Whereas previously the discipline had seemed "far removed" from the real world for her students, Dr. F. saw "incredible results" from her experiment. Two engineers taught electricity to students in the public schools, a banker set up computer systems and trained staff at a child and family service agency. Dr. F. said that placements like these caused discussion in class to turn to questions of justice. When we interviewed her, Dr. F. coordinated a program that included nine courses requiring some community service.

Another innovation Dr. F. was contemplating in her curriculum was setting up "everything that a student needs in a course" on computer disks. In a campus development workshop, she learned about a software project designed by a faculty member at a Western university. She was investigating a means to obtain the software inexpensively so as to begin offering her classes the same course resources.

Dr. F. makes extensive use of computers in her work and planned to assist a professional organization to publish conference proceedings on a website. She reported that in her introductory level philosophy courses she uses video of the character Data in *Star Trek* to help define "the human person."

Professor F.'s class consisted of 15 MBA graduate students in a course called "Business Ethics." The class we observed was toward the end of the term. Dr. F.'s plan for the evening was to have students make presentations on their research or community service, then to focus on a case study of government regulation and business. Students were familiar with the process for approaching ethical questions and making ethical decisions, which she described as "a problem-solving process."

When we met her before class, she planned to select a specific case study from a number of handouts to use as a discussion motivator. After selecting one case, she began with a review of what was covered in the last class, followed by "housekeeping" time, in which she reviewed course requirements and similar details.

Dr. F. interacted casually with the students. She smiled and laughed with them, creating a relaxed atmosphere. She used phrases such as "I agree with you" or "I hear what you're saying," along with direct eye contact with the speaker and a posture that suggested sincerity. Numerous times she injected humorous comments. She carefully watched the class to determine who was participating, and then deliberately focused on those who had not contributed by directing statements or questions to them.

She used a Socratic method consistently, accepting student comments about a particular writer and giving an honest critique of what she referred to as "abysmal existing literature." When faced with no response to a question, she led the students back to former foundation information through nonthreatening means: "You remember this stuff from your earlier classes." Once she had given the assignment, she allowed the class to interact without interfering. Willing to relinquish control, she appeared comfortable in front of the class and patient while the students were talking, making eye contact with each.

When describing herself, Dr. F. always includes her role of teacher. Her teaching methods include the use of case studies, small group work, video, and incorporating service learning into her courses. Although she has never taken any formal education courses, but rather, learned to teach "by imitating others," Dr. F. believes that her teaching differs from others in that she has the ability to present difficult material well.

Professor D. Edward Hart (Professor H.), Biology
D'Youville College, Buffalo, New York

Dr. H. team teaches a gross anatomy class of 90 students which meets early in the morning at a small private Category IIB college. The class meets for two hours a week of "slide shows" in a large tiered lecture hall, and eight hours a week for lab. Dr. H. believes the lecture method, rather than the Socratic method or small-group discussion method, is best suited to the subject of anatomy. In his slide shows he uses color-coded slides packaged with his textbook, as well as slides prepared for him by a technician at the local university and by a student assistant. He is "thrilled" with the videomicroscope as a teaching tool because it enables him to project the dissection image he is observing under the microscope so he can point out precisely where he wants students to look. The subject for the class we observed was the root of the neck, the oral cavity, and, if he had sufficient time, skull material. The greatest difficulty students have with the subject, Dr. H. said, is understanding the 3-D relationships among the anatomical features they are observing. He explained that slides are 2-D, and skeletons have limited use because they can't be seen well in large classes. Professor H. said students also have difficulty understanding how muscles and other tissues attach to the bones to create levers and enable movement. The lever action is quite complex, he said, and students often fail to see beyond the "prime mover" to the host of other tissues involved.

This same class of 90 is then divided into two laboratory groups which have a set routine: The lab instructor does a pro-section, demonstrating how to do a specific dissection, and then the students work with cadavers in small groups to perform the same dissection. In the class we observed, Dr. H. was working to catch up to the syllabus because his slide projecting equipment was not available one class and, on another day, class was canceled due to snow. He has begun to get caught up by "chopping" some material and giving some lecture material in the lab sections.

The morning we observed his class, there was a lot of interaction between students before class. The slide lecture began when Professor H. entered the room a bit late, pushing a cart with copies of lecture outlines for the entire course on it. He arranged these on a table at the side, and then addressed the large class after chatting with students in the front row. He smiled, greeted the class, and asked them if they had enjoyed their holiday. Then he informed them that his colleague who team taught with him had undergone emergency surgery during the break. The class became hushed as he described the seriousness of the surgery and the prognosis for their teacher. He suggested sending cards and showing his colleague support. Then he circulated a class attendance sign-in list.

After setting up his slide carousel and joking about the equipment, Dr. H. told students where to begin, with their Lecture 20 notes on p. 2. He gave the students an overview of what they would learn that day: they would finish the anatomy of the neck and begin the oral cavity. Students took out their notebooks and turned to the appropriate outline. (Students said they had received the notes for this class a week earlier.) He darkened the room so that he and the slide screen were the only dimly lit area, and then he began lecturing from a set of slides on the topic of the anatomy of the neck. The slides were organized from general to particular, with a variety of views of cartilage, muscles, and nerves of the throat, the larynx, and the oral cavity.

With a warm, pleasant voice and a steady pace, Professor H. proceeded to name and locate important parts of the anatomy of the human neck. Using a laser pointer, he turned to the first slide. Dr. H. had explained to us before class that "Human Anatomy" is largely a vocabulary course. His primary teaching objective, which he does not share with students because he thinks they might slack off, is to teach them a way of learning gross anatomy, because they will have to relearn it again and again in their professional practices. Throughout his lecture, he used many descriptive analogies to help students visualize and remember the shapes and locations of specific body parts. For example, the krykoid cartilage was shaped "like a signet ring"; other parts were "bumps, like a pair of boots"; the uvula was "a tag-shaped structure" and "a little grape"; the pharyngeal opening was shaped "like a bow tie"; parathyroid glands were "sequins on the back of the bow-tie shaped thyroid"; "boot-like" cartilage was shaped "like a horn of plenty." When appropriate, Dr. H. reviewed the Latin etymology of the terms: *hypo* meant "below"; *isthmus* meant "a narrow band of land," *glossis* meant "tongue," and *os* meant "opening." Thus the *oros* was the ring around the mouth that allows us "to pucker up." He also used vivid language throughout; for example, he described some parts as "perching" on top of the cartilage, the arytenoids "pivoting" to open the glottis, and the lesser horns of the hyoid bone being "Dracula teeth." The ease with which he lectured, never referring to notes or stopping to recall the terms, indicated that he was an expert in the field. Throughout the presentation, the class was quiet and attentive, referring to their lecture outlines, while some took additional notes.

During the lecture, Dr. H. pointed out and explained key functions of certain anatomical parts by using his own body as a prop. His finger wiggling represented the vibrations of the uvula, and he demonstrated holding his nose and blowing to explain the auditory tube's function in pressure equalization: "popping his ears." To show the squeezing motion of the muscles during swallowing, Dr. H. used a vivid hand gesture, and he demonstrated palpating the hyoid bone by performing on his own throat. As he discussed the operation of the vocal folds, he pointed to the muscles on the slide to show them tightening, and he pitched his voice much higher to show the effect on the voice. This was a light, humorous touch that he reinforced by making an analogy between the vocal muscle's tightening and a musician's tightening a guitar string, thus raising the instrument's pitch.

Dr. H. announced they had concluded Lecture 20 on the neck and were moving to Lecture 21, the nose and mouth. Skipping to the second page to make up some of the lost class time, he had the class focus on the oral cavity. On the screen a large open mouth with tongue, teeth, and so on was displayed, and Dr. H. joked that it was either a portrait of Rush Limbaugh or Howard Stern, "as you prefer." Checking his watch, he determined that class time was up so he announced they would stop there but continue in the lab the next day.

After class we interviewed Professor H., focusing on some techniques he uses regularly. He discussed the importance of lab work in courses such as anatomy, which requires understanding of spacial relationships. He is resisting a proposal to reduce lab time and substitute computer media because he does not believe that virtual reality is good enough for students to learn the 3-D concepts. He reported that when students perform the dissections themselves and teach their peer groups, they learn the material better than if they were only passive members of the group. He believes that some kind of tacit learning occurs while students are performing the dissections. The physical act of operating on the specimen keeps students focused, he believes. One of the most time-consuming parts of his class preparation is trial runs of labs. He believes students become frustrated when lab experiments fail, so he tries to identify all the pitfalls and eliminate them prior to the labs. He said that students unfortunately do not have time to learn lab techniques in his courses, and that perhaps that should be a separate goal.

One of the major difficulties students have in learning anatomy is the large number of terms to be recalled. The course largely requires rote learning, and Dr. H. says that students typically become overwhelmed or "burned out" in the middle of the course. He has developed techniques and learning strategies to help students past this hurdle.

Dr. H. explained the sources of other instructional techniques he uses regularly. The printed lecture outlines and the procedure for organizing the human anatomy lab were learned from a faculty member in the medical school at the local state university where

Dr. H. took a course after learning he would be teaching gross anatomy for the first time. He had never had a course in human anatomy before. Professor H.'s extensive use of analogy (and *homology*, or similarity of structure) is a traditional technique, as is the use of mnemonics. ("PT's Love Sex; however, Can't Take Time" is an example of one he uses for students to recall the names of the carpal bones.) When teaching physiology, he uses flow diagrams and many visuals.

One of the learning techniques Professor H. shows students is how to use the anatomy atlas or manual to make copies of visuals, which then become the drawing board for muscles or nerves. He suggests that students make many copies and draw the anatomical features repeatedly so that the visual image replaces the huge descriptive definitions in their memories. He tells students not to purchase flash cards, but to make their own cards for maximum learning value. However, he warns that making flash cards is a time-consuming prospect that may not have equal benefits in terms of learning.

During labs Dr. H. monitors student learning and makes adjustments in lecture plans accordingly, as he sees where students are having difficulties. He believes that the informal environment enables students to feel comfortable asking questions, and it is there that he learns most of his students' names. Dr. H. tests frequently: four lab tests, three midterms, and a final that is 25% comprehensive, but based on the previous test questions. He anticipates that as many as 25% of the class will not get a grade of C or higher, and thus will have to repeat the course to remain in their major programs.

However, when a student who is doing poorly asks for help, Dr. H. told us that he is extremely generous with his time, often meeting for 15 to 20 minutes each with as many as 10 students after each test. For example, during one summer session when the course met four days a week, he worked every Friday, his free day, for four hours with one or more students. Often he uses an empty classroom or lab and has several students draw their understanding of key anatomical features or processes on the blackboard. This enables him to pinpoint where their misconceptions are and to correct them. Together the remedial group revises the original student's drawings. Dr. H. tries to teach students how to learn better by having them focus on positive achievements when they study rather than negative (what they haven't done). For example as a way of learning a disciplined approach to study, he instructs them to create check lists and a timetable with time allotted for loose ends. He urges them to take breaks when learning terms "to defer the anxiety." He said, "The mind practices 30 seconds residually when diverted from a task."

Most of his classes are homogeneous, with students of the same college experience and major. However, in the anatomy and physiology course (which he was not currently teaching) he often had students who were freshmen nursing majors and sophomores who were physical therapy or occupational therapy majors. To monitor the difficulty of this introductory-level course and assure that it was not overly demanding for the freshmen, he kept separate class averages for the two groups. He told us that he did not believe that the current instructors were monitoring this and, consequently, the freshmen were having difficulty. For other introductory courses in biology, which are smaller, Dr. H. makes use of essay exams and term papers to assess students' learning. With a group of students whose performance on the essays showed them to be weak writers, he wrote his own model essay answers to each test question, then gave them to the students and asked them to revise their own answers for a higher grade (averaged in). One technique Professor H. uses for his own encouragement is to keep a "good feelings" file with notes and letters from former students (because so many students experience difficulty in his courses).

A typical lab section in another course, "Human Anatomy and Physiology," meets for two hours a week. We observed Dr. H.'s work with a lab group of nine students who were instructed by other professors. He gave the group 20 minutes at the beginning of class to complete course evaluations, as required by the college. Then he asked the group whether they had started the nervous system. Only two out of nine had, so he opted to lecture to them for the first part of the session.

Students were seated on lab stools behind lab desks as they watched Professor H. explain the nervous system by using numerous models. He used etymology, analogy, and vivid diction, as he had in the anatomy class, to explain the location and function of parts of neurons. He demonstrated the videomicroscope to show students a nerve cell, but the equipment didn't work too well so he used a model of a neuron to explain key concepts. Throughout the lecture, Dr. H. referred students to appropriate sections of the lab manual. Again with a steady, slow pace, he used his body to illustrate anatomy—for example, a knee jerk for a reflex demonstration, and a toddler's waddle to show how muscle groups coordinate to produce complex actions like walking. Dr. H. made references to examples from life throughout. For example, he said that ice skaters and ballet dancers program their cerebellums so they can do complex things without thinking.

Dr. H. closed the class by advising students that their fourth lab practical exams would be the following week, and he told them to see him to gain entry to the laboratory so they could study and review. Then he gave the class time to examine the models or prepare, as they chose, for the exam. Two students chose to do a dissection, four talked and worked with models, two students studied the lab manuals alone, and one left the room. As they studied in their favorite ways, Dr. H. traveled among them responding to questions.

Overall, Professor H. has a friendly, low-key presentation style. His extraordinary ability to describe anatomical features and functions vividly, his use of gestures, and his knowledge of Latin etymology seem to be his greatest presentation strengths. He uses a variety of visual aids well and understands their limits. His class outlines and willingness to work with individual students outside of class make students aware that their professor is eager for them to learn. He has been the winner of a Sears & Roebuck Teaching Excellence and Campus Leadership award, and he has served two times as chair of the Division of Mathematics and Science.

Professor Georgia B. Pyrros (Professor G.), Mathematics
University of Delaware, Newark

Professor G. teaches mathematics at a large university and has won the student-selected campus teaching award twice and the outstanding advisor award once. She has also been nominated three times for the teaching award given by the College of Arts and Sciences during her 11 years of service. She regularly teaches calculus to large sections (100–180) of undergraduate students. Professor G. claims that "the will to put a tremendous amount of energy into teaching" is the primary ingredient behind her having been recognized for her excellent teaching. She also indicated that she tries to identify what is bothering students about their learning and then "show them the way out." For the discipline of math, Dr. G. said, professors have to be very sensitive with students who don't have the ability to picture relationships. She believes that language and math abilities go together, and she typically performs error analysis of a single class's work and then attempts to clarify those errors.

A native of Greece, Professor G. describes her typical class behavior as "Socratic"; she establishes a dialogue with students as she moves up and down the auditorium. Despite a warm, charming demeanor outside of class, she said that her classroom style is authoritarian and she expects absolute silence as she teaches. She described her teaching as "very intense work." Her European educational background was responsible for her teaching style, Dr. G. said. At her university, she was taught by "super professors" for whom "style and performance," the "art" of teaching, was important. Dr. G.'s non-native status gives her a unique perspective on American culture. She finds it interesting that the U.S. higher education system distinguishes between applied knowledge versus theoretical knowledge—between "teaching" and "education."

When we interviewed Dr. G., her teaching load at the university included 10 hours a week of class time as well as coordination duties: two courses in calculus, one hour of a women's study course, and one hour of a problem solving course. Dr. G. had been teaching more than 20 years, having first worked at a community college. When we observed her she was also developing a new course with the women's studies faculty entitled, "Women in Mathematics."

We observed one of Dr. G.'s three sections of calculus. The class was held in a midsized tiered lecture hall that seats approximately 250 students. Of the 120 students enrolled, only 36 were in attendance on this Good Friday. Neatly dressed in a dark suit, Professor G. was in the front of the hall five minutes prior to class and informally interacted with the students as they arrived. In preparation for the class, she had prepared two overhead projectors with blank transparencies on a roll (so students could roll back to information) to review for an upcoming test using first and second derivatives.

Professor G. constantly asked questions and entered into dialogue with students (or herself) in a problem-solving manner. She would ask a question, give the answer, and then ask "why" rhetorically, answer her own question, and then explain the answer. She did all this while working the problem on the overhead. The students, meanwhile, were working the same problem on their calculators. She continuously maintained a conversation while working the equation: "It's looking up (the curve). Who is looking up? Concave up, concave down?" She accepted a response from a student, complimented the answer, and then used it as a springboard to explain further.

During the class, Professor G. moved about the lecture hall, up the levels and right into the rows of students. When a student responded, "I don't know," she immediately responded, "Sure you do. I'll wait." She then initiated a conversation with the student as she walked him through the problem. She stayed right next to him and talked to him (almost as though having an intimate conversation) while also scanning the class. As she cruised through the rows, she looked for students who were on the right track. When she found someone, she complimented the person and asked him or her to draw a version of the solution on the overhead at the front of the class: "He's got a good point!" "She's absolutely right." "Could you sketch it for us?" All went willingly to the front of the class and presented their work. There appeared to be no fear of being incorrect. Next Dr. G. reviewed a sample test question from a previous test and went through each possible answer, discussing why it was either correct or incorrect and acknowledging that many of the problems were confusing.

During the class, Dr. G. used humor frequently. As she explained an expression, she offered, "For 3 points. We're running an auction here. You know it. You just said it!" She called on various people and saw that they were having difficulty with a particular type of problem: "Who has 'no clue'?" Several students immediately raised their hands (no one had any problem revealing their 'cluelessness'). Two very large male students in T-shirts and baseball hats worn backwards who indicated they were having trouble were asked to take their places at the overhead. As she bounced back and forth between them (while the rest of the class were working on their own calculators), she encouraged all to work in their own way. As they reached certain points in the equation, she would ask the class if they agreed with the direction the problem was going. She emphasized that both were correct methods, though different. She encouraged students to help one another by spotting one who was correct and asking her to go to the front of the room and help. Soon there were two students working at the overheads, and Professor G. was back in the rows checking work. "If you don't agree, speak up. If you see a mistake, go down and help." When a student was asking or responding to a question, she went to talk directly to him or her. She was patient while the student worked on a problem: "I'll wait for you. Take your time." Rather than accept no answer, she waited, then talked and demonstrated. Never did she rush through material. At the end of class, she thanked them, and then students brought completed problems for her to initial (meaning they received extra points on the test).

We went to Professor G.'s office informally (with no appointment) again in May. There was a line of students waiting to see her. She acknowledged us warmly and asked if we would mind if she saw the students first, a small action which nevertheless dramatically revealed her priorities.

Professor Josiah B. Gould (Professor J.), Philosophy
State University of New York–Albany

Professor J., a Distinguished Teaching Professor of Philosophy at a large state university, has been teaching at the college level for 35 years. He is also a two-time recipient of the Chancellor's Award for Excellence in Teaching, and he believes that it is possible to be both an award-winning teacher and a scholar.

We observed Dr. J. teach a class of approximately 22 undergraduate philosophy majors in a 300-level class on Aristotle. The class met in a miserable, narrow, rectangular classroom. Windows that were open to the busy outside quad framed one end of the classroom, and the door was open for adequate ventilation to a busy and noisy hallway. In order to see the professor, one would have to sit directly in the center of the class. Most students sat in the two rows next to the door (these filled up with latecomers).

Professor J., a stately man, entered the class exactly at the appointed time wearing a sport coat and tie. Immediately he began reviewing previous material, which consisted of quotes from the textbook. Chapter by chapter, he highlighted important concepts, compared and contrasted various philosopher's views or interpretations, and posed insightful questions to a less than enthusiastic crowd.

Dr. J. used a lecture method most of the time, but did switch occasionally to a Socratic approach. His interactions with the students were serious and respectful. He asked thoughtful questions but did not press anyone to answer. When someone did offer a response, he entered into a personal dialogue with that individual. Frequently he presented concepts to ponder rather than posing direct questions.

Dr. J.'s lecture was well-organized, with prepared notes and frequent references to specific pages in chapters. His voice was rhythmic and very melodic, almost lending the impression that he was having a conversation with himself and including the audience on occasion.

After class we asked him if he ever had any problems with the students. He indicated that he had one student who was coming to class but doing miserably on the exams. For that student, he had created writing assignments designed to test his comprehension in an alternative manner. Dr. J. gives the impression of being an incredibly bright person who is deeply immersed in his subject and very interested in assisting students achieve. Although he is not a spellbinder, he is reported to "take the discipline seriously, without turning people off." He considers his role as teacher as "profoundly" important to his self-image and told us that he would find it "difficult to imagine doing anything else."

Dr. J. reported that his distinctive teaching methods vary from course to course. In his history of philosophy courses, he gives an overview of the period and then discusses with the students the doctrines and arguments of the relevant philosophers, trying to help them to discover flaws and insights. In critical thinking and logic courses, he points out the kinds of arguments and the elements of arguments, and then discusses methods of validation. He said that he stresses the philosophical side of logic with particular focus on the idea of logical necessity and other modalities such as consistency. He learned to teach by observing his own teachers and feels that his teaching differs from others in that he values clarity more highly than do some of his colleagues.

Professor Donald F. Peters (Professor D.), History
Niagara University, Niagara Falls, New York

Dr. D. is a 31-year veteran of teaching history at a private comprehensive university where he received the Excellence in Teaching Award for what he believes is "a combination of adherence to rigorous standards and dynamism in the classroom." He believes that it would be difficult to be both an award-winning scholar—if that is based on publication—and an award-winning teacher, because both demand a concentrated amount of time and because "student contact outside of class is essential to good teaching." However, that would not preclude an individual faculty from excelling in both areas over a period of time, Dr. D. said, but "too often researchers get so into their research and writing that the other aspects of their job—in this case, teaching a minimum of four sections with three to four preparations each semester—suffer."

Professor D. teaches a variety of courses, including Writing 100, a course he accepted after English faculty "lost control" over the freshman writing component, and, as he said, other faculty were unwilling to antagonize them. He believes that any professor ought to be able to teach writing if given some orientation to the process approach. He said that he enjoys the course now and has organized the first half of the course to focus on argumentation and debate. He told us that he chooses controversial subjects, elicits student opinions, and forms them into small groups to debate and present the group's conclusions to the whole class. To his delight, he says, the groups' decisions seldom match any one individual's original responses.

We observed Professor D. as he team taught an evening section of a university studies upper-level core course, "1950s–1990s, Deja Vu," with a literature professor. The course is required of juniors or seniors and is designed to challenge students to integrate knowledge from two different perspectives. In previous semesters, he had team taught with another historian, with one playing the role of a U.S. foreign policymaker and the other presenting the Soviet view. He incorporates written assignments to force the students to synthesize the different views, a task which "makes them go crazy, because they've never had to do that before," Dr. D. said. The semester we observed him he had a new teaching partner, so they met every Saturday morning for four or five hours to talk about the plan for the next week's class. "It's fun," said Dr. D.

Materials for the course consisted of readings from the 1950s in literature, culture, and politics, as well as contemporary issues students raised in class. For example, students read Ralph Ellison's *The Invisible Man* in class in conjunction with discussion of the O. J. Simpson verdict.

This evening class of about 35 students met in a typical classroom. The class was divided into two parts: During the first half, students took an essay test; after a break, Professor D. lectured on the political climate in the Middle East in the 1950s. The professor was extraordinarily well-organized, with materials (the test) and visual aids (maps of the Middle East) ready.

The class was noisy after they returned from break. Dr. D. was dressed comfortably in a sweater and pants and he laughed, leaned on the podium, and chatted with students as they returned. As he began, his teaching partner sat to one side of the class, and he included her as a special member of his "audience." He introduced us to the class and said we would be asked questions too. He and his colleague began by discussing the test, pointing out students who did well, and listening to complaints about the length of the test. One student asked for the answer to a short-answer question, and Dr. D. gave it to him.

Professor D. then began to review background material on the Middle East, asking students to identify the non-Arab nations. Carrying an unlabeled map around the classroom, he asked individuals to list as many nations as they could in the Middle East. Few could identify the countries, and he joked with one who planned to become a teacher as he showed her the opposite side of the map that was labeled with appropriate names.

As he began his lecture, Professor D. moved quickly around the room, posing questions of students as he recapped a previous lecture of U.S. foreign policies in the 1950s: "(1) brinkmanship, (2) massive retaliation, (3) liberation." These three concepts became themes around which he built his lesson. He reviewed the political contexts in the USSR after Stalin died, trying to get students to recall and connect what they had learned five lectures earlier. Throughout his lesson, he used vivid language to describe the events. The Middle East was "a mess, a tinderbox;" the Hungarian revolt was "a slaughter"; and an assassination was "splattering his brains against the wall."

Professor D. describes his teaching method as "Socratic," and indeed he flung questions out like a machine gun at a furious pace, always giving students information and asking them to anticipate the outcome. For example, he asked students whether Egypt was a rich or poor country, and joked that they had a 50–50 chance of being right, and the worst that could happen if they were wrong was that they would help their classmates. He constantly challenged students to deduce the behavior of nations based on what they knew about the countries' geopolitical climate and previous policies. If a student answered incorrectly, he would say "No," and explain, or go on to ask the next student. Calling on each student by name, and joking with them about previous responses or attitudes, he role-played various nations and political leaders. Gesturing vividly, varying his voice from loud to intimate, and changing his facial expressions, he alternately became Eisenhower, Dulles, and Nasser. Comparing the Aswan Dam project to a nearby power plant, Dr. D. drew upon what students knew to help them understand the material. During his dramatic performances, students were riveted and asked few questions, as if afraid to interrupt the show.

Professor D. referred often to a large map taped to the blackboard. He also frequently wrote out names and key terms. At one point he distinguished between "nationalism" and "nation(ality)-ism," another key concept of the 1950s (and 1990s). As he neared the end of the class, Dr. D. announced, "It's quiz time!" and asked students to imagine Dulles' reaction to the Anglo–Egyptian Treaty of 1954, based on what they knew of Dulles' Presbyterian character. Using vivid parallelism, Dr. D. summed up the outcome: "Israel gets the Sinai, Britain gets the Suez, and Egypt gets the shaft."

Several times during the lesson, students asked for more details, especially of names involved in historical events, but Professor D. resisted, telling them he wanted them to focus on concepts. One particular student did this several times, and Dr. D. turned to the class to see whether they too wanted more details. They replied loudly in a chorus, "No!" However, he told the student to see him afterward, and he would give him the information.

Near the end of the class period, Dr. D. summed up the Soviet perspective vividly by asking students to imagine how it felt to be in a Russian classroom in 1957, with the U.S. surrounding them in an effort to "contain" them. Even though they said their policy had changed, Dr. D. recapped, Dulles and Eisenhower really continued the "containment" policy, although they spoke of "liberation," "massive retaliation" and "brinkmanship." Thus Professor D. brought the class back to the original key concepts, showing how they were only new words that were not reflected in U.S. actions. The class ran over by 10 minutes on this evening before a holiday break, yet students did not complain.

After class, several students lingered to discuss comments Professor D. and his colleague had made on drafts of their papers. Dr. D. told one man that he had the problems of style typical in a nontraditional student; that is, "he had forgotten how to write simply and clearly, and had instead written in a stilted style." The student remarked that there were a lot of red marks on his paper, but Dr. D. assured him that he would catch on if he attended to the instructors' comments. He tried to assuage the student's anxiety, and the young man left the room somewhat skeptical but apparently ready to try again.

Professor D. is an extraordinarily gifted lecturer and fun to watch—moving smoothly from topic to topic, focusing attention on important concepts through dramatizations, forcing students to pay close attention and be prepared to respond, and treating each of his students as though they were special. We did wonder if his style might not intimidate some quieter students, but his playful attitude seemed to make answering wrong in class acceptable.

Like the other distinguished teachers we observed, Dr. D. is very introspective about his teaching role. He splits his self-image in two: how he views himself, and how others view him. From his perspective, his role as teacher is extremely important: "[Teaching] is one of those professions where you can make a difference, and while you can see the change, the frustration of never knowing the final impact keeps life interesting. I would like others to see my 'role as teacher' as one which is lofty, and most people do, despite the on-going 'jabs' about my having a 'part-time' job."

Dr. D. speaks of commitment:

If one has to take the time to determine how much time one spends on teaching, I would suggest he/she is not teaching. You are a teacher 24 hours a day, and it seems you draw on every-thing—from the classroom to the most casual of encounters—to teach. Contrary to what may be believed by some, I do not be-lieve this total commitment to teaching is difficult as long as you can honestly say that you are truthful. By that I mean, be your-self: Permit the student to see you, warts and all, admit to faults, and work to improve, but do not be anything other than what you are. I believe students will respond to this whether they wish to emulate "who you are" or whether they reject that model. However, they will always learn from your constant striving to be true to yourself and improve.

On flexibility and organization, Professor D. writes,

My goal is always to teach "from the class".... I try to spin off from whatever comments and/or questions the students may have, often not answering the direct questions, but explaining what the question is asking and then returning to the students for responses, which are often more questions. Perhaps one student got closer to the "method" than any other when asked on a departmentally prepared course evaluation to respond to: "Were lectures clear and informative?" The 9-point response scale allowed the student anywhere on the scale from "often confusing and uninformative" to "always clear and informative." The student circled, "often confusing and always informative," and then noted that "the combination was excellent." You can always lead a student to a synthesis, but he/she has to accept or reject on her/his own accord.

As for his models for teaching, Professor D. said he stole the best traits of several professors who taught him and molded these to his own personality. Never enrolled in an education course, Dr. D. claimed, "I am still learning...[how to teach better]." He believes that teaching well is a gift and not a learned behavior: "We can teach others how to teach adequately, but I believe that, above that level, it is a gift and we should remember to say, 'Thank you.'"

Professor William T. Harris (Professor W.), Economics
University of Delaware, Newark

Dr. W. (aka "Crazy Willie") has won the University Excellence-in-Teaching Award, the Outstanding Teaching Award from the College of Business and Economics, and the University Excellence in Undergraduate Academic Advising Award at the University of Delaware, a Category I research institution. He was also voted "Best Professor" by the student newspaper during his 14-year stint there.

Dr. W. is notorious for wearing a dancing condom tie when he introduces the concept of market demand (focusing, of course, on condoms as the goods in question), but when we observed him, he was very conservative in his dress and his approach to teaching. Youthful in his movement and energy, he sported a button-down shirt and tie as he conducted class. His notes and rules are regimental. His combination of playfulness and rigor are a magnet for students who fill his classes to capacity every semester.

During observations of an introductory economics course (each of two sections had enrollments of 260), his legendary organization, energy, and provocative teaching style were evident. For example, his syllabus is organized in a two-pocket folder labeled "Economics 151–Important Stuff." Enclosed is an assortment of information—ranging from his biography, office hours of his teaching assistants, and informal introductory remarks—followed by a formal syllabus. Colorful reprints of university attendance regulations, an academic calendar, and a form to complete if a student misses a class when a graded assignment or examination is due, confirm his seriousness about class attendance. In an attempt to run his large classes efficiently and assure that he and the students accomplish their "economics mission," he enforces "strict and inflexible" rules, and is explicit in presenting his expectations and requirements. Warning students who cannot follow rules or accept sanctions, he advises, "Do not enroll in this course." To further underscore his serious commitment to students' understanding the rules, he asks them to sign a duplicate copy of the syllabus acknowledging that they understand the class policies and procedures.

As is his usual custom, we were told by the students, he appeared in the class well before starting time and began informally interacting with them. A large portion of the tiered lecture hall was filled when he arrived. One student informed us that many others believe that if they arrive early and sit in the middle, they won't be called on, "But," she laughed, "They're wrong!" Bantering with students as he tested the overhead projector and they moaned about the topic, "monopolies," he retorted, "What did you expect, *The Little Mermaid?"*

Checking his watch at precisely 12:20 p.m., he signaled his graduate assistant who sat in the back of the classroom and had responsibility for conferring with students who had class related questions. The assistant rose to close the doors so that the class could begin. Chatting with students as he walked to the back of the class and distributed a problem set color-coded by class section, he acknowledged us and jokingly admonished students to "be on their best behavior." Students are required to buy a "Micronotes" workbook that is keyed to correspond to Dr. W.'s lecture notes. He works from a highly organized notebook containing lecture notes and corresponding transparencies. The blank pages of the student workbook are labeled with dates and topics, but students have to fill in lecture notes and label graphs and diagrams from the lecture overheads.

Professor W. began the lecture by stating the Latin derivation of the term *monopoly*. Then, using rhetorical questions and real world examples, he developed key concepts of trademarks, copyrights, and patents. Using examples such as the invention of soft contact lenses, computer software, and cable TV, he illustrated the impact of the monopoly on pricing. To further emphasize the rationale behind profit-maximizing decisions to empower one supplier, he provided additional examples such as DeBeers' exclusive rights to market South African diamonds, Reynolds Aluminum's control over bauxite, and Dupont's development and trade rights to nylon and Teflon.

The highlights of Dr. W.'s presentation were his interactions with students to engage them in analyzing two monopolies: ownership of the Panama Canal, and the market demand for cable TV. Drawing a freehand map of the Western Hemisphere on the overhead, he inserted a line for the Panama Canal along with a "stick" boat. He informed the students that it saves 6,000 nautical miles and 10 days' time when a ship uses the canal. Playing a game of "trivia," he asked a student to "take a guess" at the toll for a ship to pass. "Two hundred dollars," was the student's response. "Two hundred dollars!!" he repeated. Using this response to make the point of expense and savings, he began to explain that the average ship pays $35,000 or more to pass through the canal, in contrast to $100,000 for going around Cape Horn. Continuing to make vivid illustrations, he pointed out that the range of fees is based on a Panamanian ton: "About $2 for a swimmer, and $100,000 for the largest ship, a cruise ship." His remarkable gift for assisting in the visualization of the concepts also included the use of humor: "My mother went there, not swimming but on a cruise ship—and not the Love Boat." Emphasizing why no one broke up that monopoly by building another canal, he jokingly used students' vernacular: "Notice where they built that 'sucker'." Then he engaged students in a discussion of the expense of construction and the limited number of ships on the seas that make the building of another canal unprofitable.

Expecting more interaction from the students, he began to walk among them and call on individuals. Referring to the students as "ma'am" or "sir," he used another example of monopoly and market demand—cable TV—to enable students to apply the concepts to their own experience. Asking one young woman where she was from and directing her to go up to the overhead, he told her to draw a map of her region. She balked at first, and he challenged her by saying, "Hell, I just drew the whole Western Hemisphere!" provoking a round of laughter. Encouraging her to take a risk, he said, "Just make it up!" Dr. W. then began probing with questions about the population of her city and the cable services available, leading into a discussion of market demand. Wandering up into the rows, he randomly chose another student to give the definition of market demand. The student was unable to respond, so Professor W. waited until he found the information in his text. "What's demand? Say it loud and proud. What page? Sounds like a church service, doesn't it?" He grinned as he made his way to the other side of the lecture hall. Asking another student to repeat the correct response, he prompted him to compute the demand for cable service in the woman's home town based on the formula. When the answer was incorrect, he repeatedly asked other students for help, and then calculated on the spot. Bouncing and dancing dramatically between students, encouraging responses by sincere requests such as, "Help me, sir!" he elicited laughter with an absurd example of monopolized market demand: "How many would pay $700 a month to watch a Tractor Pull Channel?" Testing their understanding of the concept of market demand, he reverted to the Panama Canal example using different numbers and asking students to compute market demand again. This time he met with success.

As the end of class approached, one student made the mistake of closing his book and Professor W., with his proverbial "teacher's eyes in the back of his head," reproached him. "What did you do to your book?" he asked. "Open it up, sir! I've got four more minutes. I'm going to give you all the education your parents paid for," he told them. Distracted by three students in the very back of the room, he continued lecturing while walking and used his proximity to control their chatting. One student nonchalantly attempted to get to the right page without attracting attention, but Dr. W. "nailed" him and told him to "Keep turning, sir." Lightening up, he asked, "What are our visiting professors going to think—I can't control this class?" Noting that class was officially over, he announced the time: "It's 1:20, and it's Miller time!" As students filed out, they stopped to ask questions and turn assignments in to the graduate assistant.

Our observation of Professor W.'s classes confirmed that he was especially successful in making dry material interesting. He told us, "It's not like a fun class with sex. It's economics. Yuck. You have to work exceptionally hard to get people's attention. I use a little bit of humor through pop culture to break the ice," he says, referring to his use of clips from movies like *Top Gun* and *Animal House*. But he warns his students, "Like the rules of engagement in *Top Gun*, my rules are not flexible."

5

Distinguished
Teaching

*A New Way of Viewing
the Character of Excellence*

A professor who has been recognized for distinguished teaching is like a symphonic conductor, responsible for paying attention to each instrument in the orchestra individually while attending to the whole. The conductor demands a standard of excellence and makes clear what is necessary from each performer, and the outcomes are evaluated by the both the conductor and the audience following each piece and at the end of the season.

After observing the excellent teachers in our study in their classrooms, we came away with the impression of artistry, an appreciation for the beauty of the patterns they created through repetition and variation of instructional elements. When we attempted to analyze our research findings using the methods of previous researchers, we became frustrated. Therefore, in this chapter, after examining the reasons for evaluating teaching and the difficulties of measuring teaching effectiveness, and reviewing the history of criteria of excellence, we conclude with a holistic appraisal of our participants' teaching and use that to propose a comprehensive theory of teaching excellence. This chapter shows how we experienced an "epiphany" with respect to the nature of distinguished teaching: Like others before us, we had been like the blind men and the elephant, touching on aspects of teaching excellence but unable to see the whole. We found that for excellence in teaching, the whole is far more than the sum of the parts. (See Qualters, 1995.) When we observed and/or interviewed the professors for this study, we found we were reacting not to the intensity or duration of individual "notes" of their performance, but to the melodies and harmonies the teachers produced. Consequently, to show our respect for the sophisticated "music" of teaching, rather than to perform a task analysis and present fragments of their teaching as has been done before, we provide our holistic impressions of these masters from a multi-perspective theory of intelligence.

The first section in this chapter presents a rationale for this part of our investigation and reviews the literature about common characteristics of faculty who have been acknowledged as distinguished teachers. It also looks for relationships between educational and psychological research on characteristics of excellent teachers and personality traits, and calls for the standards for evaluating teaching excellence to include character.

What's the Point of Evaluation?

Why is teaching evaluated in the first place? Administrators and faculty alike do not dispute that faculty evaluation, particularly evaluation of teaching effectiveness, is a minefield. Twenty years ago, administrators wanted to be able to make distinctions about faculty teaching effectiveness in order to "deliver a better product" as part of the business philosophy called "total quality management" (Cornesky, 1993; McDaniel, 1994). They subscribed to the theory that

> accountability is a basic consideration in effective management, and an important area of application is faculty performance. Since accountability requires some precision and a systematic means of gathering, analyzing, and evaluating data, [they asserted that] demands for improved methods of evaluating college faculty [would] be forthcoming. (Miller, 1974, p. 5)

Yet against today's calls by students, parents, and employers for better teaching, administrators increasingly see the faculty as protecting "a culture in which bad teaching goes unnoticed and unsanctioned and good teaching is penalized" (Sykes, 1988, p. 5). Unwilling to share the responsibility for having created a culture in which prominent faculty research agendas are rewarded over teaching (e.g., faculty advancement leads to release time from teaching), higher education administrators have instead sought a quick fix—better evaluation tools and criteria primarily to make better personnel decisions. With few tools and criteria forthcoming, they have overly relied on student ratings as their primary source of data (Aleamoni, 1987b; Cashin, 1990; *CHE Almanac,* 1995, p. 33) because these ratings have been studied more and have proved more reliable than other measures (Lowman, 1995). Student ratings are also relatively inexpensive, easy to administer, and quantifiable.

The faculty, on the other hand, question the motives and the tools of administrators. As professionals regularly required to provide evaluation feedback through grades to their students, they wonder why administrators are so quick to attach importance to a simple survey and give it supremacy in determining faculty teaching performance. They reject the corporate model of faculty as employees and students as customers, and they (rightly) suspect that successful teaching is far more complex than the standard 5 point Likert-scale student surveys reveal. Most faculty insist that assessments be sophisticated enough to distinguish between faculty who merely perform activities, those who are very competent, and those who excel. (And there probably are some faculty who reject evaluation of any kind because they are worried whether they will personally measure up.) Those who are most thoughtful about teaching refuse to accept simplistic behavioral models of instruction or to settle for a single classroom observation as valid measures of the teaching/learning experience (Cox & Richlin, 1993; Menges, 1990). Intuitively, faculty know who the outstanding teachers among their faculty are, and many are willing to admit that more definitive research could reveal what distinguishes those teachers who excel from those who are merely competent. However, faculty often resist such efforts to make distinctions because they do not accept the usual goals of the evaluation: to decide whose contract is renewed, who is tenured, and who will win the annual teaching award.

We contend that an improved definition of teaching effectiveness has not yet evolved because the primary use of previous models has been summative evaluation, not formative evaluation; that is, criteria have been used to grade faculty, rather than to enhance their teaching performance (Cox, 1994; Ramsden, 1992). Furthermore, most faculty have had little or no guided preparation for their teaching role and are therefore very nervous about and inexperienced with assessment of their teaching. In a casual investigation of the preparation of graduate students for teaching college classes, for example, we found that 46% of 59 teaching assistants from 42 different universities who responded to an on-line survey posted on the national TA listserve had had fewer than six hours of orientation for teaching, and more than half had no formal observation of their teaching. The same percentage of beginning teachers reported that the only means of feedback about their teaching was from student ratings. Abbott, Wulff, and Szego (1989) concluded that feedback that includes standardized ratings and other forms of feedback about student perceptions can be useful in helping TAs improve their teaching, yet Gil (1987) has shown that it is not often a regular part of TA development programs. We believe that the view of the classroom as sacred ground where the professor practices his or her art independently without critical feedback begins in graduate school. Subsequent invasions of this sacred turf for evaluation makes the faculty under review feel naked and exposed before their peers. Also, in our experience, senior faculty who have not kept their pedagogy current or those who may have succumbed to burnout or other signs of lost youthful enthusiasm are also unlikely to welcome evaluation of their teaching.

Complicating the matter are pressures and rewards today for "dumbing down" the curriculum in both secondary and higher education classrooms (Gatto, 1992). American education generally has been pushed to return to more rigorous standards, as evidenced in New York State by the recent move to require all students to pass statewide examinations (Regents exams) for high school graduation. However, too often in the college classroom today, with the diverse student population we described in Chapter 2, "an unspoken bargain between students and faculty [exists]. 'Don't ask too much of me, and I won't ask too much of you'" (Sykes, 1988, p. 86). Gatto suggested two origins of this attitude in high school students—schooling and television: "The children I teach are materialistic, following the lead of schoolteachers who materialistically 'grade everything' and television mentors who offer everything in the world for sale" (1992, pp. 31–32). Junior faculty, who often are assigned to teach introductory courses, confront the dilemma of students' resistance to rigorous reading, writing, and research requirements (Gatto, 1992; Sacks, 1996), and they are often ill-prepared to work with the new range of college students from diverse cultural backgrounds or impoverished learning environments. Though senior faculty may tell junior colleagues to ignore these problems, untenured faculty do so at their peril. We know of occasions where disgruntled students have unfairly complained to administrators about the demands of young professors, and the instructors were forced to modify their expectations or face rebellion and possibly lose their jobs. (See Sacks, 1996.)

The unfairness of our current evaluation system is paralleled in a recent study by a British researcher: "It is one of the Mysteries of the Universe why the almost complete lack of a definition of excellence *in research* [our emphasis] has not stopped researchers from being promoted" (Gibbs, 1995, p. 18). Yet she found that despite 96% of all higher education institutions in the United Kingdom including teaching excellence in their criteria, only 11% of promotion decisions were being made on the grounds of teaching excellence. Although these institutions described excellence in teaching as their primary goal and offered training and support for new lecturers, biennial appraisal of teaching (classroom observations), annual review of all courses, funding for development in teaching, and support from the vice chancellor—still, Gibbs found, "It is devilishly difficult for members of the committee to recommend a good teacher ahead of a good researcher, or to tell two good teachers apart" (p. 20). In order to elevate the status of teaching, Gibbs recommended that institutions take the following steps.

1. Define what they mean by excellent teaching.
2. Distinguish competence from excellence and leadership by having reasonably well-defined criteria about excellent teaching and standards for weighting and rating of teaching/research/service.
3. Weight teaching more heavily.
4. Increase the sophistication of teachers.
5. Promote excellent teaching, not just excellent teachers.
6. Not treat promotion as a separate issue.
7. Not underestimate external levers (research funding). (p. 20)

Learning Outcomes: Higher Education Goes "Back to the Future"

Although the focus of this chapter on evaluating instruction has been on the teacher, not on student outcomes, we feel obligated to reflect on a cyclical pattern in the history of education whereby the performance of the student has been used to verify the competence of the teacher. Fuhrman and Grasha (1983) reported that in colonial colleges,

> each student [was] questioned orally in public by anywhere from five to twenty examiners.... Marks were not given, but judgments were passed on both the student and his tutor. The performance of his students was also an evaluation of the tutor. It was therefore to the tutor's advantage that his students performed well. (p. 5)

The past few decades in higher education can be characterized by evaluation of teaching through measurements of student satisfaction rather than student performance. And, although systematic attempts have been made to develop teaching methods and practices based on various theories of learning, these reforms have not had much impact (Fuhrman & Grasha, 1983, p. 13). In fact, on many college campuses, we have strayed further away from the legitimate assessment of teaching effectiveness through the measurement of learning than our eighteenth-century counterparts. With the reintroduction of the concept of "outcomes assessment," however, higher education has come full circle back to the colonial system of evaluating instruction by measuring students' learning. Classroom assessment techniques are becoming more sophisticated and professors are being urged to conduct research as part of their regular evaluation of students' learning (Angelo, 1991; Banta, 1996). But this form of evaluation is not without its pitfalls, especially if you take it one step further and attempt to use outcomes to assess teaching. Blackburn and Lawrence (1995) outlined the problems inherent in evaluating teaching effectiveness through assessment of learning outcomes. They discussed the problems of the pretest/posttest method, including variables of entrance behavior, students' learning from peers or other sources, designing equivalent tests, and agreeing on a standard for "effective" outcomes (p. 180).

Although we acknowledge the importance of investigation in this area and encourage future research, we have chosen to limit the scope of our research and to focus on excellent teaching, leaving the thorny and complex task of evaluating learning outcomes to others.

The Soul of Excellence: A Chronicle of the Educational Perspective on Character

We believe that excellent teachers are the embodiment of the interface of natural abilities (innate character tendencies) and nurture (learned aspects of personality and acquired knowledge as evidenced in teaching behaviors). Here we will review the history of inquiry into the nature of character as it relates to excellent teaching.

In fact, we have discovered that character is often the silent criterion today for evaluations for renewal, promotion, and tenure in higher education across the nation, as evidenced by data gathered from the on-line bulletin board of the American Association of University Professors (AAUP). In addition to the three usual criteria of teaching, scholarship, and service, for example, faculty at the University of New Mexico are evaluated on personal characteristics. These are defined in the *University of New Mexico Faculty Handbook* as

> all traits which contribute to an individual's effectiveness as a teacher, as a leader in a professional area, and as a human being. Of primary concern here are intellectual breadth, emotional stability or maturity, and a sufficient vitality and forcefulness to constitute effectiveness. There must also be a sufficient degree of compassion and willingness to cooperate, so that an individual can work harmoniously with others while maintaining independence of thought and action. This category is so broad that flexibility is imperative in its appraisal. (B. Woodfin, personal communication, April 22, 1996)

Contractual issues stemming from the inclusion of the criterion of personal character, such as the one described above, are being reported by faculty at universities nationwide, with growing concern over the ambiguity of such a criterion. At Tennessee Technological University, according to departmental bylaws at its website, faculty continue to be evaluated annually on the basis of teaching, creative activity, service, professional development, and character. They define character as "those qualities of mind and spirit which merit emulation by the students and faculty: fairness, open-mindedness, objectivity, tolerance, patience, enthusiasm, and a fascination with and commitment to the field." In the evaluation criteria, the category of "personal factors" requires that faculty demonstrate "competency, initiative, personal growth, cooperativeness, adaptability, dependability, [and] effectiveness of communication" (http://www.tntech.edu). In addition, the Tennessee Technological University *Faculty Handbook* requires that assessment of collegiality also be a specific requirement in personnel decisions.

The AAUP Task Force on Tenure has recently begun to investigate the prevalence of the practice of evaluating performance based on character traits and collegiality (W. W. Roworth, personal communication, June 13, 1996). Anecdotal evidence suggests that such evaluation is far more common than anyone has suspected, underscoring the need to expose and evaluate the potential use or misuse of this criterion to assess performance.

The discussion about character has had a long history. In a dialogue with his student Meno, Socrates explored the meaning of human excellence or virtue. Through the conversation Socrates was able to guide Meno to a conclusion: justice and temperance are universal qualities of excellence. In his *Nichomachean Ethics*, Aristotle discoursed on two kinds of virtue or excellence—intellectual and moral: "Intellectual excellence owes its birth and its growth mainly to teaching, and so requires experience and time, while moral excellence is the product of habit," he wrote (in Wheelwright, 1951, i, 7).

Whereas Socrates and Aristotle defined human excellence more holistically, Hippocrates, the father of medicine, divided character into four temperamental types: melancholic, choleric, phlegmatic, and sanguine (Adler, 1928/1968, p. 181; Pervin, 1984, p. 272), which served as a model for personality types which persisted in literature until the twentieth century.

Alfred Adler, an early twentieth century psychologist who first studied under Freud and then broke away to develop his own theories, was among the first to begin a modern inquiry into character, which, like the ancient Greeks, he equated with "soul" (1928/1968). Based on his observations of "expressions of character," he established a precedent for the imprecise methodology and terminology of character traits which continue to present a dilemma to those who use them today to evaluate teaching.

The criterion of character as a basis for effective teaching has been addressed broadly since the 1970s by a bevy of education researchers who list personality characteristics to describe outstanding teachers. As with many professors, educational researchers often disagree whether it is possible to define distinguished teaching (Cronin, 1992; Weimer, 1993) and even if excellent teaching is an art or a set of teachable skills (Cronin, 1992). Yet scores of researchers report characteristics, tendencies, or qualities of teachers which they use to classify, analyze, or evaluate teaching. (See Lowman's 1996 review of this research and McCabe & Jenrette, 1990, for example). In fact, whole systems of faculty development and evaluation which impact decisions for renewal, promotion, or tenure are based on an imprecise lexicon resulting from this research.

Researchers have routinely generated and sorted a proverbial laundry list of teacher characteristics. The lists continue to consist of general, unmeasurable descriptors upon which major life decisions rest. We believe this imprecision is due to the lack of a theoretical framework that would tie together empirical findings and suggest new relationships that would hold true under defined conditions. Yet while recognizing the limitations of this type of research, we believe that it provides a useful starting point. Table 5-1 compares the general characteristics of excellence identified in a sample of studies conducted over the last 15 years.

Most recently, Lowman (1995) attempted to categorize and code characteristics of excellent teachers. He highlighted four categories—intellectual excitement, interpersonal rapport, commitment to teaching, and organization of the course—as being common among the professors he studied.

The following additional traits were also identified in at least one of the above studies: being a good speaker, sparking interest, being a good listener, having integrity, plus being hopeful, available, humble, respectful, charismatic, and disciplined.

Education researchers seeking to identify traits of excellent college teachers have been interested in the relationship between experience (maturation) and distinguished teaching (Abbott, Wulff, & Szego 1989; Boice, 1992; Nyquist & Wulff, 1996). The question is what part of these traits are givens, inherent in the character of the

TABLE 5-1 Characteristics of Excellent College Teachers as Identified by Education Researchers

Centra (1979)	Jarvis (1991)	Cronin (1992)	Weimer (1993)	Lowman (1995)
likes students	interested in students	knows students	interested in students	interested in students
organized	organized	organized	organized	organized
clear	clear	clear	clear	clear
—	enthusiastic about subject	passionate	love for subject	—
knowledgeable	—	knowledgeable	mastery of subject	knowledgeable
enthusiastic	excited	—	enthusiastic	enthusiastic
encourages independence	enables students to learn on own	shows how to learn	—	—
flexible	—	flexible	—	frequently makes changes
—	sparks participation	uses active learning	encourages class participation	—
—	—	caring	—	caring
—	—	compassionate	—	understanding
—	conveys significance of subject	makes material meaningful	—	—
—	—	rigorous	—	challenging
—	—	fun loving	—	fun, humorous
—	—	committed	—	committed

professor, and what part are learned behaviors developed over time?

Cronin argued, "Some things can be taught; others must be learned through experience. College teaching falls into the latter category. Learning to be an excellent teacher is a career-long undertaking, because a great teacher is never a finished product but rather always in the process of becoming" (1992, p. 150). And Sherman et al. (1987) offered the caveat that "it is clearly possible to improve as a teacher, but improvement does not always result in excellence" (p. 43). As early as 1974, Miller pointed out that "best and worst teachers engage in the same professional activities and allocate their time among academic pursuits in about the same ways. The mere performance of activities associated with teaching does not assure that the instruction is effective" (1974, p. 9). Clearly, the controversy over a definition of teaching excellence is compounded by the question of whether excellent teaching can be taught. Palmer argued,

> Good teaching cannot be equated with technique. It comes from the integrity of the teacher, from his or her relation to subject and students, from the capricious chemistry of it all.... They [good teachers] discover and develop methods of teaching that emerge from their own integrity—but they never reduce their teaching to technique (1990, p. 11).

Although we disagree with Palmer's reduction of teaching to "caprice" or "chemistry," we do agree that integrity or character is the foundation from which excellence can be developed, and that without this fundamental virtue, truly distinguished teaching is impossible.

Trait Theories of Personality

Paralleling the education research on traits of excellent teachers, psychological research throughout this century has attempted to distinguish personality traits by measuring, identifying, and classifying similarities and differences in personality characteristics (Plotnik, 1996, p. 424). As we have noted, 60 years ago Adler attempted to define character. As behaviorism gradually came to dominate psychological theory, researchers in the area of personality began to adopt more objective methods and reject self-report or introspection as a valid way of studying human traits. Habitual patterns of behavior (previously defined as character) began to be examined as responses to stimuli or goal-directed behaviors.

Concurrent with the development of behaviorism, personality researchers began to seek to codify a list of traits or "broad disposition(s) to behave in a particular way" (Pervin, 1984, p. 264). This strand of research runs parallel to much of the educational research that has been conducted on teaching excellence, although it has previously been ignored as a conceptual framework. Psychologists, in fact, faced the identical problem which has plagued education researchers: the absence of an established taxonomy of traits. Nevertheless, we believe that research based on trait theories of personality over the past 30 years—including the latest work of Goleman (1995) on "emotional intelligence," which we discuss at the end of this chapter—suggests a very useful direction for those interested in defining teaching excellence.

Three leading trait theorist researchers, Gordon W. Allport, Hans J. Eysenck, and Raymond B. Cattell, agree that human behavior and personality can be organized into a hierarchy: (1) responses, (2) habits, (3) traits, (4) types (cited in Pervin, 1984, p. 267). Like Eysenck, Cattell employed factor analysis to classify traits, from which he developed a 16 PF (16 personality factors) questionnaire. These psychologists were also interested in determining which aspects of personality were likely to be genetic and which were learned. Unlike Eysenck, Cattell tried to understand the relationship between personality, maturation, and growth (cited in Pervin, 1984, pp. 280–290).

From the 1960s to the 1990s, researchers continued to use factor analysis and reduce the list of 16 traits to the "Big Five"—a five-factor model of personality (John, 1990; Wiggins, 1996). Openness, conscientiousness, extroversion, agreeableness, and neuroticism (OCEAN) are now viewed as "supertraits," continuua of behaviors which have been used extensively to describe individual personality differences:

- *Openness to experience*—a measure of curiosity, receptivity to new ideas, and the ability to experience emotions
- *Conscientiousness*—degree of organization and stick-to-itiveness regarding personal goals

- *Extroversion*—tendency to seek interactions with others and feel joy and optimism
- *Agreeableness*—the extent to which someone shows both compassion and antagonism toward others
- *Neuroticism*—proneness to various forms of psychological distress and impulsive behavior (Costa & McCrae, 1995, p. 190)

Although many researchers in the field of personality see the five-factor model as a tremendously powerful advance in defining individual differences, other psychologists point out the flaws in the model: It is a static conceptualization of personality which neither accounts for growth and change, nor for variation based on the contexts of the behavior. Therefore, it has limited value for predicting behavior (Pervin, 1984, p. 300).

Trait theorists counter with data to show that personality traits are relatively fixed by age 30, that usually changes follow a particular theme and are responses to environmental pressures, and that personality traits remain relatively stable across time "because they are influenced by genetic factors" (Pervin, 1984, p. 427). C. Robert Cloninger, for example, published research in 1993 which led him to conclude that "individuals largely inherit their temperamental styles, which are triggered by perceptions of their surroundings.... Temperament orchestrates the habitual behavior that a person carries out unthinkingly throughout the day..." (cited in Bower, 1994, p. 190). The nature versus nurture debate continues with another group of St. Louis scientists who argue instead that behaviors are strongly affected by motivation and intention: "Character development leans heavily on a conscious sorting out of one's memories and experiences" (p. 190).

We propose that a line of investigation based upon trait theory may afford educational researchers a fruitful new way of understanding teaching excellence. Collaborative research with psychologists may allow them to discover whether outstanding teachers differ measurably on any of the "Big Five" traits from those who are merely competent. Of course, this research would be subject to the same limitations as previous trait theory studies.

The previous section provides a context for our discussion of teacher excellence. As we have suggested, much of the research on traits of excellent teachers parallels the psychological literature. If psychologists are correct that such traits are largely genetic and fixed by age 30, the time when most academics launch their professional careers, then what is the point of focusing on these traits? We believe that the major value of these numerous studies comes during the selection or screening process for new hires as well as the years before the tenure decision. Faculty personnel committees might be called on to design strategies that will probe the character of interviewees during academic searches, as well as to discover fair ways of analyzing and documenting character indicators for purposes of renewal, promotion, and tenure. We assert that assessment of character is essential at these key points in faculty careers. (See Boice for a model which incorporates the character issues previously discussed. He offered an assessment tool which could be used to screen candidates and new faculty [1992, pp. 333–338].) Although it is extremely important for institutions to identify those with the potential to become excellent teachers, we feel compelled to underscore the point that *that* is not where we must end our quest.

Conducting the Emotions: EQ Theory

From the review of the literature and our own research that investigated characteristics of teaching excellence, conducted through peer evaluations and self-reports of professors who had won teaching excellence awards, we identified six "supertraits" which were consistently cited as characteristics of excellence by researchers in classical philosophy, education, and psychology. In the order of their frequency of occurence, these "supertraits" are: (1) enthusiasm, (2) sociability/friendliness, (3) organization, (4) conscientiousness, (5) optimism, and (6) flexibility. (See Table 5-2, " A Comparison of Characteristics of Excellence.")

As Table 5-2 indicates, the education research, our peer reports, and teacher–scholar self-reports agree on these additional factors: (7) love of subject, (8) ability to inspire, (9) rigor, (10) availability/generosity with time with students, (11) emphasis on active learning, (12) knowledgeability/scholarship, (13) being a good listener and valuing student ideas, and (14) teaching/use of problem solving. Several of the award winners also mentioned (15) creativity as a distinctive factor in their teaching. So far, nothing in our findings is new or surprising.

Even though our observations and data indicated that all of these traits characterized our research subjects, we will show in this section that an analytical approach is too limited to adequately describe the *complete* distinguished teacher. Although we would expect all educators to enter the profession with the best intentions—namely, commitment, interest in students, and deep involvement in their discipline—distinguished teaching professors are set apart by another marker, character, a combination of innate personality dispositions and learned social behaviors which are reflected in our list of traits of excellent teachers. We view character as the soul of excellent teaching. It is the authentic spirit of the teacher which infuses the pedagogy with significance.

An exciting new approach to the study of character development is outlined in Daniel Goleman's groundbreaking book, *Emotional Intelligence* (1995), which broadly reviewed the research on the development of intrapersonal and interpersonal intelligence, a term the author equates roughly with character. Building on the work of trait theorists in psychology and 10 years of scientific studies of emotion, Goleman presented a theory of social intelligence derived in part from the powerful new methodology of brain-imaging technologies.

The "emotional intelligence" which Goleman acknowledged could also be called character includes "abilities such as being able to motivate oneself and persist in the face of frustrations; to control impulse and delay gratification; to regulate one's moods and keep distress from swamping the ability to think; to empathize and to hope" (1995, p. 34). As with the classical Greek philosophers, Goleman was concerned with the development of moral virtue; however, he placed its origins in the interaction between the emotional circuitry of the brain (the amygdala) and the experiences of the individual. He contended that those who possess the character he defined—who manage their own feelings well, and who read and deal effectively with other people's feelings—are more successful in every arena (p. 36).

Goleman argued that the difference in life success rates can be explained more accurately by emotional intelligence (EQ) than IQ, that EQ skills can be taught early in life, and that ethical behaviors derive from these "underlying emotional capacities." He argued that impulse control, which is the basis of will and character, is necessary for moral behavior, whereas empathy, the ability to read emotions, is the source of altruism (1995, p. xii). His analysis of recent studies of emotions described the subtle interplay of heredity

TABLE 5-2 A Comparison of Characteristics of Excellence

Classical Philosophers	Education Researchers	Trait Theorists	Emotional Intelligence Theorists	Peer Reports (DeWaters & Baiocco)	Self-Reports (DeWaters & Baiocco)
lively	enthusiastic	—	enthusiastic	enthusiastic	enthusiastic
sociable	friendly	agreeable	—	personable/pleasant/nice	warm
reliable	prepared	conscientious	—	good campus citizen	prepared
easygoing	flexible	—	flexible	—	flexible
optimistic	—	optimistic	optimistic	—	optimistic
—	organized	organized	organized	—	organized
—	sensitive	—	sensitive	sensitive to students	—
—	passionate	persistent	passionate	—	passionate
—	—	open/curious	persistent	—	perseverent
—	—	—	—	open contact	open/accepting
—	fair	—	—	strict but fair	fair
—	love of content	—	—	loves subject	loves the discipline
—	demanding	—	—	rigorous	challenging
—	stimulating	—	—	inspiring	inspiring
responsive	caring	—	—	—	caring
—	emphasizes active learning	—	—	involves students in learning	creative & active learning
—	—	emotional	expressive	—	conveys affection
—	knowledgeable	—	—	scholarly	knowledgeable about discipline

values student ideas
energetic/dynamic

has integrity
wants to help them learn
lecture skills
available
diplomatic
understanding

humble

concerned

empathic
clear
exhibits leadership
likes students

has clear and specific goals
encouraging

engaging
listens to students
active

motherly

omnipresent

mature
popular with students

exhibits leadership

addresses student problems

charming

self-controlled
masterly

mature
popular

egoless

socially perceptive
empathic

self-motivated

extroverted

is a good listener

masterly
has integrity

excellent speaker
generous with time

collaborative
concern for students

clear

likes students

teaches problem solving
encouraging

active
even-tempered

and environment in producing what the Greeks defined 2,500 years ago as "virtue" or "excellence": "Our genetic heritage endows each of us with a series of emotional setpoints that determines our temperament. But the brain circuitry involved is extraordinarily malleable; temperament is not destiny" (p. xiii).

Goleman's forerunner Howard Gardner, author of *Frames of Mind* (1983) and *Multiple Intelligences: The Theory in Practice* (1993), first conceptualized two primary types of intelligences: interpersonal intelligence, "the ability to understand other people"—what motivates them, how they work, how to work cooperatively with them," and intrapersonal intelligence, "a correlative ability, turned inward" (1993, p. 9). Gardner classified interpersonal intelligences into four categories: (1) leadership, (2) the ability to nurture relationships and keep friends, (3) the ability to resolve conflicts, and (4) skill at the kind of social analysis Goleman calls "social perceptiveness." Gardner (1993) agreed with Salovey that teachers are likely to be empathetic, and to be individuals with high degrees of interpersonal intelligence, skilled in reading social cues that reveal others' needs and desires.

Peter Salovey and John Mayer (1990) took Gardner's concept one step further by using brain studies as a means of understanding human behavior. Together, Salovey and Mayer coined the term "emotional intelligence," and defined it as a set of five domains: (1) knowing one's emotions, (2) regulation of emotions, (3) motivating oneself, (4) recognizing emotions in others (empathy), the fundamental people skill, and (5) handling relationships.

We believe that Goleman's synthesis of these definitions of emotional intelligence is exceptionally useful for understanding the characteristics and behaviors of excellent teachers. In particular, his categories of (1) motivation and optimism: hope, (2) empathy, (3) expressiveness, and (4) organizing and managing groups: leadership seem to correlate superbly with the characteristics of excellent teachers as defined by other educational researchers and our own study. Because these definitions are based on brain studies, they may provide the key to the better evaluation system which faculty and administrators have been seeking. We may, for the first time, have access to a physical model of character.

With a view to elucidating the art of teaching, we approached our case study observations and interview data from the perspective of character as defined by Goleman, Gardner, Salovey, and Mayer. Using their definitions of character as the conceptual framework from which to examine the excellent teaching which we observed, we reorganized the "supertraits" we listed at the beginning of this section under a new taxonomy. (See Table 5-3.) Under "intrapersonal intelligences" we have included the "supertraits" of "optimism," as well as "enthusiasm," and "sociability/friendliness," (the latter two fall under the intrapersonal intelligence subcategory Goleman defined as "expressiveness"). Under "empathy," we included the traits of "availability/generosity with time with students" and "being a good listener and valuing student ideas." Under "interpersonal intelligences," we have placed "organization" and "leadership," and finally, we have concluded with "the ability to inspire," "rigor," and "conscientiousness," additional traits of emotional intelligence and certain markers of character which we see as the soul of excellence. Chapter 6, "The Scholarship of Teaching," addresses the remaining characteristics previously identified by education research as "love of subject," and "knowledgeability/scholarship," and subsequent chapters explore and refine the characteristic which education researchers call "flexibility," a trait we think often overlaps with "creativity" and which excellent teachers demonstrate during instructional problem solving.

TABLE 5-3   "Supertraits" of Excellent Teachers: A Taxonomy

Intrapersonal Intelligences
    Optimism
    Expressiveness
        Enthusiasm
        Sociability/friendliness
    Empathy
        Availability/generosity with time with students
        Being a good listener and valuing student ideas

Interpersonal Intelligences
    Organization
    Leadership
    Ability to inspire
    Rigor
    Conscientiousness

The remainder of this chapter will illustrate how our case study participants demonstrated the emotional intelligences in this taxonomy.

Intrapersonal Intelligence: "Cockeyed Optimists"

As we have seen in the psychological studies of personality, hopefulness or optimism seems to be a personality trait which has genetic roots, although environmental factors also operate as a child develops (Schier & Carver, 1993, p. 28). This is the characteristic which Goleman calls "the master aptitude," because it is the wellspring from which self-motivation and joyful expressiveness flow. Snyder et al. (1991) described hope, a behavior which they viewed as similar in some respects to optimism, as involving both a sense of agency and a sense that pathways are available to achieve one's goals. People who have high levels of hope, who are optimistic, routinely have higher perceptions of psychological and physical well-being because they are more action-oriented, more effective at coping with stress, more willing to confront, more likely to put a situation in the best possible light, and more able to grow personally from difficult experiences (Scheier & Carver, 1993).

Snyder et al. concluded that optimism is a predictor of academic success, and that enthusiasm and persistence are markers of optimism (cited in Seligman, 1991). One can infer that those who have achieved the greatest academic success, who have been awarded the highest scholastic degree, the doctorate, are more likely to be both optimistic and persistent. Indeed, our findings supported this previous research—all of our case study professors exhibited outward signs of positive views of the future. In fact, we explicitly identified optimism as one of the six "supertraits" of outstanding teachers which we listed earlier.

One of the most prominent signs of optimism among distinguished teaching professors is their zealous belief in the power of their teaching. We found that, although they acknowledged that students can learn without a teacher, our teacher–scholars believed that they could enhance the learning process. Describing their roles as "learners," "catalysts in learning," and "cooperative–artists, who, like the farmer or physician, can produce powerful results that might not occur naturally," they exuded confidence and optimism. Another optimistic metaphor for the role of teacher was expressed by Dr. R., who saw the role of the teacher as a midwife (as in Plato's *Theaetetus*) who "tenderly assists the pregnant woman with the delivery of her offspring. So too, (he reported), the teacher assists the inquiring mind of the learner to give birth to knowledge and to facilitate discovery." Dr. R. said that college teachers are responsible for educating prospective leaders "not to worship knowledge, but to question it!" As an English professor, he stated that his role was to participate and interact creatively with his students to provide them with the ability to use language "to access their humanity through their most powerful, creative and stimulating thoughts and emotions...to search for new ideas, to challenge old ones, and to wrestle riddles."

Implicit in such views are the assumptions that everyone has the power to be creative and powerful, that new ideas exist, and that riddles can be solved. Through their language and their actions, our teacher–scholars constantly projected beliefs that life can improve, that students can learn, that human progress is possible. As Professor D. said, "Teaching is one of those professions where you can make a difference, and while you can see the change, the frustration of never knowing the final impact keeps life interesting. I would like others to see my 'role as teacher' as one which is lofty, and most people do."

One of the simplest, most direct ways in which our excellent teachers displayed optimism was by trusting their own ability to improve as teachers. Many of the distinguished teachers spoke of working diligently on their own performance. Dr. D. wrote, "I believe students will always learn from your constant striving to be true to yourself and improve." Others asked students to help them to become better teachers and said that they listened.

Inevitably, teachers encounter human weaknesses and limitations. However, the outstanding teachers we observed did not attack students when they were not prepared. Instead they guided them toward positive behaviors such as studying more, attending class, or trying new techniques. When students were apprehensive about trying new methods, they offered assurances and positive predictions. For example, Dr. C. told students: "This should take only 30 seconds, and you'll get better at it as you gain experience." And Dr. D. assured one man who was concerned about "a lot of red marks" on a draft of a paper that he would "catch on if he attended to the instructor's comments, and that he had the typical problems of style of a nontraditional student; that is, he had *forgotten* how to write simply and clearly, and had instead written in a stilted style." The implication was that the student already knew how to write well, and that the ability would return.

One eternal, universal truth about education is that some students fail—that not all students will sufficiently grasp the material in the time allotted. Our award-winning professors seemed to have reached an uneasy truce with this fact of life. Some were philosophical, offering advice and "pearls of wisdom" to students, though they understood that a large part of students' learning was "up to them." Dr. H. found this to be the hardest part of his teaching. He anticipated that as many as 25% of his human anatomy classes would not earn a grade of C or higher, and thus would have to repeat the course to remain in their programs. When students who were doing poorly asked for help, Dr. H. was willing to spend hours with them. For example, he taught them how to stay optimistic while learning the huge lexicon of anatomy by focusing on positive achievements rather than negative (what they hadn't done) when they studied. With a group of students who were weak writers, he wrote his own model essay answers to each test question, gave them to the students, and asked them to revise their own for a higher grade to be averaged in. This unwillingness to accept human limitations is a mark of the excellent teacher.

Another quality of those who possess the intrapersonal intelligence of optimism is self-motivation, or "initiative." Although most faculty are called upon at some time to develop new courses, our teacher–scholars appear to relish the opportunity to create something new. They can often be found among those who are engaged in curricular "visioning" and "re-visioning." Curricular reform appears to be fun for them: It stimulates their creative juices and pushes them to explore new territories, to become the engaged learners that they seek to create. Recall, for example, that Professor E. was the founder of a university department; Professor F. had initiated a university-wide program in service learning and was generating a computer resource disk; Professor H. took the initiative to enroll in a medical school anatomy course in order to prepare for his course in human anatomy, and he had developed another new course and a computer software anatomy atlas in the past few years; Professor G. was breaking new ground with a course on "Women in Mathematics"; Professor C. was the creator of a university apprenticeship system for lab assistants; and Professor D.

taught a new university studies interdisciplinary course, "1950s–1990s, Deja Vu." Several of our case study subjects had also traveled all over the world on sabbaticals; Dr. R. had his own consulting business; and Dr. F. was busy professionally, assisting her professional organization in publishing proceedings of a conference on a website. All of these activities are evidence of initiative. These creative teachers could not resist the opportunity to play with the curriculum, to stir up the existing structures, and to push the boundaries of their disciplines, their professions, and their lives.

Intrapersonal Intelligence: Self-Control and Expressiveness, Markers of Emotional Maturity

According to EQ theory, emotionally intelligent individuals are capable of understanding and describing what they are feeling, expressing feelings appropriately, and coping with negative emotions by adapting successful methods for soothing themselves (Goleman, 1995, p. 57). Self-control and expressiveness are two sides of this emotional spectrum which the award-winning professors we observed demonstrated in abundance.

As for self-control, the outstanding teachers we observed had comfortable demeanors as they moved among students, exhibiting confidence that the students would do as they expected when they turned the class over to the students. In their smaller classes, they showed that they had gone beyond the stage where they had to be the center of attention; instead, they purposely shifted the spotlight to the students. (See our discussion of stages of teaching development in Chapter 11, and Ramsden, 1992.) After they set up the framework for learning in a given course or class, they allowed the class to interact freely. Setting their egos aside, they appeared to make learning "student-centered." The students knew that they came first. We believe that this willingness to relinquish control and to be patient while students practice or apply what they have learned is another mark of distinguished teaching. Like parents watching a child learn to ride a bike, the teacher–scholars we observed appear to know when to support and when to let go.

We believe that outstanding teachers also know how to control their own negative emotions. For example, Dr. H. kept a "good feelings" file of notes and letters from former students that he kept for his own encouragement, and Professor G. worried about burnout in her non-tenure track position, one in which she is not eligible for sabbaticals. And, although teaching is very important to Dr. R., he told us that when he finds himself taking things too seriously, he "stops and listens." Then he "hears the panpipes in the distance and views the satyrs leering and laughing at [him] from their wild places." This ability to self-monitor and manage the natural stress and frustration of the educational process is a key sign of the emotional health of distinguished teachers. Although, admittedly, our sample was small and our presence may have had an influence, throughout our study, we observed no angry retorts or outbursts between them and students or colleagues, nor any signs of abruptness or impatience.

Enthusiasm: A Passion for Teaching

The enthusiasm which is mentioned so frequently in the education literature as a characteristic of distinguished teachers can be understood as the natural expressiveness of a person with high EQ. We found that this liveliness is often expressed in their responsive movement and their language, rather than the usual stereotype of someone bounding around a room like a cheerleader. And the enthusiasm was for the total act of education: They loved to learn, they loved students, they loved their field, they loved teaching. Such people are harmonious, "fully actualized" human beings; in a very real sense, they teach *who* they are, not just what they know.

To elaborate, we describe enthusiasm among our case study participants in terms of movement and energy, the topography and intensity of their behavior. They were very much in control of the pace of their interactions with students. As in a dance, the shape of their movements appeared orchestrated: They moved purposefully according to the feedback received from the class, and they knew when to vary the rate—to slow down, to speed up—with changes in the subject, the students, and the setting (time and place). Although not all enacted observable, external enthusiasm, we saw some who moved athletically in front of the classroom and among the rows of students, and others who were physically emphatic, using dramatic gestures and strong variations in rate, volume, and pitch, and flinging questions out like machine guns. One worked with up to four students at a time on two overheads while she cruised among the rows, assisting the students in problem solving.

Another maintained a rapid volley of questions and responses among students. Like a tennis player, he "served" a question, stepped aside awhile to umpire, and then returned the volley of responses with backspin.

In addition, the emotional language the teacher–scholars we studied used to describe their teaching, their disciplines, and their students reflected an intensity which is a marker of their "passion" or expression of joy in what they do. We found that our outstanding teachers had a rich vocabulary to describe their own emotional states. For example, to explain their commitment to teaching, they described themselves with such expressions as, "fully devoted to [their] efforts as a teacher," and said that they "genuinely like students and enjoy teaching." They reported that teaching was "profoundly important" to their self-image, and they spoke of "finding it difficult to imagine doing anything else." Dr. C. reported that his self-image was "Vital!" to his role as a teacher: For 30 years he had listed his profession as "not professor, not researcher, not college professor—but teacher." Some described their teaching as "theatrical," "intense," and "dynamic," and they frequently used superlatives to describe their intense pleasure when their teaching was successful: "To my delight," Dr. D. reported, "the groups' decisions seldom match any one individual's original responses." Dr. F. reported "incredible results" from an experimental teaching method, and Dr. H. told us he was "thrilled" with the videomicroscope as a teaching tool.

In every case, the award-winning teachers we observed also displayed enthusiasm through the use of humor. They employed jokes, sarcasm, characterizations, emphatic facial expressions and gestures, parodies of institutional icons, anecdotes, puns, and demonstrations to relieve anxiety, to attract attention, and to create pleasant associations that would enhance students' long-term retention (learning).

Many of the award-winning teachers we observed also approached learning as a kind of play: Dr. R. wrote,

> The statue of the young girl [in front of a European university] symbolizes how students should approach learning: with a ragamuffin, barefoot irreverence for certainty and with a childlike appreciation for creative inquiry and play. My role as teacher is to facilitate combinational play and childlike curiosity. Teaching is *play* of sorts!

And Dr. D. told us that he had a new teaching partner for the inter-disciplinary course they team taught, so they met every Saturday morning for four or five hours to talk about the plan for the next week's class: "It's fun!" he exclaimed. His excited approach was no-ticeable in the vivid language he used to describe historic events: The Middle East was "a mess, a tinderbox"; the Hungarian revolt was "a slaughter"; and an assassination was "splattering [the vic-tim's] brains against the wall." Gesturing vividly, varying his voice from loud to intimate, and changing his facial expressions, he alter-nately acted out the parts of Eisenhower, Dulles, and Nasser. Simi-larly, twice in the course of his lecture Dr. E. used an awestruck tone to describe photosynthesis as a "miracle."

Dr. B.'s teaching philosophy sums up the gusto with which teacher–scholars appear to approach their life's work:

> Teachers who truly have a "calling" love both their subject and their students. That means, in the case of an English professor, that she read literature, attend plays, and actively engage in speaking and writing. All of these I do, although I rarely have the time to read novels during the academic year. It is easy to love one's field of learning. I have always felt fortunate to be teaching English, for the range of material is vast and less likely to become boring to both teacher and students. "How can the professor down the hall who is teaching molds compete with the mystery of Greek tragedy, the lush beauty of Wordsworth's poetry, the raw power of *Moby Dick*?" I ask. "Perhaps molds can be mysterious, beautiful, and powerful, too," I speculate.

Empathy: Teachers as Emotional Tuning Forks

According to EQ theory, enthusiasm is contagious as is its social counterpart, sensitivity, or empathy. This observation is based on brain studies that have found some people to possess an increased sensitivity that makes their autonomic nervous system "more easily triggered" (Goleman, 1995, p. 116). Goleman wrote that persons who know how to soothe themselves often are excellent at comfort-ing others, and that these individuals become the friends others seek out for help, because they know how to make their friends feel good about themselves.

Empathy directed outward becomes sociability or friendliness, another "supertrait" identified by previous research as a characteristic of excellence. In this regard, we found that award-winning professors were adept at creating naturally inviting atmospheres. For example, they responded quickly and thoughtfully to our request to participate in our study. That they did this for strangers suggested to us that their friendly demeanor was an aspect of their customary behavioral repertoire. When we came to observe them, they smiled warmly, welcomed us, and included us in their classes, just as they did their students, with whom they chatted before or after class. Between classes, we observed lines of students outside their doors. Some held celebrations for their students. Known as "popular" on campus, these teachers often held campus leadership roles.

The rhythm and flow we described in our musical analogy of teaching at the beginning of this chapter is an external sign of the harmonious relationships these friendly, outstanding teachers had with their classes. Bernieri and Rosenthal (1988) have suggested that interpersonal coordination, especially synchronous movement, is related to social rapport. Their studies of movement coordination showed a positive correlation between movement synchrony of pairs of high school students and affective ratings of students' interactions as friendly, happy, enthusiastic, interested, attentive, cooperative, humorous, and easygoing. In general, they concluded that a high level of synchrony in an interaction means that the people involved like each other (Bernieri & Rosenthal, 1991).

Indeed, one of our teacher–scholars reported that her colleagues sometimes saw her as a "Pollyanna" because she always found something to like in her students. We observed this rapport, which was similar to the interaction between a mother and infant, repeatedly between the students and the teachers in our study. Goleman (1995) might have been describing our subjects in this passage:

> Setting the emotional tone of an interaction is, in a sense, a sign of dominance at a deep and intimate level.... The forcefulness of a good speaker [*teacher*]...works to entrain the emotions of the audience. That is what is meant by, "He had them in the palm of his hand."...Emotional entrainment is the heart of influence. (p. 117)

In a section of his book entitled "Neurobiology of Excellence," Goleman (1995) described individuals who achieve mastery in a given activity as entering into a state of "flow," a condition akin to Maslow's description of "peak-experiences" (1968). The elegance of our distinguished teachers in lecturing, in dealing simultaneously with individuals, groups, subject matter, the environment, and their own needs, seems to exemplify this exalted state of performance which Csikszentmihalyi described as "optimal experience":

> a sense that one's skills are adequate to cope with the challenges at hand, in a goal-directed rule-bound action system that provides clear clues as to how well one is performing. Concentration is so intense that there is no attention left over to think about anything irrelevant, or to worry about problems. Self-consciousness disappears, and the sense of time becomes distorted. (1991, p. 71)

When our award-winning professors spoke or wrote of this transcendent state in their teaching, they spoke of "being on a roll," "knowing when [their] teaching was a hit," or "entering into an eloquent mode where [their] every word and the students' responses were beautiful." They frequently used the word "love" to describe their feelings about students and their work, which we believe relates to the educational power of "flow" which Goleman described. We suspect that the excellent teachers we studied found the passion for their disciplines in much the same way as the child in the description below, and that one of the reasons that they chose to become academics was because they had had happy learning experiences:

> The flow model suggests that achieving mastery of any skill or body of knowledge should ideally happen naturally, as the child is drawn to the areas that spontaneously engage her—that, in essence, she loves. That initial passion can be the seed for high levels of attainment, as the child comes to realize that pursuing the field...is a source of the joy of flow. And since it takes pushing the limits of one's ability to sustain flow, that becomes a prime motivator for getting better and better; it makes the child happy. This, of course, is a more positive model of learning and education than most of us encounter in school. (1995, p. 95)

The wonder of the teaching–learning experience is that some teachers like our award winners relive the joy of learning as they teach, and so model the pleasure of learning their disciplines for their students. This is why our respondents told us that they believe that scholarship and curiosity about their subject as well as the world are essential ingredients for the excellent teacher. Apparently, the desire to continue learning, to keep experiencing the pleasure of discovery, the "life of the mind," is deeply engrained in the distinguished professor. Not only does the joy of learning enrich and revitalize the professor, but, like a tuning fork set in motion, it begins a parallel resonance among students.

Empathy: A Path to Leadership

The distinguished teaching professors we observed were constantly scanning the classroom, monitoring the impact of their words and actions on students' faces, and observing the posture, the tone of voice, and the eye contact of their students for cues of successful communication. The "radar" which was present among them is a sign of another highly prized aspect of emotional intelligence. This ability to read nonverbal cues is an innate ability, a "given of biology" according to Sternberg's review of the literature (1985, p. 261). There are enormous benefits for those who possess the ability to read nonverbal signals: better emotional and social adjustment, popularity, and sensitivity. Empathy is the outer-directed equivalent of self-awareness.

Over and over again, the distinguished professors in our study showed signs of being empathic and uncommonly sensitive to their students' feelings. For example, they showed kindness, patience, and humor to relieve students' anxiety.

This became obvious in how they responded to students' errors or silence in class. Dr. D. joked that "they had a 50–50 chance of being right, and the worst that could happen if they were wrong is that they would help their classmate"; Professor G. patiently waited while a student worked on a problem, saying, "I'll wait for you. Take your time." Rather than accept no answer, she waited, then talked and demonstrated. When a student responded, "I don't know," she immediately responded, "Sure you do. I'll wait." Later, turning to the class, she announced, "We're running an auction here. You know it. You just said it!" Similarly, Professor R. 's interactions with the students were serious and respectful. He posed insightful questions but did not press anyone to answer. When someone did offer a response, he entered into a personal dialogue with that individual. He reinforced student responses, whether they were completely accurate or mere approximations, by redirecting them. If the answer was inaccurate, he redirected the response by having the student find the problem with the response and then helping him or her find the solution logically. When faced with no response to a question, Dr. F. led the students to formerly learned foundation information through nonthreatening means: "You remember this stuff." When Dr. R. began questioning his introductory literature class and discovered that many had not read the assignment, he synopsized the story. However, we have known one professor to close his book quietly, announce that he would be available to meet with them again when they were prepared, and exit the room. This individual told us that such a dramatic tactic has only to be used once.

As part of a generic plan, excellent teachers appear to monitor 100% of the time formally and informally. They verbally quiz, they watch for signals of confusion on the faces and postures of the students, and they listen to the types of responses or questions of the students. Some monitor formally by using active learning techniques such as asking students for one- to ten-minute written summaries of course material and quizzing them about areas of confusion at the beginning, middle, or end of class. Another method of systematic monitoring is the use of student response journals.

In other ways, we repeatedly witnessed behaviors that revealed the extraordinary empathy our teacher–scholars had for their students' needs. Dr. R. reported that he "shares his life with his students, doesn't stress answers, and demands, in the most tender way, more than the students think they can give." Dr. E. described the teacher's responsibility "to share feelings, and to be sensitive to the moods and reactions of the hundreds of young persons who depend on the total quality of the teaching effort." In his class, he modeled this behavior by focusing the overhead with care (which was neatly typed and easy to see from the back of the hall), announcing that he would post an answer key as soon as a few late tests were completed, and explaining that besides regular office hours, he would have additional office hours if there was a need. Dr. F. was striving to develop new software inexpensively so she could offer her classes additional resources within their budgets. Others described their actions of monitoring of students as "getting a 'read' on their problems so as to address them." They did so by such methods as keeping separate class averages for freshman and sophomores to "assure that the course was not overly demanding for the freshmen," and by creating alternative writing assignments "for a student who was coming to class but doing miserably on the exams."

Another marker of empathy is outstanding teachers' possessing both a knowledge of and vocabulary for the range of emotions that students undergo in the process of learning their subjects. They spoke of students' "frustration," sense of feeling "overwhelmed" or "burned out" in the middle of a course, and "anxiety," as well as techniques they had developed to help students overcome these emotional hurdles. Professor G., for example, told us that she tries to identify what is bothering students about their learning, and then "show them the way out." She added that math professors "have to be very sensitive with students who don't have the ability to picture relationships," and agreed with the class that "many of the problems were confusing."

Two of the professors we observed were particularly sensitive to students who were planning to become teachers. To build rapport, as well as to underscore that the student had to master the material, Dr. D. joked with her as he showed her how to remember the geography of the Middle East by using a map with the answers keyed in on the opposite side. In Dr. C.'s course for lab instructors, he relentlessly questioned one student who said she was worried about students' not attending. She wanted to know how to tell if a student had resigned. Dr. C. questioned her for what seemed like a long time to discover her motives, and when she confessed that she was worried about a student, he praised her commitment and told her it was right to be concerned.

Because researchers have found that nonverbal cues—facial expressions, speech, and body cues—are major influences on the perception of emotional messages (Ekman & O'Sullivan, 1991), and that emotions must be managed successfully in order for learning to occur, it follows that teachers who can accurately read the emotions of their students will be better at communicating, building rapport, and helping students to appreciate the joy of learning while overcoming the frustrations of not learning. The capacity to imagine how it feels to be in another's shoes, in this case the student's, gives these teachers an edge in motivating them. This is why excellent teaching professors may deal very differently with students who experience the same problem: They know that some students react to praise, others to independent work, others to cajoling. They listen to the unique voice of each student, much as a conductor would the instrumentalists in the orchestra.

In summary, the outstanding teachers we observed were consistently measuring, evaluating, and responding to their students' nonverbal communications. Add this empathy to the previously identified emotional intelligences of optimism and expressiveness, and then cap them with the organizational talents we will describe next, and it becomes clear why the teacher–scholars we studied are dynamic in the classroom!

Social Analysis: The Key to Successfully Organizing and Managing Groups

We believe that a person may possess all the emotional intelligences we have discussed, though lacking the ability to organize and manage groups—an essential leadership skill—still not be an excellent teacher. Because teachers most often meet with students in groups (only two of our subjects, a music teacher and a studio art professor, reported working regularly with solo performers), they must be skilled at negotiating, sustaining relationships, and detecting others' motives and concerns. They must be sensitive to the politics of groups and be proactive in the classroom. Goleman calls this ability "social analysis," and says that those who are gifted with it "can be excellent teachers." These individuals are natural leaders who sense and articulate the consensus of the group and make people enjoy being in their company (1995, p. 119).

Our interviews with 30 award-winning professors revealed that they had been elected an average of three times each for such leadership positions as Faculty Senate and department chairperson, and nearly one-third had been elected president of the faculty governing body. Many reported holding these campus offices for long periods. Further evidence of their leadership comes from our case studies, in which we found that two of the ten award-winning professors had served as deans of undergraduate education, one had been an officer in the military, several had served as officers in a collective bargaining unit, and two had held administrative appointments heading special campus-wide programs. There is no doubt that the qualities that students find inspiring in these professors also make them leaders among their peers.

Our case studies also provided us with many examples of the analytical abilities which Goleman states are essential to those who manage groups. First, the professors in our study were inclusive, assimilating newcomers into the group almost effortlessly, and they often modeled the social sensitivity they sought to teach. The way we were accepted into their classroom was revealing. Dr. R.'s class held up handmade signs and sang "Welcome!" on cue. During one class, Dr. C. provided us with special handouts he had located on his teaching technique. After another class, students waited in line to speak with him. When they asked him for clarification, he leaned forward and focused attention directly on specific students, a behavior he repeated during our interview with him later in his office. Although he was very busy, he listened and responded to our questions with curiosity and full attention. Dr. D. made sure to introduce us to his teaching partner, who sat to one side of the class, and he included us in his "audience" with a warning that we would be asked questions too.

During classes, the distinguished professors we observed often monitored the behavior of the group. They noticed, though did not always acknowledge, latecomers; they changed activities in response to their questioning of students who were signaling; and they noted when students were engaged and when they were apathetic. When Dr. C. developed a raspy throat, he considerately removed his body mike to clear his throat—a small behavior that marked his habitual way of recognizing and adapting to the needs of others.

Another significant marker of the excellent social perception of outstanding teachers in our study was their ability to identify and reward positive student behavior with praise and suggestions. Dr. F. used phrases such as "I agree with you," or "I hear what you're saying," along with direct eye contact with the speaker and a posture that would suggest sincerity. She carefully watched the class to determine who was participating and then focused on those who had not contributed yet by directing statements or questions to them. Dr. G. was also a model of positive reinforcement. She accepted responses from students and complimented the answers: "He's got a good point. She's absolutely right. Could you sketch it for us?" Not only did she reward individual students for good performance, she encouraged students to help one another by asking the stronger students to correct errors for others: "If you don't agree, speak up; if you see a mistake, go down and help."

In a similar vein, Professor H. provided a role model for being supportive during the serious illness of his team teacher. He first set an upbeat tone by greeting the class and asking them if they had enjoyed their holiday. Then he informed them that his colleague who team taught with him had undergone emergency surgery during the break. The class became hushed as he described the seriousness of the surgery and the prognosis for their teacher. Before beginning his lecture, he ended on a positive note by suggesting that they send cards and show their professor support.

All professors today have to be sensitive to diversity among their students. Whether they agree with "political correctness" or not, professors who ignore the cultural differences among today's student population do so at their peril. Dr. H. displayed an example of sensitivity to students' political leanings when he joked about a slide of a large open mouth with tongue and teeth exposed, remarking that it was "either a portrait of Rush Limbaugh or Howard Stern, *as you prefer.*" And Professor C. demonstrated very explicitly to his teaching assistants how to deal with the potentially explosive problem of course requirements and religious holidays. He advised his students, "Do not announce this policy, but *say* to anyone who complains, 'No religion prohibits this; there are no make up exams'; and, 'It's been on the syllabus from day one.' " If students in the course still objected, he recommended, "Tell them to write a letter stating that they did not take the exam for religious reasons. The grade will not be counted." He advised them not to tell students this in advance, or the students would not study. Other evidence of sensitivity to individual differences was Dr. H.'s openness to different students' learning styles as they studied in their favorite ways for a laboratory exam.

Nearly every classroom has one or two students who enjoy monopolizing class time. Dr. D. used group pressure to quash the behavior of one student who interrupted the class several times by asking for more detailed names of historical events. Dr. D. resisted, telling them to focus on concepts. When the student persisted, Dr. D. turned to the class and asked whether they too wanted more details. They replied loudly, in a chorus, "No!" However, Professor D. also told the student to see him afterward for the information. This vignette captures the essence of group management. Dr. D. refused to allow the student to derail the focus of the lecture, but he also gave him the dignity of an alternative way to satisfy his curiosity and receive attention.

To reiterate, a talent for social analysis is the heart of group management. The award-winning teachers we observed used it constantly to shape their plans and to organize and maintain smoothly functioning courses. We believe it is the source of the "supertrait" education research has labeled "organization." Careful analysis of the audience for their courses allows excellent teachers to design effective curricula, methods, and assessment to meet the needs of groups and individuals. Without exception, we found that the excellent teachers we observed used pre-assessment of students' abilities and interests to shape their plans. For example, Dr. L. uses a basic set of questions at the beginning of each semester to determine whether students know the background information necessary to be successful in the course. During the first class, with one graduate group whom she found underprepared for the rigors of the upcoming condensed semester, she stopped, gave a 20-minute break, requested the assistance of two students, went to her office to retrieve materials with the missing information, and sent other materials to the library to be placed on reserve. Returning to class, she verbally redesigned the timetable around the background information. In other words, she did not punish the students for what they didn't know. She reorganized on the spot.

This is one example of how the professors in our study were flexible; they had plans which allowed students to influence the plan at any time. Their agendas included a pattern or structure of presentation strategies which varied depending on the size of the class, the level of student knowledge, the personality of the group, the approach (theory-based, survey, or seminar), level of student interest (upper-level majors, or fulfilling a general education requirement), or the time frame of the course (a three-hour evening course, a 50-minute class, or a four-week intensive summer course).

They developed routines whereby the students knew what to expect, and they taught the students *how* to learn the subject, often by modeling the process of learning. Students took a certain comfort in trusting that the professor wouldn't throw them a curve ball; however, this did not imply rigidity in the classroom. Environments were created within their courses which allowed students to trust, to take risks, to ask "dumb" questions, to make mistakes without being chastised, and to receive help to find the solution.

For example, each of our award-winning professors maintained fully developed policies and procedures which were built into their syllabi and applied consistently. The students knew what they needed to do to earn particular grades, and they knew the professor's expectations for attendance, punctuality, and behavior. They were aware of what they needed to do to be successful in the course. One professor, for example, handed out individual folders at the beginning of the semester. Included in these folders, labeled "Important Stuff," were very detailed syllabi, policies, and procedures, all presented on bright paper in a humorous tone. (See Chapter 6.) Many others distributed outlines of each class, or they displayed outlines on transparencies and frequently referred to them during the class ("we are *here*"), while others verbally reviewed what would be covered at the beginning of each class ("what we will do today"), then summarized at the end of class ("what we just did"), and finally introduced what would be covered in the next class.

Clarity is probably the most consistently reported marker of organization. The ability to make difficult material understandable appears to be very important not only to students, but to the professors themselves. Repeatedly, distinguished teachers self-reported that their teaching differs from others' by its clarity. Clarifying is a critical skill that enables the teacher to sort information into levels of importance and allows the students to sift through what is nonessential and focus on what is significant. One of the most frequent ways of clarifying material used by our distinguished professors was a wide variety of audiovisual aids: charts, drawings, lists, outlines, formulas, equations, maps, models, computer software, videos, films, and demonstrations.

Another remarkable feature of distinguished teachers' skill in clarifying was their ability to use analogy. Some professors, Dr. H. for example, used analogy in nearly every sentence. Every time he introduced a new term in anatomy, he described either its shape or its function in terms of what the students already knew. This ability to see similarities and convey them through analogy to students seems to be at the heart of what students mean when they report that a professor "makes difficult material clear." We might venture that our distinguished professors would score high on Miller's Analogy Test or on an open-ended test of their inventiveness.

To sum up, the outstanding teachers we observed had in common optimistic outlooks, emotional self-awareness and control, expressiveness, empathy, and the ability to organize and manage groups. If ethicists are correct, this collection of emotional intelligences is the source of integrity (Kurtines & Gerwitz, 1984). Individuals who know themselves, who express their emotions positively and sincerely, and who understand the feelings of others are the people we want for friends. We admire their authenticity and appreciate their concern: In a word, they inspire us.

Personal Integrity: The Essence of Character

Someone has described integrity as "what you do when no one is looking." The award-winning professors we studied described themselves as "honest," as individuals with "a sincere interest" in students, and as people who "take the discipline seriously, without turning people off." Professor D. wrote eloquently about his devotion to teaching and the need for authenticity, which is a characteristic of excellent teachers:

> You are a teacher 24 hours a day, and it seems you draw on everything—from the classroom to the most casual of encounters—to teach. Contrary to what may be believed by some, I do not believe this total commitment to teaching is difficult as long as you can honestly say that you are truthful. By that I mean, be yourself: Permit the student to see you, warts and all, admit to faults and work to improve, but do not be anything other than what you are.

In a similar vein, Dr. B. wrote,

> As for loving students, I believe a teacher must *respect* students even when they show ignorance, arrogance, or anger. It is too easy to blame students when they fail, rather than to look at our teaching and find it deficient. It is not as easy to *love* all students. However, the way a teacher handles difficult students may distinguish one who is a "great" teacher from one who is merely "good." I think I am a good communicator, a sensitive counselor. My candor about myself opens the door for student honesty. Once we develop a relationship, the possibilities for learning are

limitless, for there is no greater motivator than love. Schmaltzy, yes, but true.

Supporting this philosophy of openness, Morgan, Phelps, and Pritchard (1995) suggested that self-disclosure leads to trust and promotes credibility, factors that surely enhance teaching and learning. These professors said that they developed honest relationships with their students and their classes by scrupulously adhering to policies and procedures and avoiding the kinds of deceptions that some faculty with less integrity use, such as posing trick questions on tests. They were not afraid to reveal their own values, as when Dr. E. pointed out to his oceanography class that "science and religion are complementary, as I told you before." Obviously, this view is a theme throughout his course. They spoke of the "tremendous responsibility" which instructors accept when entering the profession of teaching, and of the many elements of good teaching that are "more ethereal and cannot be 'learned' although they may evolve with experience, maturity, and wisdom." They were not above admitting the limits of what they knew or revealing their spiritual beliefs. Dr. D., for example, concluded our interview by saying, "I believe that above the level of competence, teaching is a gift, and we should remember to say, 'Thank you'."

One of the markers of integrity we observed in excellent teachers was their knowledge of when to resist external pressures and risk offending colleagues, administrators, and students. Like Thoreau's self-reliant individual, they marched to their own drummers when it came to ethical decisions. For example, Dr. D. agreed to teach a freshman writing component even though he risked antagonizing the English faculty on campus, who were angry because they had lost control over that part of the curriculum. Dr. H. reported that he was resisting a proposal from faculty in a related discipline to reduce lab time and substitute computer media, because he did not believe that "virtual reality" was good enough for students to learn the 3-D concepts of anatomy.

As for academic standards and integrity, these professors were adamant. Dr. B., for example, described herself as "relentless" if she suspected a student had plagiarized. Several of the distinguished teachers expressed disdain for faculty who dishonestly manipulate student ratings of their performance by inserting faked responses or changing others. Although he was pressed for time in the course,

Professor H. gave his class 20 minutes at the beginning of class to complete instructor evaluations, as required by the college. As for allotting primacy to teaching, Professor G. illustrated how she dealt with competing demands on her time. When we paid her a surprise visit, she acknowledged us warmly, but asked if we would mind if she *first* saw the students who were waiting to see her during her office hours. In another example, as Dr. C. mentored his lab assistants, he described himself as "cruel" for enforcing a policy to award extra credit: "But this is the way to handle the workload. The assignments must be done in their handwriting to discourage copying. Notes should be fleshed out, not just the outline. Record the grade in your gradebook/spreadsheet." Warning his graduate teaching assistants that there were many ways for their students to cheat, he concluded, "The value derived is worth the slop in the system."

Another marker of excellence we observed was the rigor with which our teacher–scholars set and adhered to standards. A common evaluative statement refers to these individuals as "strict, but fair." For example, they might insist upon punctuality for class, a high quality of work presented to the professor, appropriate behavior in class, and academic integrity. Although a common misconception exists in academe that those who win teaching awards are usually liberal graders, we found that the distinguished teachers we studied were unusually rigorous and demanding with their students, a finding consistent with previous studies (Beidler, 1986; Cronin, 1992). They did not cave in to students' requests for high grades, but rather, had the ability to assert their own expectations in a manner which students perceived as fair. Like those Goleman described as highly skilled in social interactions, they were not afraid to confront students if that was deemed necessary for the student to learn. This ability to balance their true selves and values against the need to make others happy was another mark of their integrity: The peers in our study reported that award-winning professors had reputations for excellence, quality service, and humanistic values.

Another aspect of the integrity of the distinguished teaching professors we studied was that they "practiced what they preached" about professional responsibility. The work ethic of the excellent teacher is embodied in the "supertrait" of conscientiousness. Our distinguished teachers had many years of experience in teaching. One professor reported that he had not missed a class in

43 years. They referred to themselves as learners and took responsibility for continually expanding their knowledge. They looked internally when there was a problem with student learning; instead of blaming the student for not learning, they attempted to identify the teaching problem. They approached evaluation (testing) of students in terms of finding out what the student *knows* as opposed to what the student *does not know.* They spent an extraordinary amount of time both in preparation for classes and with their students, making themselves available and putting their students first. Professor G., for example, claimed that "the will to put a tremendous amount of energy into teaching" was the primary ingredient behind her having been recognized for her excellent teaching: "Not everyone can afford it; not everyone is willing [to devote the time]." In addition to their daily commitment to teaching, we also observed that many excellent teachers assumed a broader responsibility for the quality of students' education beyond the classroom by serving on college committees, taking on administrative roles, and initiating reforms campuswide.

Reforming the Evaluation of Teaching

Let us return to our initial question of why evaluation is necessary. Is it any wonder that the evaluation of teaching and the development of criteria for judging teaching excellence have been so slow in coming? Administrators and faculty have different agendas and have refused to acknowledge each other's legitimate needs. Yet there may be a middle ground. If criteria for effective teaching and standards of excellence were developed and used first to refine hiring procedures, then to support faculty professional growth, and later for evaluative purposes, then both needs would be met. Faculty who were assisted early on in their careers would be more comfortable with regular evaluations, would improve their performances as a result of the regular feedback, and therefore, would be more likely to meet the standards for renewal, promotion, and tenure.

Research has suggested that professors make the best effort to improve *before* they are evaluated for personnel actions and that feedback during instruction is more useful than a single final assessment (Boice, 1992; Gil, 1987). So it is, we contend, that faculty are most willing to work on their teaching performance when they receive assistance throughout their teaching careers, not solely during reviews for renewal, promotion, tenure or post-tenure.

We believe that it is important to make distinctions about teaching effectiveness so that teaching assistants, junior faculty, and even senior faculty who are experiencing difficulties will have the opportunity to improve—a radical idea. This improvement in teaching effectiveness has a ripple effect: When teaching is improved, learning is improved. The happy results of this endeavor are students who are better educated citizens and faculty who make steady progress professionally, gaining promotions and tenure along the way.

What is needed is a standard of excellence which is powerful enough to meet both the agenda of administrators who say they want better teaching and faculty who want better learning. The standard should derive from a theory that is broad enough to accommodate a variety of styles and to describe a range of phenomena. This theory should encompass the art and the science of teaching; the professor's character, knowledge, and actions; and the learning of the students. It should provide the basis for judgments about institutional effectiveness as well as judgments about hiring, promoting, and firing.

Toward a Theory of Teaching Excellence

We believe that so much confusion over how to define distinguished teaching exists because research on teaching excellence to date has been very rudimentary, focusing primarily on the identification of "characteristics" or "traits" that mark the outstanding teacher. Some of these traits, as we have shown, are personality descriptors, though others point to teaching behaviors and practices. Only recently have studies gone beyond vague, general terms to describe the professors, their knowledge, or their actions. Few researchers have adequately addressed the need for an overriding theoretical framework to explain the relationship of the traits excellent teachers are said to possess, and no one seems to have investigated how or why some faculty develop these characteristics, behaviors, and notions about teaching, and others don't.

We have chosen to approach a definition of teaching excellence from a more global perspective. Based on a broad review of the

literature from the ancient Greeks through contemporary educational theory and modern psychology, as well as our interviews
with award-winning professors and their peers and actual classroom observations of excellent teachers, we propose a theoretical
definition which includes four elements:

1. The *character* of the professor (values, personality, and social
   intelligence)
2. The *knowledge* of the professor (disciplinary and pedagogical
   understanding)
3. The *actions* of the professor (problem-solving behaviors)
4. The *responses* of the students (learning outcomes).

In this chapter we have examined who distinguished teachers are,
and in subsequent chapters we will explore what they know and
what they do. We recognize, however, that these are artificial categories and that, in reality, they continually interact during instruction.

We acknowledge that aspects of our theory are not original, and
that each of its parts has been articulated or suggested elsewhere.
What *is* new, we believe, is the theory's comprehensiveness, its use
of current psychological research to refine the term character, and
its analysis of teaching behaviors from the perspective of problem
solving. We believe that this multifaceted approach to defining
teaching excellence finally does justice to the complexity of teaching, incorporating as it does both the *art* of teaching which has been
the subject of philosophers since Socrates (see Highet, 1959; Decyk,
1996) and the *science* of teaching, a view which includes the behav-
iorists' mandate for objectivity and reliability as well as brain researchers' biological approach to behavior.

Conclusion

In the absence of interdisciplinary communication and lacking a
theory of teaching excellence, higher education has been recycling
the same old attempts to evaluate teaching and not getting very far.
We believe that the way out of this mire involves collaboration
among researchers from such fields as psychology, humanities, cognitive science and education. We also believe that such research
could prove valuable for faculty personnel committees, some of

which already employ vague criteria of "collegiality" and "character" in their decisions to hire, retain, and tenure.

In this chapter, we have addressed the question, "What are the characteristics of excellent teachers?" from a variety of perspectives, ultimately integrating them into a model of character based on a theory of emotional intelligence. Our focus now turns to a discussion of precisely what teachers know about their subject and about teaching. To date, the literature connecting teaching excellence with "knowledgeability and scholarship" has been superficial at best. Based on our research, in the next chapter we will explore the minds of teacher–scholars—what they believe about teaching, their methods, their plans, their policies, and their assessments of instruction.

6

$$\boxed{}$$

Scholars of Teaching

Early in the twentieth century, institutions of higher education in the U.S. were in transition from the traditional British university to the German model of the research institution. The shift from a values-laden system of education towards a values-neutral scientific approach to knowledge resulted in the elevation of research (the discovery of new knowledge) and in the decline in the prestige of the teaching of the "wisdom of the ages" (Boyer, 1990). The ideal of the teacher–scholar arose as a compromise between these two competing philosophies of education. This significant change in the mission of education led to the belief "that the promising scholars promoted to tenure were really good teachers" (Huber, 1992, p. 125). Some studies have suggested that the concept of the teacher–scholar is a myth (Massey & Wilger, 1995, p. 16), whereas others have found a positive correlation between scholarliness and ratings of effective teaching (Bok, 1991). We agree with Boyer, however, that we need to go beyond the tired old teaching versus research debate and give the term *scholarship* a "broader, more capacious meaning" (1990, p. 16) which encompasses both research and teaching, as well as the integration or application of knowledge. Boyer implied that good teaching is the key to good scholarship, and that distinguished teachers are the agents of great scholarship—that scholarship does not just happen, great teachers make it happen. To quote, "In the end, inspired teaching keeps the flame of scholarship alive" (p. 24).

As our research shows, distinguished professors often define their own scholarship as contemporary and having application to the classroom. They view the teacher–scholar roles as variables in an equation whose sum cannot exceed the constants of time and energy. Their view is consistent with education research, which shows that distinguished teachers use broad knowledge across disciplines to make their subjects meaningful, and analogies and examples from a variety of sources to make difficult material clear (Brandt, 1988; Menges & Weimer, 1996). Moreover, they reported that their commitment to students' learning requires an extraordinary expenditure of energy and time, often leaving little room in their lives for the in-depth pursuit of narrowly focused scholarship in their disciplines.

Of our 30 distinguished professors, 92% agreed that it was possible for a faculty to be both an award-winning teacher and award-winning scholar, but many of them qualified those responses. In their own words, our distinguished teachers reacted to the teacher–scholar issue:

- "It's extraordinarily hard to be excellent *simultaneously* in both [teaching and research], as both take more than full time."
- "Teaching and research skills are different talents. A person is lucky to have one, much less both!"
- "Scholarship involves refreshment of one's intellectual inventory. Writing for publication is not the only way to do this."
- "Over a period of time one individual could be both [teacher and researcher].... Too often (if not always) researchers get so 'into' their research and writing that the other aspects of their job, in this case teaching, will suffer."

At the heart of this debate is how one defines scholarship. The distinguished teaching professors we studied suggested a broad interpretation of the term. They spoke about connections and relationships between what they study and what they want students to learn, a kind of scholarship which Rice (1991) calls "synoptic capacity," the ability to draw together various areas of an academic discipline and to place concepts in the larger context of the discipline. This is similar to Shulman's notion that:

> several kinds of understanding and skill...underlie a teacher's expertise and distinguish it from the mere subject matter expert['s].... The teacher not only understands the content to be

learned, but comprehends which aspects of the content are crucial for future understanding of the subject and which are more peripheral and are less likely to impede future learning if not fully grasped. The teacher comprehends which aspects of the content will be likely to pose the greatest difficulties for the pupils' understanding. (1988, p. 37)

In addition, our distinguished teaching professors were interested not only in *what* is taught, but equally, *how* it is taught; they possessed the knowledge that Rice (1991) called "pedagogical content knowledge" and "knowledge about student meaning making." For them, the classroom became the research laboratory for the observation of student learning, with the professor actively but informally investigating, and discovering means of improving instruction (Angelo, 1991; Schön, 1987). We believe that the distinction between "scholarship" and "pedagogy" can be resolved by acknowledging that excellent teachers possess a range and depth of expertise about teaching that surpass the norm, although they may not be able to articulate this knowledge. Ronkowski (1993) and Hatton (1989) described such professionals, who practice without a theoretical model and researched principles, as *bricoleurs,* those who learn by trial and error. This do-it-yourself approach is a consequence of academe's failure to recognize teaching as a form of scholarship, according to Ronkowski (1993) and Drummond (1996). It is these teachers whom Aristotle was describing when he wrote, "Broadly speaking, what distinguishes the man who knows from the ignorant man is an ability to teach" (Shulman, 1986, p. 7). If the emphasis in the teacher–scholar debate is reversed so as to refer to distinguished teaching professors as *scholars of teaching,* then we eliminate the false dichotomy that has distracted us from the university's primary goal, which is to educate.

During the last 20 years, research universities across the nation have attempted to develop a "culture that values teaching" (Sorcinelli & Davis, 1996). In the mid-1970s, for example, the State University of New York (SUNY) created a rank called "Distinguished Teaching Professor" as a way of recognizing those full professors who had demonstrated "outstanding teaching competence over a period of years at the graduate, undergraduate or professional levels" (SUNY Distinguished Teaching Professorships Policies and Procedures 1995–96 Series, p. 1). For a time, this was the only "super" rank in the university, and it was bestowed upon those who had already attained the high status of full professor, with its recognition of scholarship, service, and teaching. Soon, however, two other ranks were created, those of "Distinguished Professor" (for those excelling in research) and "Distinguished Service Professor" (for those excelling in college service) (C. Herreid, personal communication, March 29, 1996). Accordingly, over time the status of these ranks has been informally inverted, once more relegating teaching to a lower rung of the ladder, so that the rank of "Distinguished Professor," not "Distinguished *Teaching* Professor," is now viewed by the dominant campus culture as the higher rank. One AAUP president at a Category I (research) university, for example, expressed this opinion: "They should not give these [ranks] at a research university, because they are not given to the strongest professors. I would not consider it an honor to receive one," a view which we heard from other professors as well.

The SUNY definition of a teacher–scholar is one who "keeps abreast of and makes significant contributions in his or her own field, and uses the relevant contemporary data from that field and related disciplines in teaching" (SUNY Distinguished Teaching Professorships, p. 3). An acceptable set of criteria for distinguishing teaching excellence is listed among the policies and procedures of the document. The primary criterion for appointment is *skill in teaching*, with consideration given to mastery of subject matter, sound scholarship, service to the university and community, and continuing growth. The SUNY teacher–scholar is one who:

- Performs superbly in the classroom
- Maintains a flexible instructional policy which adapts readily to student needs, interests, and problems
- Demonstrates mastery of teaching techniques
- Is generous with personal time
- Is easily accessible (office hours, conferences, special meetings)
- Demonstrates continual concern with the intellectual growth of individual students (teaching-related services to students)
- Is a responsible student advisor
- Sets high standards for students and helps them to attain academic excellence
- Requires above average quality and quantity of work from the students

- Actively works with students to help them improve their scholarly or artistic performance
- Does not hesitate to give low evaluations to students who do poorly (SUNY Distinguished Teaching Professorships, p. 3)

The SUNY criteria advise those selecting Distinguished Teaching Professors to consider the professors' performance in the context of their instructional load—the "number of substantially different courses taught, the number of students per course, and the teaching techniques employed in the various courses" (SUNY Distinguished Teaching Professorships, p. 3). They also suggest that local selection committees consider "the quality, quantity, and difficulty of course-related work," and that they look at students' accomplishments as other evidence of excellence (p. 3).

The University of California at Berkeley similarly specifies criteria for making teaching excellence awards at the research university:

- Command of the subject
- Continuous growth in the field of study
- Ability to organize course material and to present it cogently
- Effective design and redesign of courses
- Ability to inspire in students independent and original thinking
- Ability to encourage intellectual interests in beginning students and to stimulate creative work in advanced students
- Enthusiasm and vitality in learning and teaching
- Guidance of student research projects
- Participation in advising students
- Participating in guiding and supervising graduate student instructors (teaching assistants)
- Ability to respond to a diverse student body (Sorcinelli & Davis, 1996, p. 72)

Surveys have found nearly universal use of variations of these sets of criteria at research universities (Miller, 1995; Quinn, 1994).

In recent years, researchers have provided the intellectual framework for a new view of pedagogy (Seldin & Associates, 1990). In this chapter, we will analyze from a variety of perspectives the ways in which the distinguished teaching professors we studied thought about their teaching and applied those thoughts to their practice: Shulman's (1986) academic and pedagogical knowledge,

Boyer's (1990) scholarship of teaching, Chickering and Gamson's (1991) Seven Principles for Good Practice, and Goleman's (1995) emotional intelligence. As winners of faculty and teaching awards ourselves, we have chosen to intersperse our own experiences in this and subsequent chapters for a broader range of examples. Our goals are to explore the wisdom of practice, to provide a more contextual conception of pedagogy, and to show how it relates to research on the scholarship of teaching (Menges, Weimer, & Associates, 1996).

Teaching Philosophies: A Compass for Learning

The distinguished professors we studied appear to be guided by a solid philosophical compass which points them toward a common but paradoxical destination, the independence of their students after they have been thoroughly acculturated. Although these educators all came from various backgrounds of teaching preparation (only one-quarter had a written statement of their philosophy of teaching, and most could be described accurately as *bricoleurs*), we found that when we questioned them, they had well-developed and distinctive beliefs about pedagogy and shared the overriding goal of creating independent learners.

In the remainder of this chapter, we will describe what these professors believe and how that impacts what they know and do as teachers. Because they are reflective experimenters, using the classroom as their laboratory, their research is informally conducted at every class meeting, during office hours, and in discussion with colleagues. They know how students learn. They are able to identify what information is important for the students to learn, where the difficulties in learning that material usually arise, and how to clarify material through a rich array of techniques.

Here is how one award-winning professor, Professor I., described a defining moment in his education. When exposed to "two different and in some ways antithetical pedagogic methods," he chose the tutorial over the traditional lecture format:

> The first [method] was very much a legacy of the British university system: a don, usually clad in a black habit, would preside in Moses-like fashion from his Mount Sinai of a podium over a lecture theater crammed with hundreds of blank, bored, and often unconscious young faces. For a whole excruciating hour, we

would watch the don conduct a private and often inscrutable conversation with himself about the Higher Truths of whatever it was we were studying. Each don may have had his individual quirks or peccadilloes, his prosaic or polemic habits of literary interpretation, but the expectation was always the same regardless of who he was: We students were to record in our notebooks the frequently incomprehensible Higher Truths handed down to us, and faithfully regurgitate them come examination time, hoping vainly that Enlightenment would appear in some form during the interim.

In addition to the mandatory lectures, however, we were also able to attend weekly, noncompulsory tutorials which provided forums for discussion and debate between small groups of students and a teacher. The tutorial was evidently considered inferior to the lecture, as the star dons almost invariably delegated the task of teaching them to graduate students and junior professors. But to my young mind, the tutorial was without doubt the considerably more rewarding educational experience, in contrast to the lecture, from which I almost invariably emerged with a notebook full of doodles and a head full of empty phrases.

Another, Professor R., believes that it is his job to teach students to "think differently." He connected his classical university background with his belief that students enter the learning environment (the university) with preconceptions that are:

Aristotelian or Western in nature—an either/or way of thinking, as opposed to the Eastern or Zen concept of "mu," "no thing," or "ShoShin," which suggests a beginner's mind, an empty mind, a ready mind, a mind like a child's. For [students], thinking is a function, learning is like math...considering things concretely rather than looking for a range or a balance. They read a poem and comment, "That poem stinks!" unwilling to look at that poem as having a variety of qualities or messages. Some poems readers will like, others they will not. They need to get rid of their judgmental attitudes,...of things being only black or white. *They must be taught to think differently.*

Expanding that concept, Professor L. suggested that in order to *think* differently, students must also be taught to *see* differently:

They must learn to withhold judgment, to place no limits on what they observe, to view things objectively before making subjective assumptions, to identify what they see as opposed to what they don't see. They must eliminate judgmental or limiting language such as "just," "only," "simply," et cetera. They may only make assumptions if they have gathered sufficient and valid data. A rule of thumb in the initial stages of learning to record concrete impressions is, "If you can see it, hear it, count it, or measure it—only then may you write it."

For example, returning from an observation in a school, students were describing a student who happened to have a severe physical disability. When required to describe what the student did, they wrote, "He only sat there." Digging for what really was observed, the professor refused the response and relentlessly grilled the students for information about what he did do—not what he did not do. It turned out that the student did sit in a wheel chair, did localize with his eyes, did vocalize "yes" and "no," did laugh at jokes, and so on. According to Professor L., the students needed a new focus. They needed to break the mold of how they had previously seen individuals.

Professor M.'s philosophy of teaching is based on her belief that education is values-laden. She acknowledges three values which have evolved as central components of her teaching: relevance, integration, and ownership. These interdependent values dictate her classroom goals and the means by which she attempts to achieve them. She writes,

> Clarifying my values and becoming conscious of how they manifest in my classroom behavior, in my choices concerning course content, and in my evaluation of student work is ongoing:
>
> *Relevance*—Preparing for any class requires actively choosing what material will be covered and what information will be relegated to the periphery. The more challenging choices involve the question of how to present the information so that it meets students' needs and interests. I attempt to ask myself from the students' perspective, "What does this theory, this research result, or this anecdote, have to do with my life?" The effort to relate course content to students' actual life experiences facilitates their engagement in the material.

Integration—Students are asked to reflect back to some other point in time when a similar theory was covered and how it would explain the current phenomenon being discussed.

Ownership—Effective teaching is a shared enterprise, where both the teacher and student take some degree of responsibility for the learning process and establishing work standards. The process may be initiated by the teacher, who outlines the expectations for the students, but it continues to emerge over time through mutual feedback. I am far more inclined to "set someone up for success" than to play "stump the student," and believe that this attitude motivates students to rise to my expectations.

Professor B. also believes that teaching and learning are cooperative acts, and writes, "The teacher establishes ownership of the teaching process which includes not only imparting the knowledge, but also preparing and motivating the students to accept it." She focused on student outcomes as the only measure of successful teaching and identified her role as model learner:

If a student doesn't learn, has the teacher taught? No. Ideally, each of us should be able to "turn on" our students to the material to be learned, so much so that other factors such as personal problems, poor textbooks, or prior unpleasant associations with the material cannot distract students from their goal. "Teachers" who continually go through the motions of "teaching" despite their students' poor performances have missed the point. They are *not* teaching.

I always tell my students that they are two-thirds responsible for their learning, and I, one-third. In other words, I expect them to put twice as much effort into the process as I, for I already know the material. However, I have found that when I work very hard, students feel guilty when they do not match my effort. If I set a good example with regard to preparation for class, they usually follow suit. When students fail to prepare for class, I do not humiliate them; I move on to the next student. Their own guilty consciences will do the rest. When we all take responsibility, we become a community of learners.

Our participants acknowledged that an understanding of human behavior is essential for good teaching. Dr. B. suggested that her background in education awakened her desire to experiment in the classroom:

> Having received both my doctoral and master's degrees in education, I feel I have an advantage over faculty who have never formally studied education. It is common for people to ridicule what they don't know about, such as education programs. However, I find it fascinating that the very same faculty who perceive teaching *only* as an "holistic art" are often the faculty who teach the scientific method. I wonder, "Why do they exclude human behavior from scientific inquiry?" I have found my courses in the psychology of learning to be very useful in the classroom. Believing as I do that human behavior is goal-driven, I encourage students to set their goals higher than they believe they can accomplish. Then, when they are in this uncomfortable stage between what they know and what they are beginning to know, I reward them with as much help and encouragement as I can muster. I do not punish them with bad grades, but rather, work with them on improving their initial responses, a practice which works particularly well with writers. In educational jargon, this strategy is known as "shaping."

Another example of the integration of one's self and one's philosophy into teaching is Professor R.'s use of a statement of values and a code of ethics as an introduction to his courses. His values are expressed in a handout entitled "Life 101: Ten Rules for Being Human," which provides students with information on what lies at his core. He lets them in on his interpretation of the secrets of life so as to demystify and humanize both the material and himself, once again showing how authenticity and values are central to excellent teaching. Sharing a comic code of ethics which is, nevertheless, sincere, he distributes a set of "Will Rogers-esque" quotes from "Don't Squat with Yer Spurs on! A Cowboy's Guide to Life by Texas Bix Bender" (1994). Using this code of ethics—"The Code of the West"—Dr. R. sets an irreverent, playful, and iconoclastic tone:

> "If you find yourself in a hole, the first thing to do is to stop diggin'. Commentary: Simple mistakes become serious offenses when we persist in denial and cover-up." [Or,] "The easiest way to eat crow is while it's still warm. The colder it gets the harder it is to swallow. Commentary: Ordinary, small errors become

compounded by time; the longer we wait, the harder it is to apologize or admit error—and the bigger the problem becomes."

Dr. R.'s commentary and tone convey a set of traditional values: humility, self-awareness, common sense, awareness of the influence of one's behavior on others, thoughtfulness, and individuality. Another "Life 101" handout, "Ten Rules for Being Human" (anonymous), further reveals Professor R.'s values about growth, introspection, and self-reliance: "There are no mistakes, only lessons. Growth is a process of trial and error, experimentation. The 'failed' experiments are as much a part of the process as the experiments that actually worked." These common sense axioms (variations on the elements of emotional intelligence which we presented in Chapter 5) can be applied to almost every educational experience.

Foremost, Dr. R. sees his role as a college teacher as "educating prospective leaders not to worship knowledge, but to question it!" He reported that his role is to participate and interact creatively with his students "to search for new ideas, to challenge old ones, and to wrestle riddles." He said, "A teacher is essentially a learner! Therefore, it becomes imperative [for him] to know how each [of his] student[s] thinks. And communication—both written and spoken—is the obvious means for his learning how students think." His role as teacher, therefore, is "to provide students with the ability to use language to access their humanity through their most powerful, creative and stimulating thoughts and emotions."

With a doctorate in rhetoric, Professor R. naturally looks to the classics for guidance: He described the sources of his ideas about teaching thus:

My teaching philosophy and style have been shaped by the great teachers I have encountered in real life and in books (especially the classics). My approach to learning is as old as Plato, a guiding influence in my teaching career. Socrates metaphorically viewed the teacher as a midwife (see Plato's *Theaetetus*) who tenderly assists the pregnant woman with the delivery of her offspring. So too the teacher assists the inquiring mind of the learner to give birth to knowledge and to facilitate discovery. The path to learning is through sustained, creative and systematic inquiry.

Drawing upon a well-developed set of metaphors, Dr. R.'s own words reveal a carefully thought out definition of the college teacher's roles:

In many respects a teacher is like a farmer or a physician. Plato compares the teacher to the healer and compares Comenius (in the *Great Didactic*) to a farmer who cultivates the soil of the mind. I view my role in a similar sense. Plants can grow without a farmer; people can heal without a physician, and students can learn without a teacher. But the teacher as a cooperative–artist, like the farmer or physician, can produce powerful results that might not occur naturally.

As a teacher my role is to emphasize the importance of doubt and uncertainty. Doubt is the key to education! At the University of Göttingen (in Germany), made famous by the great physicists Max Born and Werner Heisenberg, the symbol of the school is an iron statue of a barefoot girl standing beside a goose. The statue is not in front of the library, but outside the rathskeller (pub)—another place of learning! At graduation all students kiss the statue. The statue of the young girl symbolizes how students should approach learning: with a ragamuffin, barefoot irreverence for certainty and with a childlike appreciation for creative inquiry and play. My role as teacher is to facilitate combinational play and childlike curiosity.

Teaching is play of sorts. It's like riding a raft: you pile everybody on board; you get swept up in the swirling current of the classroom; you steer the best you can; you never really sink; and you always have wet feet!

Methods of Implementing the Philosophies: So What's New?

With the exception of technology, most of the award-winning professors reported using methods that, when analyzed, would not be considered new. Although their practices in the classroom may have current buzzwords attached to them, they are in fact as old as Socrates and as "new" as Dewey. In other words, the methods used by these teachers were not unique in and of themselves; however, the difference lies in the manner in which they selected from this array to suit the multitude of learning needs they encountered. They applied the wisdom gathered from their experiences in an almost compassionate manner. In a monitoring mode, their "radar" was always attuned to how their methods and materials were affecting individuals or groups of students.

The philosophies we have presented suggest that our distinguished professors possess an abstract level of knowledge, a belief system which informs their choice of teaching strategies. At the experiential level, this translates into what they know and what they do about teaching. This pedagogical knowledge includes when to use different techniques, when to choose particular materials, and when to vary the pace. They demonstrated that they knew how students were reacting to the material, how students could best learn the material, how to clarify it, what the pitfalls to learning the material were, what was important to emphasize, how best to present the information, and what differences existed in student learning styles.

To sum up, as we have already shown, the practices of award-winning teacher–scholars we interviewed exemplified the six "supertraits" of emotional intelligence cited in Chapter 5. Their planning, interactions with students, and methods of evaluating reflected an extraordinary degree of conscientiousness and organization. These behaviors could also be described from the perspective of Chickering and Gamson's best practices (1991) as "encouraging student–faculty contact" and "giving prompt feedback." Their materials and manner often displayed a playful, irreverent, or creative approach to the subject which could be interpreted as "enthusiastic," and their behaviors suggested in other ways a maturely developed EQ or set of intrapersonal and interpersonal skills that they used in their drive to help students to excel as learners. There were no pessimists about human development in this group. Instead, they optimistically viewed themselves as "works in progress," always striving to improve their teaching and their students' learning. They diligently planned, prepared, and revised their methods as they encountered instructional problems, as if possessed by some vision of human potential shining before them like the Holy Grail. Sure of their goals, they reported that they confidently experimented with "new and improved" ways of clarifying and conveying concepts and skills, and when students failed, they took it almost as a personal wound or affront.

Because they were scholars with breadth as well as depth, the outstanding teachers we observed took leadership and responsibility for global learning on the part of their students: for example, they saw writing, speaking, cultural literacy, values, and professional behavior as their legitimate domains, regardless of the subjects they taught. Although other faculty may throw up their hands at the extent of students' deficiencies, these professors roll up their sleeves and begin the challenging task of educating in the broadest sense. Even though their classes might be very large, they often continue to require some essay responses and/or papers; and they frequently connect their teaching to current events. Viewing synthesis as an important cognitive goal for their students, they purposely design courses that force students to cross knowledge boundaries and discover connections. In other words, once again they demonstrate Rice's (1991) synoptic capacity of integrating and connecting discipline knowledge to larger contexts.

Master Planners

In this section, we will provide a window into the planning minds of teacher–scholars, and while there might not be a "hard copy" of their mental processes available, when prompted, they were able to articulate these planning processes, which appear to be deeply embedded in their teaching lives. The planning methods our distinguished professors employed surfaced at all levels: campus-wide curricular initiatives such as grant writing and institutional planning; international, intercollegiate, and interdisciplinary program development; program additions and revisions; new courses; and new lesson plans. We found that they were planners *par excellence.*

At all levels, the distinguished teacher–scholars we studied frequently exploited wide professional and social networks to enhance their planning efforts. Often the award-winning faculty we studied were involved in writing grant proposals that served the entire campus, such as service learning, computer laboratories designated for writing, and faculty development. They initiated feasibility studies for international student and faculty exchanges, as well as articulation agreements, consortia for sharing resources, and partnerships between colleges, high schools, elementary schools, business, and the community. At the course level, they might engage in collaborative planning with a teaching team, or they might schedule a series of speakers to enrich their courses. Like "stars" in the business world, they demonstrated high levels of initiative, networking, self-management, and communication skills (Kelly & Caplan, 1993).

At the course planning level, the outstanding teachers we studied reported that good courses "need to have a plot or a narrative," a dominant theme or set of key ideas repeated throughout the course. Through experience, they developed a sense of the limits that the students would most assuredly encounter, so they planned interventions which sometimes resulted in major revamping or restructuring of courses. For example, students are notorious for miscalculating the amount of time a term paper requires and therefore meet roadblocks when trying to use library materials late in the semester. One professor, Dr. B., decided to break the task into segments and move it to the beginning of the course. The first assignment consisted of reading, summarizing, and citing several sources; the second paper investigated a research topic and organized it into a draft outline; and the third task was the extended research paper. He planned for it to be due in mid-semester to eliminate the competition for library resources and continual requests for incompletes at the end of the year. Professor B.'s intervention is a successful solution to a "core idea that is particularly challenging to teach and learn" within the usual content domain of the English classroom. His techniques serve as a useful illustration of Shulman's merger of academic content knowledge and pedagogical knowledge (Sparks, 1992).

Within their plans for structure in their courses, we found that the teacher–scholars we studied often created a variety of rigid frames or routines for their classes, but inside those frameworks, they were flexible. An examination of sample syllabi with instructor policies demonstrates the kinds of rigid frames they employed to shape the learning environment. The syllabus represents a protocol for the course—the operating rules of explicit course procedures and policies which continually redirect the responsibility back to the student. Hammons & Shoock (1994) reported that an effective syllabus serves a variety of purposes: to communicate information that students need at the beginning of a course and that instructors need to have in writing, to model good planning, and to demonstrate that the instructor cares about teaching and students (1994, p. 7).

Through the syllabus some of our distinguished teaching professors also provided a preparation for the feelings the students were most likely to encounter while taking the course. They articulated the normal way learning the material worked: "This particular material may be difficult to understand at first, but trust me that after we reach a certain point, it will become clear. Don't get overwhelmed, just hang in with me."

An examination of a syllabus prepared by an excellent teacher reveals a depth and comprehensiveness essential for clarity. For the teacher–scholars we studied, each element of the syllabus was considered essential in preparing the student to approach the course independently and to be successful. Professor L.'s syllabus stated the traditional means of contacting her, and reinforced her availability so that conflicting schedules could not be used as an excuse for failing to seek assistance: "Individual assistance is always available by appointment." In addition, however, she was explicit in the inclusion of her email address and explanation of how students could use it, a message machine that directs students to leave specific information so that she could respond appropriately and in a timely fashion, and a procedure for guaranteeing that a written message would reach her. Similarly, her course objectives were explicit and behaviorally oriented.

The student will:

- Summarize general information, through in-class discussion and term paper, pertaining to _____.
- Demonstrate knowledge, through examination procedures, of each area of _____ in regard to definition, prevalence, etiology, characteristics, diagnosis, and remediation.
- Become familiar with _____ literature through independent reading and in-class discussion.
- Participate in field observations.
- Demonstrate skill in observation and recording _____ through written reports.

We found that when teacher–scholars were assigned a new course, they sought out those with expertise and gleaned the best from existing course materials, assignments, and methods; in other words, they conducted teaching research on best practices for that course. The vast majority indicated that they learned to teach by observing professors they admired and avoiding practices that they found less valuable. Dr. H., for example, went back to school, literally, and retooled himself to teach gross anatomy by attending a medical school course so he was not simply studying the content, but focusing on the process of instruction—the pedagogy—for this very sensitive, peculiarly physical and factual subject matter.

Over their lifetimes, award-winning professors appeared to have sorted out those course policies that were essential and discarded those that were unenforceable. The result was a set of policies which some could construe as rigid, while others might say that they demonstrate one of Chickering and Gamson's (1991) best practices of "communicating high expectations." For example, in her syllabus, after her content outline and methods of evaluation, Dr. L. focused on course policies regarding deadlines, presentation of work, and ethical standards. They are emphatic, clear, and rigid, designed to encourage a sense of the quality and conscientiousness she expects:

- *All work must be typed.*
- *Late assignments:* There will be *no* work accepted beyond the agreed upon date.
- Any work not submitted in class must be handed directly to a secretary in the Office (first floor) before the end of the due date. It is your responsibility to be sure that the secretary initials, dates, and notes the time of receipt. *Under no circumstances are you to slide papers under an office door.*
- *Incompletes:* There will be *no* incompletes given in this course.

She reports being comfortable with her apparent rigidity in late assignments because, at the beginning of each course, she puts the responsibility for choosing due dates on the students. Thus, she promotes time management and advance organization skills through the students' review of their total semester requirements—other course exams, projects, or paper deadlines—and allows them to determine a reasonable time frame in which to prepare her coursework. Handing work in to the secretary emphasizes the value the professor places on students' work, and prevents work from being misplaced, damaged, or "missing."

Other examples of clear and emphatic communications are Professor G.'s statements of policies in each syllabus, with the caveat, "No exceptions will be made," and Professor W.'s distribution of an

"Important Stuff" folder that thrusts responsibility clearly upon the student and which includes the following strictures:

- You should not make travel plans before this date (last exam date).
- If you believe that these rules are too harsh, unreasonable, or unacceptable to you, do not enroll in this class.
- Punctual (i.e., on time) classroom attendance is required. Arriving late to class is distracting and diminishes the educational attainment of those attending class in accordance with the University Policy. Personally, I think it is rude and inconsiderate to obstruct the serious pursuit of learning that students are entitled to and expect. Therefore, students enrolled in this course are required to attend class on time or not at all. In plain English, this means that if you cannot for any reason whatsoever get to class on time, do not enter the classroom after the scheduled start of class. Arriving late to class will automatically lower your course grade by one letter grade. [Professor W. refers to this as a "meaningful sanction."] There will be no exceptions to this rule, so please do not ask. If, for any reason, you cannot comply with this policy or find it unreasonable or unacceptable, do not enroll in this class!
- Please be advised (warned) in advance that I frequently conduct classes in an unusual manner (that's why they call me "Crazy Willie"). At times I will call on students or make comments that are intended to make the lectures a little more lively and interesting. These remarks are *not* intended to embarrass, harass, humiliate, or offend anyone. If you think this behavior will be unacceptable to your sensitivities, do not enroll in this class. Otherwise, chill out, loosen up, and let's have some fun.
- As you realize by now this class is obviously very *large*. In order for such a large class to be successful, it is necessary for everyone to cooperate and follow a few simple classroom procedures. For my part, I will present organized, clear, and hopefully interesting (and at times entertaining) lectures. I will provide you with supplemental handouts dealing with the lecture material. In addition, you can count on me to begin and end each lecture on time and to devote the class time to explaining and presenting the material I expect you to learn. I require, however, an

equal effort on your part to make the class successful. Specifically, I expect you to attend class punctually, prepared, and attentively. You are encouraged to ask relevant questions in class, but you are *not to distract your fellow classmates with unnecessary talking during the lecture.* If you insist on talking in class and disturbing others, I will ask you to leave the classroom.
- Students are expected to sign an acknowledgment that they have read the rules.

With a similar focus on the responsibilities of both student and teacher, Dr. R. softened the approach to orientation by providing a "Guide to Success in My Course" that outlined what students could expect from him and what he expected from them. He defined the student and teacher roles using a metaphor: "This course is like a restaurant. You order and pay for the food. I serve it. I can't and won't make you eat it. That's up to you. However, I want to serve you the most appetizing and nutritious food I can. I won't hound you if you're not hungry." Other expectations, which conveyed Dr. R.'s values as well as emphasizing that students should spend "time on task," another of Chickering and Gamson's (1991) best practices, included:

- Take your education seriously.
- Your education is your responsibility.
- Ask a lot of questions.
- My courses require a lot of reading.
- Writing is required in this course.
- Get involved from the start and keep me posted.
- Get to class 15 minutes early whenever possible.
- Become results oriented.
- Keep up with assignments.
- Take pride in your work.
- Respect classmates and me.

Concluding with a pep talk, he underscored his investment in their success and reaffirmed their share of the responsibility by saying, "If you do poorly in my course, I fail as a teacher. I gain nothing when my students do poorly. Therefore, I will make an effort to help you succeed. However, if you don't show any initiative, I can't help you."

Oddly, the effect of such dicta is often to increase enrollment in the professors' classes. As the research on student ratings of courses shows, it appears that many students like a challenge and give higher ratings to professors whose courses are more difficult (Beidler, 1986; Cronin, 1992); others simply want to be able to claim the experience of having taken a course from such a demanding character. But for the outstanding teachers we studied, the rules only began with the syllabus and policy statements. All of the excellent teachers we observed created routines which enabled their classes to function efficiently and fairly. Implicit in their daily presentation were structures which they frequently shared with students in the forms of lecture outlines, overviews, summaries, and previews for the next class. Students entered the classroom and they knew what to expect that day. A sample of the routines we observed included the following repertoire of activities.

- Three-hour evening class—30 students:

  1. Housekeeping—attendance, upcoming assignment reminders
  2. Administration of an hourly test, feedback from students on test
  3. Review of previously presented information
  4. Assessing the knowledge base of the students on the new material through dialogue
  5. Role-playing of historical figures
  6. Review of class content via oral quiz at the close of the class
  7. Final summary of the three main ideas presented during class
  8. Remaining after class to meet with students

- 50-minute class—200 students:

  1. Housekeeping remarks on how to study for the upcoming test
  2. Introductory remarks about what will be covered in class
  3. Lecture–film–lecture
  4. Concluding remarks about what was covered and what would be introduced in the next class
  5. Remaining after class to answer questions

- Two-hour science lab—9 students:

  1. Instructor demonstrates pro-section
  2. Students imitate instructor model in small groups, dissecting
  3. Each group takes turns presenting to the rest of the class

- 50-minute class—400 students:

  1. Motivational activity involving the entire class
  2. Presentation of the central question underlying the lecture
  3. Alternative theories that provide possible answers to the scientific question
  4. Concluding remarks leading back to the essentials of scientific inquiry
  5. Remaining after class to respond to students

As we have said previously, these routines are not unique. What *is* unusual is the professor's uncanny ability to select the best routine for a particular class, and to vary that routine at just the right point so that students do not become lulled into complacency. Note, too, that they incorporate many of Chickering and Gamson's (1991) best practices: encouraging student–faculty contact, cooperation among students, and active learning; giving prompt feedback; and respecting diverse talents and ways of learning.

Motivational Planning

When it came down to the level of daily preparation and presentation of the material, the teacher–scholars we observed incorporated a wide array of effective methods. Whether or not they would label their actions as such, they were, in fact, following a lesson plan, a recipe for each class. Like your Aunt Peg's instructions for making her special brownies—"a teaspoon plus a tad more"—they may not use the education jargon, but they nonetheless had a well-developed plan, and whatever you call them, the ingredients were always there. That is, they had a continuous system for identifying and monitoring the level of students' knowledge and skills (status assessment). They had clear and specific objectives with criteria for success. Uniquely, they paid extraordinary attention to what motivates students to learn their material. They followed logical procedures, taking care to identify any limiting factors related to either the students, environment, or material, and they planned solutions to overcome the limitations (interventions). Rather than having a single option, they were prepared if necessary to tap their creative resources for alternatives. Throughout their in-class time with the students, they used informal evaluation continually (formative assessment) as well as diverse means of more formal testing (summative assessment).

Status assessment is essential at every level of planning. The award-winning professors we studied used an ongoing process of monitoring students' level of comprehension of prerequisite as well as newly presented material. They identify the skills and knowledge essential to success in their course. Beginning with assessing the students' entrance behavior/current level of knowledge, they adapt to the needs of the students as they develop their course plans and daily plans. Their skills in monitoring student behavior within each class allow them to slow down or move ahead based on their assessment of the students' comprehension. For example, Professor L. began a graduate course by quizzing the students to establish a baseline and identify gaps in their backgrounds. After reviewing their responses, she distributed resources for them to close holes in their knowledge base. In the first class of another outstanding teacher, she asked students in her writing courses to write about their previous positive and negative experiences as writers, and then she used that writing sample to identify their attitudes as well as their skill levels. For a weekly science lab, Professor H. began by asking students what they had covered in their lectures which were taught by other faculty in order to determine whether he had to backtrack to "level the playing field" before proceeding to the current procedures.

Many who teach in a discipline that is organized around skills acquisition (such as science, math, health sciences, engineering) use a specific planning procedure on a class-by-class basis in order to cover objective material ("Using Lab Sheet 12, students will work in teams of three to follow the lab protocol to complete Experiment X within the allotted lab time"). Others declare that their daily class *objectives* are frequently values-laden, and they have difficulty melting them down to behavioral terms because the language doesn't come naturally. In several discussions about specific objectives with award-winning professors, we found that we had to change our language in order to dig through the deeply embedded layers of strategies that actually constituted their objectives. (We hypothesize that perhaps this is the reason for the common resistance to outcomes assessment.) It is possible that one reason students do not learn may be related to the failure of many faculty to consider, articulate, and specify their expectations and objectives. Outcomes assessment forces academics to become student-centered. This may be uncomfortable for them, because they have been acculturated in a traditional system that has fostered a teacher-centered model where students passively receive information. Traditionally, college faculty teach as they have been taught. We believe that the higher one moves up the educational ladder, the more teachers make the assumption that students ought to have acquired foundational knowledge and skills previously and that, until recently, academics have been educational snobs, deflecting responsibility as demonstrated in an attitude which translates to the refrain, "You should have learned this in undergraduate school…high school…grammar school."

We also found that the distinguished teachers we observed were exceptionally skilled at motivating their students to meet their learning objectives, regardless of how murky their teaching objectives were. We found that these professors translated their passion for their subjects into a repertoire of behaviors that engaged the students to change their values and assumptions. In higher education, many students come in with an aversion to certain subjects; they have been exposed to overanalysis, dull presentations, or defeat. Their past professors have somehow failed to connect the material to their lives in meaningful ways. By contrast, the scholars of teaching we studied personalized instruction by addressing students by name and attempting to build relationships with individuals and groups. Even those with large numbers of students in one class made attempts to cross the barrier by moving among the students. Recall that Professor G. cruised among the aisles and rows, interacting with individual students, and that Professor P. asked students through his "A. L." technique to interact individually with him through writing. Professor W. sent letters of congratulation to anyone in his large introductory classes who received an A, encouraging them to become economics majors. Other professors shared their own work with students to model both the process and product of their scholarship. Together these examples convey to students the professor's sincere concern for them.

We found that our award-winning professors were also skilled at motivating learning by finding their material's relevance to students' experiences. Their illustrations included metaphors, stories, allusions, and even simulations, evidence of their having achieved a "Stage Three" level of teaching development at which they were primarily concerned not with the academic content or with their pedagogical skills, but with the students' learning needs (Ronkowski, 1993, p. 84). Some, like Dr. I., made antiquated subjects meaningful through regular references to pop culture (TV, film, and music), references which were not meant to dumb down the primary material, but to remind the students that, for instance, plays in the Elizabethan period were themselves part of popular rather than high culture. Others used dramatizations which "contemporize" literature by encouraging students to create scenarios demonstrating their comprehension of the plots, style, and characters. For example, students of Professor B. imagined and enacted a "bedroom scene" between Oedipus ("Eddy") and his wife Jocaste ("Jo") as they disclosed their secrets. Another group of students portrayed the saga of *Romeo and Juliet* in rap style. Professor R. identified problems with his students having aversions to reading literature written before the twentieth century, so when he assigned Thoreau's essay, "Civil Disobedience," he related it to his own personal dilemma during the Vietnam War. He highlighted the theme by recalling, "Your actions must flow from your conscience. If the laws are unjust, then it is your duty to transgress them." He told how he felt about his decision today and cited the historical figure Cassius Clay (now Muhammad Ali) as an example of a famous conscientious objector.

Another illustration of the choice for contemporary materials follows. Rather than using a traditional reader (a collection of essays) in her first-year English classes as a stimulus for class discussion and writing, Dr. B. had students subscribe to *Newsweek* in order to give them information and exposure to issues that face U.S. society today. She reflected on how students' attitudes about foreign affairs changed from apathetic to keen interest during the semester in her communications course preceding the Persian Gulf War. The class had been avoiding discussing news stories from *Newsweek* relating to the conflict in the early fall, but gradually, as the political tension grew and call-ups of reserves were mentioned, they perked up their ears, read the stories avidly, and discussed the issues passionately. At the close of the semester before the war, the class divided into sides and argued for and against military action. Dr. B. recalled that students' discussion and writing grew intense:

> Our class vote, a narrow majority favoring war, was subsequently paralleled in the Congress. Students who had shown no interest in the topic were well-informed when the issue came before the country, and, as their friends and family members were shipped to the Gulf, they thanked me for forcing them to learn about the issue.

The following semester, during the bombing of Bagdad, Dr. B. began teaching the research process by assigning topics related to the Persian Gulf War. A whole research paper project evolved that culminated in students' presenting oral reports on their research in a "teach in" to which their friends were invited.

Another professor uses a visualization activity to make students appreciate the significance of her subject. Dr. L. described an activity that she introduces to students preparing for a career in teaching. In a class prior to their student teaching experience, she asks them to close their eyes and envision a classroom. She tells them to look around, see the organization of the classroom, "check out" the materials, notice the students and so on. Next, she directs them to focus on one child, either a boy or a girl. She tells them that the child they have chosen is very special because it is their own child. This usually brings a few chuckles. Then she asks them to focus on the teacher and informs them, "That teacher is you."

Asking them to open their eyes, she begins a discussion centered around what parents want for their children's education. The final question of the activity is, "Would you want *you* to be the teacher of your own child? And, if not, why not, and what will you do about it?" Thus students are forced to shift their perspectives and appreciate the parents' view as well as to look at their own shortcomings as teachers and begin the process of addressing them.

Designing Materials

As part of their planning, distinguished teachers use materials and presentations that are creative variations of the standard. When standard texts, equipment, or resources do not meet the needs of the students or the environment, they design their own. Disgusted with the exorbitant price of textbooks, several professors downloaded the most current public domain information from web sites and compiled a set of readings for a graduate course; another collected resources on a computer disk and sold them to the class for the price of the disk. When inadequate space in the laboratory prevented all students in the class from viewing a cadaver dissection, two professors collaborated to produce an interactive human anatomy atlas in hypertext. Others provided written examples of successful papers, projects, essays, and reports as models for students. Some carried all of their lecture resources for an entire course to every class on a cart, giving themselves the option to jump back or ahead based on the class performance and schedule. One professor, Professor V., dismayed by the lack of wiring or equipment for on-line exchange for faculty or students at his college, took matters into his own hands. He installed phone lines in his home, hooked up four computers, appropriated the needed software, and for a $20 fee, provided the faculty and students with the software to get on-line. He took a major problem and created a solution: in one academic year he provided service to over 200 students and faculty.

Limits and Interventions: "The Best-Laid Schemes O' Mice and Men..."

No matter how carefully a course may have been planned, the logistics of working with people, space, and materials often cause disruptions in the flow of learning. Professors in certain disciplines often run into problems with equipment and time constraints. Several professors in the sciences reported that they hire students (or use TAs) to do trial runs of laboratory experiments. They noted the problem areas encountered and developed realistic time frames within which to adjust the content and procedures before the students entered the lab. These efforts were made so that the students had every opportunity to experience success within a reasonable time frame. Again, the intent was student-centered. The planners were attempting to run interference so that the students had an optimal learning environment. Our experience leads us to conclude that many forms of these informal interventions eventually become codified into procedures, policies, or standards.

Distinguished teachers establish clear expectations for students not only in written assignments, but in all modes of communication. When problems and interventions become habitual, then policies are necessary to prevent crises and to promote smooth learning experiences. The following section illustrates how teacher–scholars take initiative to develop clarification techniques, as opposed to punitive measures, to resolve difficulties. In the following section, to show how problem solving becomes proactive, we will present an illustration of how one professor developed a set of policies and procedures over a period of years.

How Plans Evolve into Policy

Dr. L., who was involved in a teacher education program, found that despite providing a specific framework for her students to work within, she needed to do the same for the educators with whom she worked in the community. Although the students were clear on the approach she took to supervising their internships, the cooperating teachers were often accustomed to different policies or procedures, depending on their past experiences. After several encounters with teachers' evaluating student teachers in a negative and very unconstructive manner, she decided to provide a model of how she would like to see her students evaluated. Rather than assume that all were "on the same page academically," she provided the cooperating teachers with a sample evaluation form, complete with appropriate evaluative language. (See Appendix D for the "Sample Lesson Evaluation.")

A set of standards, policies, and caveats were developed in sequence by the same professor who saw the need to clarify the evaluation process for cooperating teachers. She had discovered that students often select fields of study with various motivations, and they enter programs with a diverse set of experiences and backgrounds. For a professor concerned with student success, this diversity becomes a challenge when the standards for a specific discipline come in conflict with the student's prior experiences.

It becomes paramount that the student learn (and be taught) the standards necessary to be successful. In an attempt to close the loopholes discovered as incidents of inappropriate student behavior occurred during off-campus field experiences, Professor L. created a set of guidelines and expectations that served a dual purpose. This "Statement on Professional Behavior" (Appendix D) set basic standards for both in- and out- of class, and was designed to begin to mold the professionalism that would be expected of them in their chosen field. Additionally, it gave an instructor a framework from which to handle unusual situations. For example, while on a series of field assignments, a student who continued to argue with the orientation guides was demonstrating what was described as bizarre and paranoid behavior. Reports from the personnel at the observation sites required that the professor deal with the student immediately. As it turned out, the student exploded with anger in an administrative office and was barred from campus. In the meantime, the professor had to repair the established relationships with the community, highlighting the importance of a proactive approach to this professional behavior issue. A policy statement on professional behavior ensued.

Although the previous policies had an immediate impact and were subsequently included in every syllabus within the department, there was cause to become even more specific by giving a series of warnings or "Caveats on Performance." Complaints from teachers and college supervisors indicated that perhaps the general policy wasn't explicit enough. The caveats which followed presented students with a more down-to-earth approach to what to do and what not to do. Additional forms provided cooperating teachers with guidelines for handling and reporting inappropriate behavior. (See Box 6-1, "Caveats on Performance.")

However, the outstanding teachers we studied did not simply demonstrate proactive planning through the development of formal policies and procedures. Whenever they met with their classes, they were ready with alternative plans. Constantly monitoring the class, the teacher–scholars we observed acknowledged the need for several backup plans—a fail-safe set of alternatives—depending on the need to remediate, to advance, or to refocus within a class. Most experienced professors admit that they incorporate these "by the seat of their pants" or without any formal planning, but in truth, these alternatives derive from years of experimenting in the classroom. The *pièce de résistance* of planning for the excellent teachers we observed, however, are their plans to evaluate students' learning. Recognizing that students' learning involves both the affective and cognitive domains, their evaluations incorporate strategies for

BOX 6-1   Caveats on Performance for the Student in a Field Experience

Discussing students, parents, or situations related to the school in which you are participating must be done with discretion and only with the teacher to whom you are assigned. Ethical and confidential treatment of all information is essential. In other words, don't get involved in teacher lounge discussions, gossip, or "war stories" with anyone. *Keep your eyes and ears open and your mouth closed!* Learn what you will do when you become a teacher as well as what you won't do, through observing.

Defensive behavior can be defined in many ways. Here are some examples:

- Responding to every criticism or suggestion made to you with a justification for why you did what you did. *Just listen!* If a remark is made by your supervisor or teacher, it usually is to correct, redirect, or improve upon something. If you don't understand what you are being asked to correct, then certainly ask questions.... But remember ...many comments do not require a response.
- Placing blame on others for things you are responsible for is immature and inappropriate.... It's fine to say, "I guess I made a mistake."

A clear interpretation of your role as a student is essential to a successful relationship with your supervisors in the field. You have been accepted into the classroom as a guest. You have entered the placement with limited practical knowledge and should be prepared to learn and be instructed by your teacher and supervisor. Problems occur when the student refuses to accept authority. This can take the form of challenging the teacher or supervisor's competence, having hostile interactions and exchanges with those responsible for your supervision, inappropriate acknowledgment of a supervisor's title and role, or refusal to follow college or school policies and procedures. Manipulating, circumventing, or subverting the policies or procedures of the field experience is unacceptable.

Predictable behavior is expected. You do not have the right to "get angry, explode, lose control," et cetera. You are expected to be in control of yourself. Age and past experience have no influence on the current field experience. Your current placement is just that—"current." You must be willing to open yourself to new approaches that may be different than those learned in the past.

© Jamie N. DeWaters (1993)

monitoring attitudes, comprehension of information, and skills. They are aware, for example, that students who merely read and regurgitate the information often produce the dull, mechanical papers teachers dread, whereas students whose emotions have been tapped create lively writing with authentic voices. Reaction papers and/or journals are evaluation strategies that excellent teachers employ. These allow students to express their understanding and application of theoretical concepts in their own words. These papers encourage students to write their views and feelings in structured and appropriate ways to develop insights. As part of their consistent monitoring, the professors we studied used both formative and summative assessments of students' emotional reactions as well as their comprehension.

We found that our award-winning professors employed countless methods of assessing student performance to provide students with informal feedback while they were learning so they could improve (formative evaluation). They commonly offered many opportunities to revise work prior to final grading. We found that some professors allowed students to practice via nongraded assignments, whereas others walked the students through the language and the techniques, and gave them assignments that simulated the upcoming graded task. These reduced the fear and performance anxiety students experience, while supporting and assisting them prior to grading, when the motivation to improve was strongest. This strategy also freed students to take risks and develop skills in self-evaluation.

The following example demonstrates this developmental approach. In a requirement for a series of observation reports in Dr. L.'s courses, students were not expected to hand in a new paper until the prior one had been returned. The professor explained that each paper was to be used to guide the development of the next one. The directives were to make new mistakes, not the same old ones. The papers were to be handed in together in a folder so that the professor could review the students' progress. Grades were determined developmentally. Thus the pressure for getting work back was diminished because the students knew that they did not have another paper due until the prior one was returned. Professor L. told students:

> Expectations rise as the semester moves along. While grading each new paper, I look back through the papers to verify

improvement. If this is not occurring, then I invite you to hand in a draft (in person) before submitting the next paper for grading.

Several of the distinguished professors we studied used some daily kind of active learning technique that gave them the opportunity to monitor student interpretations of the class material. At the end of each class, students used a 3 × 5 card to indicate the gist of the presentation and/or ask for clarification. Quick review of these responses allowed the professors to determine if objectives for that class were met, and to clarify any misconceptions in the next class meeting. This technique provides crucial information to both the professor and the student at a time when the intervention is most meaningful, and responses can be included in formal assessments.

When it came to formal evaluation for the purpose of grading (summative evaluation), our distinguished professors also reported that they assessed students on a developmental basis. They were more lenient in assessing early assignments in the course, expecting that the students would use the feedback to modify their performance as the semester progressed. Their natural optimism, which we documented in Chapter 5, led them to expect that with instruction, practice, and feedback, students would improve.

An example of how one professor combines formal assessment of students' emotional responses to a task within an objective format is as follows. In a course that required field observations followed by objective professional reports written in a very rigid style, Professor L. added a subjective component to the written report. After observing during a field activity, the students wrote their specific observations according to the stringent format, but were required to include their subjective impression in a less formal journal. The journal entry that accompanied the observation report could be handwritten and was intended to encourage the student to react to the environment and individuals encountered. The professor assured confidentiality and encouraged honesty, because for many, this was the first exposure to their selected career. The assignment was referred to as a "gimme" (as in golf when the ball is very close to the cup and opponents assume that the golfer's putt will be successful) and points were awarded for merely addressing four headings with a minimum of two paragraphs each: Good points (they had to be specific), Criticisms (they had to be specific), Suggestions (they had to address each criticism), and Things I Learned (often students confirmed or questioned their career choices). This afforded the instructor the opportunity to open dialogue about questions or concerns and to provide career guidance.

Another professor who teaches English to first-year students built some slack into her evaluation system for college freshman. Because she recognized that first-year students are novices to the college experience, and therefore often require some leeway to figure out time management or to step up their efforts, she counted class participation and effort as part of their grades. Thus, although she did not allow for makeup exams or offer extra credit assignments, she built into her evaluation system a way of rewarding students who developed the work habits which lead to college success, again emphasizing the "best practice" of emphasizing time on task (Chickering & Gamson, 1991).

After struggling with a process for doing this fairly, the professor came up with the following system: First, she gave students a "+" in her gradebook during the third week of class if she had learned their names, reasoning that students who participated the most would become the most familiar to her in the beginning of the semester. Next, she assessed class participation on random dates: As she called the roll, or while students were grouped to discuss the assigned readings, she would pose questions about the readings marking a "+" in her gradebook if their answers showed that they had done the readings. To reward students' efforts, she recorded a "+" for each draft or revised draft students submitted during the semester. Those who had perfect attendance also received a "+." Finally, she gave effort grades of "+," "OK," or "R (revise)" during the semester each time she collected and reviewed their journals. Here the focus was not on how well they wrote, but whether they completed the assignments and wrote regularly and honestly. At the end of the semester, after computing students' final averages on tests and formal papers, she counted each student's "pluses" in her gradebook, and rewarded those with the top scores by adding two or three points to their averages. This usually meant that a C– would become a C, or even that a B+ would become an A–. Thus effort had a significant impact on students' grades, and the professor was satisfied that she had matched her evaluation system to the developmental stage of her students.

BOX 6-2   Field Experience Grading

A (93–100) = Superior:
- Attendance has been perfect.
- Came early and stayed late. Attended after-school and extracurricular activities.
- Always appropriately dressed and groomed in a professional manner.
- Lesson plans, projects, et cetera were so well done that teachers and supervisors want to borrow them for demonstrations.
- Never participated in gossip or heard complaining about school assignment, teacher, school personnel, students, parents, or college supervisor. Accepted supervision nondefensively.
- Made a genuine effort to get to know the administration and staff of the school; interacted professionally with everyone.
- Typed lesson plan followed college guidelines—lessons were outstanding, as were instructional materials and methods.
- Skilled in using the experience and assistance of teacher and or aide in teaching lessons.
- Maintained an ongoing professional dialogue with these people.
- Was self-directed; knew what needed to be done and how to do it.
- Teaching included more than using teacher's guidebooks; was innovative, interesting; lessons were age-appropriate and sensitive to the needs of the students. College supervisor and teacher were amazed at the student's development of high quality, appropriate supplementary materials.
- Used appropriate Standard English at all times.
- Performance in the field was outstanding at all times. Because of this performance, the faculty would think of you as their first choice to represent the Division of Education.

B (83–86) = Above Average:
- Attempts all of the things that the "A" student does but, although the work and teaching performance are well above average, there is room for some improvement. For example:
- Has occasional lapses in Standard English ("goin, doin, don't got no").
- First one or two lessons were weak but showed outstanding improvement.
- Planned effective lessons but had minor trouble with behavior management. Improved with guidance.
- Missed teaching day(s).

C (73–76) = Average:
- Arrived on time, left on time every day.
- Lessons were always well-planned, classroom work prepared on time.
- Good rapport with school personnel and students.
- Projects completed adequately.
- Instruction was adequate but not above average or outstanding in any way.
- The minimum expectations were fulfilled adequately.

C– (70–72) = Below Average:
- This grade is considered unacceptable and can be translated as failing for an education course.

© Sheila Dunn (1994)

Other distinguished teachers monitor student progress by keeping and sharing data with students on individual and group success on tests. For example, some professors calculated pass/fail rates and correlated those with attendance. Others studied or performed item analysis on test results to determine patterns of performance. In a class with first-year students and upperclassmen, one teacher examined the scores of each group to monitor the difficulty of the material in order to assure that the first-year students would not be lost. Once again, one of Chickering and Gamson's (1991) principles of good practice, "prompt feedback," was demonstrated.

With their characteristic habit of clarifying every aspect of their expectations, we also found that the outstanding teachers in our study developed and incorporated explicit evaluation criteria for success. Their standards were not only clear but also rigorous, exemplifying a characteristic of excellence we reported in Chapter 5. For example, rather than succumb to the standard practice of assigning "pass/fail" or "satisfactory/unsatisfactory" grades to student teachers, which she believes encourages mediocrity, one faculty member, Dr. Q., developed the set of evaluation criteria presented in Box 6-2, "Field Experience Grading."

Despite their commitment to diverse, regular, and rigorous evaluations, the distinguished professors in our study were aware of the limitations of student performance evaluations during the semester or even later on licensure examinations or graduate entrance examinations. Though the current trends in evaluation are undergoing scrutiny and moving toward outcomes assessments, the question remains, "When is evaluation meaningful?"

We believe the long-term effects of learning are often revealed or measured by the students who choose a discipline, who succeed in internships, who come back to visit, who write letters, who present at conferences, and who advance in their careers. Like Boyer (1990), we recommend that promotion and tenure committees should contact alumni to assess teaching effectiveness over time. Distinguished teachers tell us that the real test of learning (and effective teaching) is the answer to the question, "Have students' lives taken positive new directions as a result of their encounter with a particular professor?"

7

Instructional
Problem Solving
Dealing with Diverse Individuals

The heart of education is the relationship between teachers and students which evolves during their academic discourse. We would define teaching as an ongoing discourse in which professors use a set of problem-solving processes in order to shape students into autonomous learners. Communication theorists generally divide interpersonal discourse into five elements: A *speaker* sends a communication *message* by speaking or writing in a selected setting (the communications *channel*) to the *audience* (an individual or a group), who respond with *feedback* in the form of nonverbal, spoken, or written language (Lasswell, 1960, as cited in Davison, Boylan, and Yu, 1976, p. 117).

We contend that the instructional environment consists of a hierarchy of communication problems. (See Figure 7-1, "A Catalog of Instructional Problems.") After years of discovering what students need to learn and how they learn, as well as how to exploit a variety of techniques and materials, the distinguished teaching professors in our study acquired the ability to analyze the learning environment, identify the type of problems they encountered, and generate plans and strategies for resolving the instructional problems. We have used the five elements from communication theory as a paradigm through

FIGURE 7-1   A Catalog of Instructional Problems

Individual Students

Attitudes: Old habits die hard
Eccentric behavior
Social misfits
Warped genius
Eating disorders
Confidence: Too little/too much
Cultural baggage
Students in crisis
Marginal ability

Groups of Students

Demographic differences
Grade-grubbing
"Enabling" behavior
Elite groups
"Required course apathy"
Bimodal abilities
Large classes
Competitive clusters/cheating
Diverse cultures
Unprepared groups
Academically weak class

Instructor Knowledge & Behaviors

Maintaining enthusiasm when
   students are unprepared
Inability to accept student failure
Handling the time commitment,
   paperload/grading
Credibility gap: TAs, junior faculty,
   adjuncts
Energy drain: Other faculty
   obligations
Matching teaching style/strategies
   with students' learning needs
Shyness/stage fright

Content or Subject Matter

Finding the appropriate level of
   difficulty
Making material meaningful/
   interesting
Presenting sensitive/controversial
   topics
Choosing the appropriate depth/
   detail
Grading

Learning Environment

Unsatisfactory classroom
Unsatisfactory time constraints/
   scheduling
Inadequate textbooks
Unavailability of materials when
   needed
Students don't/can't buy the materials
Malfunctioning equipment

DeWaters & Baiocco (1996)

which to classify the problem-solving strategies of distinguished college teachers and others drawn from our experiences. The five categories are as follows:

- Problems with instructor knowledge and behaviors (the *speaker*)
- Problems with content or subject matter (the *message*)
- Problems with the learning environment (the *channel*)
- Problems with individual students (the *audience* and *feedback*)
- Problems with groups (the collective *audience* and *feedback*)

Although novice teachers tend to concentrate on content and environment problems, we found that the focus of the expert teachers in our study shifted to students and themselves. And though outstanding college teachers continue to be concerned about the material they teach, it appears that they more often ponder why particular students are having difficulty, and what they might change in their own behavior to assist students. Using their wide base of knowledge and experience, the professors in our study explored the reasons for interference with learning. Not only were they able to label these causes, but they were also able to clearly communicate, in a nonthreatening manner, what the true issues were and how those issues affected all involved in the learning process. Following their analyses of the causes of students' learning difficulties, they developed plans and strategies for assisting students in making meaningful changes and overcoming personal and academic obstacles.

This talent for social analysis, one of Goleman's emotional intelligences (1995, p. 38), is another marker of distinguished professors' extraordinary teaching skill. But analysis serves no one if it does not proceed to actions. This chapter will examine not only the subtle, sophisticated analyses of human behavior of the outstanding teachers we observed, but it will also show, through case study examples derived from our interviews and our own experience, how all college professors select particular solutions and apply them to instructional problems. The professors discussed in these case study scenarios demonstrated superior EQ, as well as notable creativity and flexibility, two "supertraits" characteristic of excellent teachers. (See Chapter 5.)

In addition, we will show that self-awareness, a fundamental emotional intelligence we have described, operates to continually spur better performance from outstanding teachers. We hypothesize that from the beginning of their professional careers to the end, these scholars of teaching have possessed a talent for self-evaluation (awareness of the impact of their own knowledge and behavior on student learning). In this chapter, we will not identify the professors by name to protect the privacy of all involved. Unique features of the scenarios have been modified for the same reason.

Individual Students: The Challenge

"Individualization of instruction" has been a buzzword in education for decades. However, it is not simply educational jargon to the award-winning professors we observed. In surveys and interviews, they demonstrated a keen awareness of problem behavior of individual students. These we have sorted into categories of attitude, eccentric behavior, inept social skills, warped genius, eating disorders, issues of self-confidence or lack thereof, cultural baggage, students in crisis, and limited ability. This category of problem behavior is by no means limited to these examples. Although not all of the attempts to solve the scenarios we describe were 100% successful, we think they offer useful insights into managing student behavior that interferes with learning and the smooth functioning of a successful course. We hope that this listing will be expanded by future researchers.

Attitudes: Old Habits Die Hard

Professors are often faced with students who have what might be referred to as "attitudes." Translated into behavioral terms, these attitudes come in many forms and may seriously interfere with their primary goal of getting an education. The student may bring old habits into a new environment and be unwilling to accept the responsibility for necessary change. Sometimes students have mismatched expectations, and, although the language to describe this behavior varies, their expectations often exceed their performance.

Take, for example, students transferring to a four-year institution from a junior or community college. Such students may have had prior success (or difficulty) at the former school and expect that the level of work and expectations of the professors would remain the same as they moved from a smaller learning environment to a larger one, or from general education courses into a major and upper-level courses. These students may be skeptical and distrustful, or they may exhibit habitual patterns of solving problems with threats or aggression.

How do these attitudes specifically manifest themselves? A chip on the shoulder, arrogance, and defensiveness are terms describing the behaviors observed by professors and fellow students. The words of the students themselves also reveal a false bravado: "I've done this...worked in this field for years...taken this course...have a relative who...am well above this level...paid lots of money and I expect...my education in my country was superior to that here...I'm above average...you are holding me back...," and the list goes on. What these behaviors are really saying is, "I'm unsure of myself and have the need to act in this manner to defend myself." Professors often recall a litany of problems presented by individual students over the years. In each case the solution that rose to the surface seemed to center on communication as a means by which to clarify, if not solve, the problem.

To illustrate, one student with a history of inappropriate behavior among the student body as well as with the faculty used the threat of litigation as a means of assuring herself a walk across the stage at commencement. Initially, her behavior caused other professors to sigh at her boastful behavior and other students to roll their eyes whenever she responded in class. But as she encountered more difficult work, her behavior progressed from being merely annoying to combative. While the student was participating in a required internship, several incidents forced the professor to establish policies and procedures that outlined very specific behavioral expectations. Sensing that she was in jeopardy, the student accused her teacher of intimidating her, claiming that she was scared to death of him. She appeared to be setting up the situation so that if she did poorly, she could claim intimidation as an excuse.

In this case, the professor used very precise and clear feedback to identify the parameters of this student's problem. He addressed the accusation directly, saying, "If you are afraid of me, that is unfortunate. If you can give me some specific reasons why, then we can work on them." He placed the responsibility for identifying specifics on the student, yet was willing to share responsibility for working on a solution. In this case, the student realized that her usual tactics did not work and left the office angrily, yet she followed the behavioral rules from that point on. The professor thought it was important to clarify that the student would be graded on the performance of her work/behavior in accordance with the expectations of the course and internship, not on personality or anything else. He believed that she needed to test the limits to determine if there would be consequences for her behavior. After this experience, the instructor decided that it was essential to be proactive and incorporate the guidelines he had developed into future syllabi and department policies.

Large numbers of nontraditional students are a relatively new phenomenon in the college classroom. Returning to the classroom after many years of experience in the "real world," they often find the initial adjustment to academe difficult. One professor tells of a male student who entered a program after having run a successful business. He quit his job (creating what must have been a financially difficult situation) and entered as a full-time student, then landed a work study job and became a fixture in the campus office where he worked. His familiarity with faculty who used this office frequently caused a misperception on his part about his role as a student.

One afternoon the student walked into his instructor's office unannounced, plopped himself down in a chair, referred to her by her first name, and proceeded to tell her a joke. Unaccustomed to this informality with a student she barely knew, she corrected his reference to her by first name, saying that she was sure that he would understand that she would prefer to maintain a professional relationship. When corrected, he became furious and informed her that if she was to be referred to as "Dr.," then he should now be called "Mr." A misperception of the social rules of academe accompanied by a lack of EQ caused the student who had difficulty with authority (particularly female authority) to misperceive the friendly demeanor of the faculty. In this case Dr. ___ chose to ignore the outburst. If he insisted on being referred to as "Mr.," then so be it. She honored his request in class while not overemphasizing the fact. She soon discovered that he was a good worker but not a strong student, and he was used to having his personality work for him. When he no longer succeeded in charming those in authority in the college, he became restive. His unwillingness to relinquish old habits caused him to have difficulty with others (both male and female) who challenged him. He did learn to avoid and obviously ignore those faculty whom he had confronted but, unfortunately, he carried his grudges with him. Under the thumb of a strong male supervisor, the student squeaked through his field experience and graduated.

Other attitude problems challenge university professors today as well. Behaviors that were unheard of in college classrooms decades ago now manifest themselves regularly. For example, some students present antagonistic behaviors, postures, expressions, or comments, or they appear blasé. In each case, the distraction to both the professor and the rest of the class can interfere with the flow of the presentation. All of our distinguished professors subscribed to the importance of communication as a solution. In many of these cases, the students are unaware of how they are being perceived by others. Here direct communication is essential. However, directness can often be perceived by the student as an attack. When the situation is presented as a shared problem, the student realizes that the teacher is not dumping the problem solely on him or her, but is seeking to help solve the problem. On such occasions, language use is important. Our subjects recommended saying: "I'm observing (state the problem)," (such as "You are scowling at me continually," or, "You argue with me on every issue,"). Then describe your assessment or feeling: "I'm concerned that you are having a problem with either me or the material, and I find that this interferes with my teaching and possibly your learning." Use terms such as "I am uncomfortable" as opposed to "You are making me uncomfortable." This is a time-tested method for conflict resolution, because it expresses shared responsibility. Lastly, asking the student, "Please help me to understand what is happening here," enlists the student's help in finding a solution.

Dr. ___ recalls a successful experience with a student who struck a belligerent pose regularly in a freshman English class and in her assigned journal writing. The student raised her voice in class and freely expressed strong negative feelings about the readings, the requirements, and the teacher's responses to her writing. Professor ___ resisted engaging in public arguments with the student, and regularly insisted that the student meet with her privately. Nevertheless, the outbursts continued, and the student was fast becoming isolated from her peers. Dr. ___ first tried reasoning and explaining her expectations during conferences with the student, but this only seemed to escalate the behavior. After receiving a poor grade on her first paper, the tall student confronted the professor after class with an in-your-face stance, insisting that she had received A's on her writing in high school, and implying that the professor was incompetent. Dr. ___ applied her usual maxim, "When the student starts resisting, the professor starts insisting," and continued to confidently affirm her evaluation and offer private assistance to the student. After that stormy meeting, the student openly attacked the professor's teaching ability in an entry in her journal, claiming that her poor grade was the result of the professor's racial prejudice. When the professor read the entry, she became angry. She decided that instead of counterattacking, she would write a note in the journal mentioning that the student seemed very angry and that surely there must have been some reason for it of which she was unaware.

This became a turning point in their relationship, for the student realized that she could not intimidate the professor, and that the professor cared that she was "acting out." The tone of their communications became honest, and the student shared the cause of her anger: her sibling who had been involved with drugs had been raped and murdered. This became the subject of her final paper, which she worked on persistently and read to an awestruck class, whose attitude turned from disdain to grudging respect.

One method many distinguished teachers utilize when teaching students who are anxious is the use of reflective or empathic statements. Telling the students how they will feel when they encounter particular material ("You won't get this right away, so don't worry" or "This will sound very phony when you first start to say this, but soon it will become part of your language") allows instructors to be predictive. They indicate that they know the problems associated with the material. They recall how they felt when they were learning it. This utilization of EQ humanizes the process and allows the professor to "head off predictable problems at the pass."

Occasionally, a student's irresponsible behavior will have been tolerated by other professors for several semesters, and she or he will be surprised when the rules change. As an illustration, Dr. ___ maintains a semi-strict attendance policy for his classes. A student who was not attending class asked for an incomplete (although she had done less than 10% of the class work). He agreed to the incomplete. The next semester she asked him to extend the incomplete for another semester, even though there were no extenuating circumstances. He refused, and she received an F and again registered for the class. His moral: "Give a student the benefit of the doubt, but don't allow yourself to be taken advantage of."

Eccentric Behavior

From time to time, students with eccentric behavior based on pathology or psychological problems present obstacles to teaching and to their own learning. When professors encounter specific problems, there are always more than the surface issues to deal with. Unstable students or those behaving inappropriately can pose difficult situations that often must be dealt with immediately. Identifying a need for counseling, for example, and suggesting those services to the individual can be very delicate. Professors report that students have accused them of calling them "crazy" when, out of concern for the student's well-being, they had suggested that counseling was available on campus.

Furthermore, issues of confidentiality often cloud faculty decisions to advise such students toward or away from certain fields of study based on their performance or behavior. Professors must weigh how much information can be given to those who will be supervising these students while in an internship or field experience. Will withholding critical information about the student's idiosyncrasies place anyone in jeopardy? Will releasing this information violate the student's right to confidentiality? These are questions to be dealt with individually and, hopefully, wisely. The result is not always a happy one for the professor with integrity. Often he or she is forced to negotiate with or about a problem student and to consider the consequences: "Should I give a minimal, passing grade to get the student out? Should I graduate students knowing they will never get recommendations or jobs in their chosen field? Do I allow the student to continue in the course of study, knowing full well that failure is imminent?" A professor often has to consider a breach in his or her integrity after weighing the consequences. He or she must rely on convention, wisdom, and a realization that moral choices exist. The best we can do in an imperfect world is to use our good judgment to reduce harm and promote the general welfare.

Numerous professors report having agonized over decisions involving students' rights to follow career choices, no matter how inappropriate those choices may be. Students who demonstrate paranoid, neurotic, extremist, or manic behavior or who draw attention to themselves by using exaggerations, fantasy, or fundamental dogmatic positions highlight the necessity for professors to adhere to tight guidelines and expectations in both the classroom as well as in clinical or professional internships. These standards should not be designed to keep students from pursuing their goals; rather, they are vital for clarifying the essential behaviors expected.

Professor ___ reported an encounter with one student who showed many and varied symptoms of serious emotional disturbance. The student was a middle-aged man who had emigrated to the United States to pursue a vocation. Failing to meet those requirements, he began a series of attempts to discover an alternative. He first entered the school as an education major, but his paranoid reactions to others (including an incident where he threatened a lawsuit when someone touched him on his watch), earned him a dismissal from that program. He began a second program where he achieved modest success despite his difficulty with the English language. This led him to seek a dual major, until two colleagues reported that they suspected the student of plagiarism. Together they confronted the suspected offender, but this student maintained his ignorance/innocence. The tenured senior faculty reported the incident to the dean. The professor revealed that the student had later confessed his deliberate misuse of sources and thanked the professor for having enforced standards. The junior colleague allowed the student to rewrite the suspicious papers.

The student continued to "hang on" in his program, despite having failed several courses. Finally, his advisor "bit the bullet," made sure that minimal requirements were met in the last core course, passed the student, and bid him farewell when he graduated. When last heard from, the student was continuing to seek some magic elixir of a graduate program that would bring him some success. He had never come to terms with the pathology which threaded through his life, but his advisor told us that he was satisfied that the student could do no one harm, despite his suspected neuroses.

The open door policy established at some public universities and community colleges in the 1970s today has become a boon for those who were late bloomers and others who did not perform well in secondary school. It has also allowed some to enter college who are academically or psychologically unsuited for it. Here we are referring not to those students whose skills are so deficient as to require substantial remediation, but to those few individuals who do not or cannot function well in any environment.

One professor recalls a student who drifted like a leaf through the corridors of the college for several years, settling here and there briefly, yet barely getting by, usually because some faculty had mistaken sympathy for standards. The student wrote papers about having been abused as a child, and her permanent "souvenir" of the experience was a prosthesis. Dr. ___ consulted the college counselor for advice on how to deal with the student, who had latched onto her when she responded positively to the student's writing. Sordid reports about her lifestyle as a welfare recipient with a drunken and abusive husband compounded the dilemma for Professor ___. The counselor chose to risk breaching client confidentiality by informing her that the student had been diagnosed with a "borderline personality disorder," and suggested that she enforce strict limits on her contacts with the student. Eventually, the student drifted out the college door to join the cadre of the moderately dysfunctional people who constitute the U.S. underclass. Professor ___ says, "You have to know when to fold 'em. Some students are beyond our resources to help. That is where social services come in."

Social Misfits

At another degree of variation from normal behavior are those students who appear to be psychologically stable, but who initially lack the intrapersonal and interpersonal skills (EQ) to make them happy and successful in the classroom. For example, although non-traditional students may be uncomfortable when first returning to college, most adapt quickly and find their niche. Professor ___ tells about one student who was the only older student in her class. She began to hear talk among the female students that he was "hitting on" every other one of them. She decided that it really didn't concern her, until she began to notice him winking at her from the front row during class. Ignoring this behavior, she was finally forced to address the issue when she encountered him stretched across the desk in front of the class in a reclining position as she entered to teach. Neutrally asking him to remove himself, she turned to speak with a student. Returning to the desk, she found him still there. She requested a meeting with him after class and explained to him that his behavior was inappropriate. He apologized and began telling her about all of his recent misfortunes. Although she was sympathetic to his unhappiness, she reiterated her classroom expectations and ended the meeting.

However, this was not the end of the story. The student misinterpreted her directness as interest and continued to display inappropriate and immature behavior and to use language with sexual overtones with the female students in the class. What did seem to eliminate the problem was a second meeting, followed by a written account added to his student file. This written account included Dr. ___'s concern, the specific behavior, guidelines for improvement, and the consequences for the student if the behavior were to continue (covered in a professional behavior policy attached to the syllabus). The problem was eliminated for the semester, but Professor ___ reports that she received a summer phone call from him in which he reverted to his inappropriately familiar style.

Other award-winning professors told us that they too had had to deal with student crushes. There are those who view the teacher–student relationship as inherently erotic, that is, they believe that teachers "seduce" students into the academic discourse. Acknowledging a seductive element in motivating students, we found it surprising that more faculty did not report this problem of having students confuse their pleasure in learning with attraction to the professor. However, one professor, Dr. ___, reported that a student "stalked" her by waiting outside her office, outside her classes, and near her car. She discussed this type of problem with the school counselor and subtly with the student, rather than confronting and thus embarrassing him. Eventually the student graduated and the problem resolved itself.

Warped Genius

Occasionally, students who are very creative are not accepted by their peers on campus and become social isolates. To what degree is it the professor's responsibility to educate such students about social relations? Dr. ___ tells of two young men, each gifted with unusual ways of perceiving their worlds and writing about them, who were social misfits. One student, a premed major with a profound stutter, a vivid imagination, and elevated diction, caused other students to look at each other in bewilderment. He took several writing courses with Dr. ___ and soon began to share his sci-fi stories and narratives with her, as well as his plans to become a doctor. Meanwhile, he became the editor of the student literary magazine, a position in which he had to make contact with other students, and in which his lack of social skills became evident. For example, students avoided submitting their work or coming to staff meetings because they viewed the editor as bizarre.

So what's the problem? Many faculty do not believe that it is their responsibility to teach "people skills" to students. However, Dr. ___ believed that the student had genuine talent as a writer, and she knew that he would never succeed if he did not understand and relate to his audiences. She began meeting with the student to coach him on how to interact with other students to get their support, and he ended up producing an interesting edition of the magazine. Later, when he failed to be admitted to medical school, the student returned to Dr. ___ for advice. He decided to enroll in a master's degree in filmmaking, and later he sent her a postcard from—corny as it sounds—Hollywood, where he was hoping to break into the movie industry.

Another student, a nontraditional male, entered college with a history of poor social interaction. Indeed, the student was a kind of warped genius who professed his extreme religious views to any who would listen. It was clear to Dr. ___ that the student had spent most of an unhappy childhood engrossed in books, as he possessed a large but idiosyncratic knowledge about literature. Not only did the student's words antagonize his peers from the outset, but his nonverbal mannerisms made others uncomfortable. This was a problem for Dr. ___, because the student was fast becoming known for his in-class harangues and his zealous beliefs. Furthermore, he enrolled in a public speaking class, where Dr. ___ felt professionally obligated to address his public image in order for him to succeed in the course.

Dr. ___ began an ongoing dialogue with the student, listening to him and avoiding confrontation, but providing feedback on how he was being perceived. In one small class, she encouraged the student to assist others with less ability, which he generously did. There he began to receive positive acceptance from his peers for perhaps the first time. Dr. ___ reported that the student revealed that he was very lonely, that he was a member of a militia, and that he expected to be martyred for his beliefs. Dr. ___ shared her concerns about the student's stability with other faculty who knew him, and they individually encouraged him to seek counseling or medical help for the problems he disclosed, which included emotional illness.

The student is now reported to be under the care of a physician. He smiles and laughs, has several friends, and is active in several student organizations. Dr. ___ suggests that some students need to be taught a new language—they need to be given the words and the physical behaviors and shown how to express themselves—so that their statements are *reflective* of their feelings rather than *reactive*. In effect, they need a mirror through which to see themselves as others do, and the professor can provide that perspective. For example, Professor ___ wrote about the difficulty of working with those who are prejudiced or dogmatic: "Education, insofar as it liberates the mind…can be an exceedingly painful enterprise for some students. I try to 'be there' for them. In two or three cases, I have witnessed students deteriorating psychologically and have been unable to help them. It hurts me a lot."

Students with Eating Disorders

Female college students are at high risk for eating disorders, according to all the psychological research. When a professor first becomes aware of the disordered way in which some young women think about themselves, whether accompanied by anorexia, bulimia, or compulsive eating, they must decide how to approach the student, for, sooner or later, the problem will have negative effects on the student's ability to succeed in college. Dr. ___ described how she dealt with several students with the problem, depending on whether the student asked for help, and whether the student was dangerously ill.

Because Dr. ___ teaches freshman, she often sees students who are not yet ready to seek help for their physical and emotional behaviors. Newly liberated from their families, they believe that they can continue their behaviors indefinitely and succeed in college. When one student revealed in her writing journal that she was both involved with a married man and bulimic, Dr. ___ invited her to come to her office to talk about the situations. The student insisted that her behavior was not a problem, so Dr. ___ gave her a brochure from a local agency that assisted those with eating disorders, and made sure she read and understood the warnings about specifically dangerous behaviors. She gave the student the name and phone number of the school psychologists, and suggested that she call when she was ready. Meanwhile, Dr. ___ contacted the campus Health Office and asked the school nurse to discreetly observe the student. Throughout the semester, Dr. ___ observed the student becoming physically weaker, thinner, and more withdrawn, but the student continued to receive B's in her course. Occasionally, she asked the student how she was feeling, always to be assured, "I'm fine."

A year later the student appeared at Dr. ___'s door, finally ready to acknowledge that she had a serious health problem. Her romance had ended unhappily, and she saw her college career plummeting. Dr. ___ again asked her if she wanted help. Together they called the college counselor and set a date for an appointment. Another year passed, and the student dropped by from time to time to update Dr. ___ on her progress. She had a new boyfriend, a new attitude, a new plan for her life. When she graduated, she glowed with health.

Dr. ___ reports other experiences with seriously ill students whose eating disorders are signs of physical or emotional abuse. She says that if students tell her they are engaging in potentially lethal actions, she feels ethically responsible for getting them immediate attention. Although they are adults, she says, they often respond best when they are accompanied to medical or psychological appointments. As with other addictive behaviors, she says, everything depends on the student's desire to change. Dr. ___ has developed a relationship with the school psychologists, so when she calls with a student in crisis they arrange to see the student immediately. If the student must withdraw from courses due to the condition, Dr. ___ facilitates the process for the student. Beyond that, Dr. ___ recommends that treatment and counseling be left to professionals, with the professor playing the role of academic counselor.

Students Lacking Confidence

Students who lack self-confidence may be unwilling to take the risk of being wrong. For some reason, taking a chance to answer a question in class or attempt an unfamiliar assignment for such students is frightening. Perhaps they have had the negative experience of being embarrassed by a teacher, or are overachievers. Regardless, this lack of confidence creates a tremendous need for affirmation in some students, so they check in with the professor on every move. Usually the work is good or excellent in quality, but because these students cannot validate their own work, they bring every fragment to the professor for review before proceeding.

Both an excess and an extreme lack of confidence thwart the achievement of the overriding goal of education, which is independent learning. Students will never become independent learners until they can make accurate judgments about their own work. One solution to this dilemma offered by Dr. ___ is to build self-evaluation criteria into each assignment. Arranged in various forms, the criteria should demand that the student ask and answer the questions, "Is it good?" "Why?" "What makes it good?" and "What could I do to improve it?" Insisting that the students use a measurable evaluation of their work, and designating a specific number of opportunities to meet with the professor, promotes the goal of independence. When the students have used up their set times, they are on their own. This strategy solves the problem of the "campers"—students who "hang out" and absorb the time that should be available to all students.

Writing paralysis, stage fright, and excessive test anxiety are two of the most common manifestations of students who lack confidence. Several professors recommend the use of gradual desensitization through practice in ungraded contexts. For example, Dr. ___ begins his public speaking course with four ungraded speech exercises which gradually require the student to take on more aspects of speech preparation and delivery. Other excellent teachers report that requiring students to submit drafts of their papers, and/or allowing them to use their notes and textbooks during essay examinations, reduces performance anxiety for all students but particularly those who have paralyzing fears. Some faculty, such as Dr. ___, regularly provide test rehearsals for their classes by giving them sample questions from old tests, or by sharing and discussing examples of previous excellent papers.

When performance anxiety appears to be extreme, Dr. ___ recommends careful observation of the student under duress. She recalls having observed one student's writing processes in her office during a makeup exam, in order to understand why the student's writing was so disjointed. She watched the student write one or two words, stop, reread, write another word, and continue. The problem was that the student had developed a writing phobia after having been penalized severely for mechanical errors (such as spelling), and thus had become unable to write freely. Her internal editor had become overactive.

Dr. ___ tells of another young woman who froze in speech class despite his desensitization techniques. In conversations with the student outside of class, Professor ___ learned that the student was the only daughter of very successful parents, and he also observed that the student always avoided eye contact, even informally. He suspected that her desire to meet her parents' high standards and their excessive investment in her academic success was the cause of her stage fright. Sometimes fear of failure, also known as performance anxiety, can be dealt with by an instructor, but when it manifests itself in extreme behavior, our participating professors recommend sending students for counseling.

Two professors report how they solved a different problem of confidence: that bravado that sometimes accompanies student *artistes*—those with exceptional talent. The dilemma confronting faculty who teach creative students is knowing how much room to allow these geniuses as they discover and develop their giftedness. Dr. ___ recalls one talented but undisciplined student who regularly ignored the rules she had established for her music students. Professor ___ describes two writing majors, one who had an elegant eighteenth century style which he simply would not vary as necessary for different purposes and audiences, and another who was an excellent creative writer but who ignored the rules of standard English.

The confidence issue here parallels those we have described earlier. These gifted students were either too immature or too rigid to accept the standards of a new learning environment. Their previous successes had reinforced lazy, unfocused, or inflexible behaviors, and they needed firm and consistent treatment. Dr. ___ recommends the use of lots of praise when these talented students make their first attempts to meet the new standards, as well as when they are exposed to models that exceed their current levels of performance. Dr. ___ decided to be very strict with her virtuoso, grading him according to his work, not his talent, and reported that she was very straightforward about what he needed to do to be successful. In Dr. ___'s case, the student failed an honors course because he did not follow the rules. Sometimes such experiences are the shock that talented students require in order for them to accept the necessity of changing their own behavior. We believe that it is the professor's duty to teach successful work habits as well as the skills, values, and content of their disciplines. Professor ___ concludes, "Students need to understand that two-thirds of what passes for talent is simply grueling, arduous, committed *work!*"

The self-proclaimed gifted or above average student also can manifest insecurity which gets played out in the classroom. Professor ___ recalls teaching a segment of a course that centered on the exceptionality of giftedness. A student raised her hand, informed the professor that she was, in fact, gifted, and explained that if the professor needed help teaching this section, she would accommodate. She seemed to want the professor to affirm her skills. The student continually complained of the simplicity of the concepts being presented.

Soon the "puffing and tooting" began to disrupt the class. Every time the student commented, the class would react with intolerance. Professor ___ chose to deal with this behavior by ignoring the proclamations and asking the student (in private) if she would prefer more challenging material that could be provided on an advisement basis (reading lists, opportunities for the student to expand) as long as the required class assignments were complete. In addition, Dr. ___ advised that the announcement of IQ status was inappropriate.

Professor ___ confronted a similar problem but discovered a different cause. He reported that a student would repeatedly write in her papers and worksheets that she considered his assignments a "waste of time," and objected to his pedagogy. He asked to meet with her and sought clarification of their problems with assignments and methods. He knew her to be one of the better students in the class prior to her declaring war on him, so he was very anxious to find out what precisely was bothering her. It turned out that her real concern was not with him, but with the fact that she was in a very large class and felt "invisible"; the assignments, she said, didn't allow her "real talents" to shine forth. He encouraged her to meet with him to devise her own assignments. She did so, produced much better work, began contributing to discussions, and ended happy with the course.

Many professors encounter another kind of needy student—one who "sucks up" to them. These are students who lack self-confidence and who therefore demand extra attention from the professor. These students, however, usually have above-average skills and are trying to discover how to ingratiate themselves with the instructor in order to get the praise, recognition, and support they need to bolster their self-images. Dr. ___ recounts how he dealt with one such student, who kept calling attention to himself in class by asking for more information. His interest in the subject, regardless of his sincerity, continually interrupted the flow of the class, and his classmates were becoming intolerant of him. The challenge to the distinguished teacher is, once again, to encourage the student while at the same time making him aware of his inappropriate behavior within the social setting of the class. Dr. ___'s solution was to ask the class whether they wanted more details, and, when they answered negatively, to suggest that the student see him after class.

Another distinguished teacher narrated the story of two 18-year-old roommates at the high end of the ability range, honors students whose behaviors nevertheless paralleled those of the underprepared students. They were awarded honors scholarships on the basis of their excellent high school records, but during their first year at college they continually challenged their honors course professors about the difficulty of the work. Because they were roommates, they had plenty of time to whine, commiserate, vent their frustration with the academic standards in the honors program, and to reinforce each other's poor study habits. The professor conferred with the students individually, but met only with "stonewalling." The professor reluctantly decided that these students were simply not developmentally ready to accept responsibility for meeting program standards. He reflected that sometimes professors have to accept the fact that major behavior changes often require more time than one semester.

Cultural Baggage

Gone are the days on most college campuses where classrooms were filled with a homogeneous group of students who shared a common elite status and were being groomed to follow family traditions in government, education, business, or the professions. "Good riddance!" we say. Today instead, as we have already reported in Chapter 2, the student population is more diverse than ever before. But this diversity has often left faculty, however well-intentioned, ill-prepared to deal with the array of instructional problems that accompany this "new America." This category of problem behaviors we are about to describe can be grouped together by their underlying cause: the students' lack of awareness of cultural rules and expectations of them in a new social setting.

Perhaps one of the most challenging, but most common, instructional problems caused by cultural differences is the inability of non-native speakers to use standard English in their assignments and exams. Some campuses offer an ESL (English as a Second Language) laboratory where such students may obtain help, but many smaller colleges do not offer this service. As more and more new immigrants and foreign students enter higher education, this problem has grown dramatically.

Dr. ___ recalls encountering a foreign student who entered without taking the TOEFL (Test of English as a Foreign Language) exam, so he insisted that the student take remedial courses as a condition of taking further courses in his discipline. He recommends helping students form support groups, or creating campus "communities" where students can get the language practice and support they need. Advisors need to encourage students to take writing and speaking courses that are appropriate to their levels, too, and not simply to assume that their knowledge of English will develop over time. Without help, these students may naturally isolate themselves into small clusters of those who share their culture, the very people who cannot help them overcome their language difficulties.

Dr. ___ tells of how he personally assisted a recent immigrant when no formal system of support was available. The student had enrolled in his public speaking course, although his English vocabulary and grammar were at about a ninth grade level, and his pronunciation was often unintelligible. During the short, ungraded speech exercises that Professor ___ used in the beginning of the course, he became aware of the student's linguistic difficulties. When the student approached him for help, he offered to listen to audiotapes of the student preparing his informal speech exercises, to analyze the errors in pronunciation, diction, and grammar, and to begin providing feedback to the student about the most serious errors. Every class, the student dropped off a tape and the professor listened, recorded the correct forms on the same tape, and returned the tape for the student's practice. The professor also assisted the student in discovering his public speaking strengths—his unusual life experiences, his sense of humor, and his character. Together they discussed his speech topics, and the student tested his ideas on the professor. In this manner, the student soon became one of the most popular speakers in the class, and he subsequently went on to a career in business.

Another example of how one professor turned cultural differences into a strength for foreign-born students is Dr. ___'s advice to his speech students to choose topics related to their cultural backgrounds. Thus, his classroom has been enriched by students demonstrating how to cook many tasty foreign dishes, as well as offering to share their customs, dances, and music, with their classmates. He reports that the linguistic weaknesses of most of these students can be turned into strengths if they learn to exploit the audience's natural curiosity about new lands.

Many professors report difficulty in addressing students' dialect problems in written and spoken communications. This is a cultural problem which often is misunderstood, because it is often based on the student's socioeconomic or subculture status, rather than on his or her ethnicity or race. Some professors fear the accusation of racism if they address the issue with particular ethnic or racial groups. But it must be noted that this issue is not exclusive to ethnicity or race.

One professor revealed her discussions with many students over the years about the use of nonstandard English. She had taught many first-generation college students who came from blue-collar environments, with many traditional as well as nontraditional students entering college as the first ones in their families to pursue higher education. They had been exposed to speech models that reflected the socioeconomic status of their families. While being sensitive to their culture, the professor neutralized the delicate topic by saying, "In this environment, this is the expected language." The professor explained that she would be remiss in not preparing each student for options, and that they needed to learn a variety of social registers in order to have the tools to compete. One English professor suggests that faculty often can be more helpful to such students, who appear to be trapped between their backgrounds and their career and educational goals, if they gain an understanding of the rules of a particular dialect and discover that the "errors" students make are not the result of ignorance, but rather of conformity to a *different* set of language rules (Shaughnessy, 1977).

A variation on individual students' problems caused by culture occurs when foreign-born students lack the cultural basis for learning the course content. Dr. ___, for example, reported difficulty in teaching business subjects to students who did not grow up in the U.S. economic system. In this instance, one recommendation might be to advise the student to find a way to gain the essential cultural background outside the course. Other content difficulties similar to this might be the clash between an English professor's feminist approach to literature for students who were born or raised in cultures where women have very different opportunities. Dr. ___ reports being sympathetic but perplexed at how to assist female students from backgrounds where women do not enjoy equal opportunity. They must find a way to cope with the enormous cultural gap between their families' expectations for them and the usual roles of women in the United States.

Another form of behavior through which cultural differences are sometimes manifested are intimidation tactics such as unfamiliar language, or charges of racism or bias, because that worked for a minority student in the past. Frequently underprepared, and sensing how out of place they are based on their former experiences, these students can become aggressive. In this case the professor needs to lay the ground rules—"On this turf, you follow my rules."

Professor ___ was on her way to class one evening when a colleague who had just finished teaching on the same floor stopped her. She suggested that she get to class quickly because one student was harassing another. Confronting them, she unraveled the heated rhetoric to find that the attacking student had demanded a research article that the other student had found in the library. When the other student didn't back down, she resorted to the use of profanity and an in-your-face posture.

Professor ___ met with the student privately and discovered that behind the attack the real person was an anxious, underprepared student who didn't really know how to use the library. Unfortunately, this student had a history of belligerent behavior, so the other student filed charges. Professor ___ felt that former professors had failed this student by permitting such behavior in any classroom. Teachers who allow intimidation in their classes because they, themselves, are intimidated by it do a disservice to all students. It is the role of the professor to protect all students from abuse and to teach those who resort to intimidation to find other means of reaching their goals.

Students in the process of recovery often present a special set of needs. They may be academically prepared, but in order to be successful, they will need continual support and encouragement. This takes time and commitment. One student who appeared very shy and fearful revealed her story during an informal office hour visit to Professor ___. She was a recovering alcoholic who had dropped out of a large university and after a period of time moved to a new city to attend a smaller school. She had focused on a major and was excited about it, but told the professor that she would need some help. A relationship was established wherein the student set up a "check-in" schedule with the professor. She would set short-term goals for herself, and the professor would help her determine how realistic they were and ways to go about achieving them. She maintained regular contact for the first year, became more independent, and eventually graduated. The major requirement from the professor, in this case, was the gift of time for the student.

When nontraditional students return to school, they often enter with a certain amount of expected baggage. Within a short time they often become stressed out, tapped out financially, or overwhelmed juggling a family, job, and school. This often reveals itself in overconscientious behavior and sometimes uncharacteristic outbursts. Dr. ___ recounts a student who was a model of consistency and mild temper. One day he wanted to speak with her during an office hour and had to contend with a number of students ahead of him. Under a time constraint but needing to clarify a point, he waited with increasing anxiety. By the time he gained the professor's attention, he exploded, yelling and waving papers in the air.

Initially shocked by his unexpected behavior, Professor ___ remained as neutral as she could. She removed eye contact and refused to listen. She suggested that he "leave now and come back when you are ready to have a calm discussion about the issue." The next morning, under her door was a humorous note of apology. He assured her that he would never "dance in public like that again," and that he was embarrassed by his behavior.

Dr. ___ suggests that whenever a student loses control, try to "cut him some slack." Later, at a more appropriate time, be reflective with the student and give him or her a way out: never close the door or back the student into a corner. Phrases such as, "I'm sensing that you are having a difficult time and more than likely didn't mean to attack. I need for you to speak to me like a human being. I don't yell at you, and I don't expect you to raise your voice to me," are clear, yet neutral.

Other kinds of cultural differences can become instructional problems. Dr. ___ addresses the problem of adapting a course schedule to accommodate students with different religious backgrounds and beliefs. In particular, he answers the question of how to deal with those who are religious and who object to the scheduling of an exam on a religious holiday. He advises, "Do not announce this policy, but *say* to anyone who complains, 'No religion prohibits this; there are no makeup exams'; and, "'It's been on the syllabus from Day One.'" If students in the course still object, he advises, "Tell them to write a letter stating that they did not take the exam for religious reasons. The grade should not be counted." He advises instructors not to tell students this in advance, or the students might not study.

Another similar problem encountered by an award-winning professor of biology was a student's moral objection to using animals as research subjects. This young anti-vivisectionist was enrolled in a required science course, but his moral beliefs prevented him from carrying out lab dissections. The professor solved the problem by pairing the student as an observer with a partner who held no such views, thus sparing one lab animal. The professor informed us that, in the future, use of computer simulations—virtual dissections—may eliminate this problem.

Students in Crisis

Beyond problems resulting from cultural differences, students today bring their personal crises into the educational setting. These can result from the student's maturation or encounter with a tragedy or moral dilemma, or they can take the form of illness, poverty, or problems caused by dysfunctional families.

One of the most common of these crises is the career crisis, which ought to be viewed not as a problem but as an opportunity, a necessary stage in the development of a person who is moving toward adulthood. Professors who are in tune with their students are often able to see a pattern in what might appear to someone else to be a one time occurrence. They may be able to see students ready to sabotage themselves. One common problem occurs as students approach graduation. The commitment to whatever field they have chosen becomes very real and very scary. For the student who has been influenced to pursue a career because Mom or Dad thought it was a good idea, this can be a time for panic. Basically, students can't fathom telling the family, "I don't really want to be a...nurse, teacher, physical therapist, and so on" and the only way out they can see is to mess up. Intuitively, most distinguished professors know they can assist these students only to the extent that the student takes advantage of the time offered. When students establish a relationship with a professor, they have someone to bounce these thoughts off (no matter how frightening they might be to explain).

Dr. ___ recalls a senior with one semester to go tearfully telling her that he couldn't go through with his plans to become a teacher. He had done an adequate job in all of his requirements, but was miserable the entire time he was student teaching. He couldn't envision disappointing his family, who had sacrificed to put him through school. What this student needed at this time was to know that his decision, though a very difficult one, was a correct one. He needed support. He needed to hear that teaching is not for everyone and that there are other career options. He needed to hear that there are enough unhappy teachers influencing children and that he was brave in acknowledging his decision. Students like this young man may find that to try out the words on someone they respect and trust can be a relief, and it can provide a dress rehearsal for their telling their families of their change in career goals.

Dr. ___ reports having to assist students with another maturational crisis: the recognition of their sexual orientation. During her work with several students, they separately revealed their growing sense of their homosexuality. Dr. ___ acted the role of the good listener for these students, providing them with accurate information to combat their fears and stereotyping, and suggesting that students not label themselves too quickly. Professors need to know, she states, that students who "come out" to them are taking a huge risk. Their efforts to communicate honestly should be met with supportive, nurturing responses. If the students' self-perceptions are accurate, they will gain tremendously from having someone they respect who accepts their orientation. Professor ___ adds that students in this maturational stage of their awkward new role may make a pass at the faculty member, and the ethically responsible action on the professor's part is to kindly parry the overture.

Since the open enrollment movement of the 1970s, more people from lower socioeconomic groups have entered higher education and many have gone on to become successful, productive citizens. But the down side of this phenomenon is that more of the problems associated with poverty have entered the college classroom too. One professor who teaches on an urban campus reports having students in her classes who have been crime victims, who are welfare mothers, who are overcoming drug and alcohol addictions, who have been evicted from their homes, or who have no network of support within the community. Marginal students who have to work full-time while they attend college often discover that they are caught on the horns of a dilemma: If they don't work, they can't afford school; if they work enough to afford school, they don't have enough time to study. Women who return to school after raising a family may be coping with disintegrating marriages. Divorced people and single parents often cannot bear the significant emotional, economic, and family stresses caused by their college attendance, even though they are doing well in college.

One all-too-common crisis among such college students, unfortunately, is depression leading to suicidal thoughts. If we look at young adulthood as a time when the cruel and undeniable realities of the world must be integrated into one's belief systems, then it is understandable that students of this age have a high incidence of suicide. Dr. ___ uses William Blake's concept of the movement from "innocence" to "experience" as a metaphor for this stage in students' development. "Sensitive human beings," she writes, "have to come to terms with the existence of evil and courageously choose to believe in the potential for goodness among humankind" in order to progress into the adult state of "organized innocence."

Dr. ___'s account of her experience with one young man who had a family history of alcoholism points to the fact that faculty can and should intervene when students reveal suicidal tendencies to them. During her freshman communications course, one young man wrote several excellent papers. One paper in particular suggested that the class clown was not what he appeared to be. She summoned him to her office for a conference and learned that he had been deeply depressed at times and was in counseling. He told her he had been an alcoholic, had made some mistakes with the law, and was on probation. He also said that he didn't worry about his health because he didn't expect to live past age 30. Toward the end of the semester, he contracted mononucleosis along with fever, pain, enlarged spleen—the works. Struggling to attend classes, he also missed an appointment with his parole officer. No sooner did he take his final exams (and score the highest grade in Dr. ___'s course!) than he was thrown into jail by an unsympathetic judge. The student's mother phoned Dr. ___ to ask her to write a letter to his parole board, which she did because she saw him as a gifted young person struggling to define himself.

In the spring, the student appeared at her office door, heavier and happier than she had ever seen him. Being in jail four months had allowed him to recover from the mono, and he was more committed than ever to completing his college degree. Unfortunately, this story does not have a happy ending. The student was killed in a hit-and-run accident, fulfilling his prophecy that he would lead a short life. But Professor ___ believes that her efforts to help the student were not in vain: The student had overcome his depression and alcoholism and had earned a place on the dean's list before he died.

Another professor describes a case involving a student who lacked a support system and whose academic career was threatened by a financial crisis. The student was a senior in a professional program when she appeared at the professor's door and meekly asked if she could request a favor. It seems her rent was past due, and she had no one else to turn to or she would be evicted. Could the professor lend her $50 towards her rent? He recommended that the student seek help from the office of campus ministry, which has a small loan fund, but the student told him that she had done that and there was no money left because it was the end of the budget year. The professor wrote a check to the student and figured that he would not be repaid. He reported that for nearly a year the student avoided him, until one day he found a thank-you note with the money in it under his door. The loan apparently had allowed the student to get through her financial crisis and continue in her program.

One of the most interesting problems our award-winning professors described was that presented by a nontraditional male student, who expressed misogynist views during class discussions of literature. Not only was he anti-women, but he also was a radical conservative. Eventually his classmates, mostly female, began to lie in wait for him to launch into a sexist tirade, and then they would gang up on him during the discussion. Otherwise a likable young man, he was fast developing a reputation among students in his program. Dr. ___ reports that her approach was to try to discover the cause of the student's disenchantment with women. In conferences with him about his writing, she challenged his views and told him they were offensive to her and why. The cause of his anger against women, she discovered, was his loss of custody of his son during a divorce.

Over the course of several years, the student gradually relinquished his anger and began to write poetry. A remarkable transformation occurred as the student began to accept his share of the responsibility for the divorce, which included his alcoholism. Professor ___ suggested that he see the school nurse for a medical evaluation, which he did, and subsequently he entered and emerged from counseling a much happier man.

Other kinds of family crises, such as the illness or death of a parent or grandparent, also enter our students' lives and can have a devastating impact. Unplanned pregnancies or abortions also create crises for students, and these may require that they reconsider their academic plans in the light of the new event. A professor reports that one semester she was advising a young couple in her class as they contemplated an abortion at the same time as she was the advisor to a young Catholic woman who decided to tell her parents about her pregnancy and to keep her child. The emotional toll of such decisions cannot be overestimated. Students in these situations usually try valiantly to continue their education, but this is the time when a wise professor can and should intervene to ask the student important questions and to give permission to the student to withdraw until he or she is emotionally able to return to academics.

Another type of personal crisis confronted a student in Dr. ___'s classes. She reported that she was having difficulty concentrating on her studies because she had been sexually molested in the residence hall. Most troubling to the student was the fact that the molester was a fellow student, and that she had failed to report the incident out of embarrassment and disgust. Throughout a semester, she returned to Dr. ___'s office to discuss her options. Eventually she did report the event and confront her molester. Thus she resolved a moral issue with the professor's guidance and began to assume the role of a responsible adult. Was this the professor's role? In our view, decidedly so, if building character and assisting students to make wise ethical choices is a goal of education.

Marginal Ability

With opportunity for special admission and financial support, many marginal students today are given the chance to take advantage of a higher education. For some of these academically marginal students, school is a cocoon, a safe haven with a useful structure. Learning may not be central for these students, compared with the built-in social atmosphere, routines, and attention available. Because of the tremendous amount of need on the part of this type of student, finding a major that is suited to the person is very difficult. This student frequently repeats many courses before finally finding a niche. He or she hangs out in the computer lab and makes clip art calendars, or becomes an expert in something other than academics. Or a student may fix on the legal system and the university's fear of litigation to threaten faculty and assure the granting of a degree.

Marginal students often seek professors who will cave in to their demands or negotiate course requirements or grades with them. The professor who is confident that the expectations set for courses are reasonable and that every attempt has been made to provide "reasonable accommodations," in addition to written policies and clear expectations, should be very helpful to this student. Careful documentation (a paper trail) early on in the student's career is essential to guidance.

Dr. ___ reports how she agonized over how to deal with a student in her graduate course whose writing and class responses indicated that he was unable to use higher order thinking skills such as analysis, synthesis and evaluation that she expected of her students. At first glance, she believed the student had a writing problem, but after she shared a draft with an English colleague, she decided that the student really had a thinking problem. She believed that the student's critical thinking skills could not be developed in the semester's time to the point of passing her course. But the young man was earnest, hardworking, and likable. She decided to meet with the student after a second assignment, to express her views and allow the student to withdraw or continue. In addition, she planned to recommend that he speak with a career/life counselor on campus for guidance as to how to adjust his career goals.

The narratives in this chapter reflect the variety of problems students bring with them into our classrooms today. We can no longer be cavalier about their concerns, believing that the students are expendable. Educating students with problems is important, not only to them but to society, and it is imperative that we understand the unique challenges individuals bring us and learn how to assist them effectively.

8

Instructional
Problem Solving

Group Dynamics

Sometimes individual students join together to create a collective problem for a professor; at other times, the classroom ecology creates discord that must be addressed. Because students are social creatures, their behavior when they gather may be significantly different from when they are approached individually. Scholars of teaching are aware of the importance of group dynamics and the potential for classes to exhibit herd behavior. These scholars develop a repertoire of tactics or interventions to prevent or redirect the problem behaviors of specific groups. (See Cross [1976], and Lowman [1995].) In this section, we will describe some of the more common problems involving groups, and show how our award-winning professors responded to them. What usually happens is that a group of students who are experiencing a similar instructional problem will band together as a result of their mutual problem, and then act collectively in inappropriate ways to attempt to influence the professor's teaching. We have found this group behavior among students at all ability levels, from marginal students to honors students.

Aggregate Student Difficulties

Different Cultural Rules

Often students who are in an unfamiliar environment (foreign, underprepared, nontraditional, or minority students) are aware of the difference and are fearful. They may take an offensive, confrontational, bullying posture, particularly with white, middle class students who aren't sure how to be politically correct. For example, Canadian students frequently attend classes at U.S. colleges and universities in border cities. Most observers would perceive no difference between these mostly white, English-speaking students and the rest of the student body. But, based on their newfound minority status on one campus, a group of Canadian students created a defensive and competitive atmosphere that immediately alienated them from faculty and the other students. Their limited opportunities to enter professional programs in their own country, accompanied by ethnocentrism, led to expectations that conflicted with the existing campus culture. Once the dust settled, Professor L___ looked at the situation objectively and saw it for what it was—a difference in cultural rules. Again, communication was the key to the solution: The faculty needed to communicate the expectations or ground rules for the new environment. She developed a brochure that presented FAQs (frequently asked questions) and made it available to all students. This not only spelled out information for the foreign students, but for the hometown students as well.

Overly Competitive Groups

One professor reported that her department used a bulletin board to display information and provide applications for various internships and opportunities for the students. She found that students were continually destroying or defacing the information or taking all of the applications so that no one else could have access to them. The students complained bitterly, implying that the department was remiss. One option was to remove all of the applications from the board and mandate that the students request them individually. Lacking the staff to accommodate this option, the professor decided to "put the ball back in their court." She replaced all of the defaced material and included a handwritten note placed in the center of the board. It read: "These materials are here for the benefit of *all* students. If you feel that you need an individual copy of one of the postings, just ask—that is the mature and professional approach. Removing all of the applications for yourself is inappropriate. Please be considerate of your fellow students." The defacement ended and the applications remained available.

A problem frequently mentioned by both seasoned and novice professors is "grade-grubbing." Grade-grubbing can take the form of whining about or challenging every question on an exam, comparing papers to others, and claiming unfair grading policies. Grade consciousness taken to the extreme can also lead to cutthroat, uncaring, "screw your buddy" practices (such as destroying library materials so that others cannot benefit from them); it suggests that for some students, getting a degree has nothing to do with getting an education. Going to school, for these students, is a means to an end. They are invested in the grades, not in the learning. Again, Professor ___ supports the concept of clarity: Spell out the grade requirements, what it takes to earn a specific grade, and how to meet criteria. Yet she told of a problem encountered whenever she returned exams to an introductory class. The students would attack (en masse) after having exams returned, each wanting to know why each question was incorrect. Tired of continually having to wear armor to fend off the attackers, she established a policy which she reviews with students before papers are returned. The following is her set of directions:

> I am finishing class five minutes early so that you will have time to look at your exams. I will pass these back folded so that your score is visible to you alone. This emphasizes that your grade is yours and has nothing to do with others in the class. Look at your own paper quietly. If, after reviewing the paper quietly, you have any questions or challenges, here is the procedure you must follow: Note!!!! I will not speak with you about your exam. You must follow this procedure:
>
> 1. Take your paper home with you and find the answer in your text.
> 2. Write out the question and the answer verbatim (include the page number).
> 3. Write out your answer (exactly as you wrote it on the test) and provide a written reason why you feel that your

answer should be considered. Label the top of this separate paper as "Request for Review."
4. Circle the item in question on the exam paper.
5. Staple all together and return it to the desk in front of the lecture hall prior to the beginning of the next lecture.
6. I will review your request and return my response by the next class period.
7. Understand that submitting a request for review does not mean you will receive any additional points.

This procedure makes students responsible for their own answers as well as validating the amount of time put into the grading process. It stresses that the professor is willing to acknowledge any error in grading and, in fact, welcomes any opportunity to raise a grade that deserves boosting.

"Enabling" Behavior

Occasionally, lack of confidence will be exhibited by small groups of students who cluster into unholy alliances, creating the education equivalent of codependency. This behavior can be found at both ends of the confidence spectrum, among weak students as well as the academically gifted. One professor described a "tag-team" couple, young adults who entered his upper-level course as transfers from a junior college. Together they struck a defiant stance in the class, complaining about the length of course assignments and the professor's grading criteria. The problem was exacerbated by the facts that they lived together, and the man had a learning disability that affected his reading speed. They had developed a system in which she read the course material to him aloud, they discussed it, then they wrote their paper drafts. Although this professor used collaborative learning strategies in his course, he was perplexed with the problem of how to assess individual learning and assign individual grades to this pair. Furthermore, he believed that the man would have to develop better reading skills if he expected to succeed in college and later in his career. Once again, the solution evolved out of regular communications. The professor reported that he confidently reinforced his expectations for performance when they confronted him in class, and invited them to meet with him. During these meetings, first together and then separately, they began to understand that he was not being mean, but rather challenging them to meet a higher standard. The man reported that he had only learned to read in the twelfth grade, when his learning disability was diagnosed, and had previously bluffed and bullied his way through high school. The student was bright and articulate in class, and the professor began a process of encouraging independent work in the pair by assigning them to different small groups during class, supporting their studying together, and insisting that their writing be their own. Gradually, the students developed their own voices in class and in their writing. At first, the separation resulted in rivalry between them but, by the end of the course, the professor reported that they were beginning to challenge themselves rather than each other. To his surprise, they enrolled in a second of his courses the following semester, with the young man informing the instructor that he was "aiming for an A" in the course.

As with the previous pair of students, sometimes a cluster of students with academic weaknesses or similar backgrounds can move beyond their dependency on each other when they are treated as individuals by instructors. Dr. ___ described the evolution of a trio of nontraditional women whose goal was to become elementary school teachers. They evolved from "the three *amigos*" to professional women. The three all had families, jobs, and busy schedules, and they formed a valuable support system for each other that only became a problem because they were all underprepared for college—a case of "the blind leading the blind." Because Dr. ___'s classes were small, she was able to confer with each student individually, so they soon learned to understand their own strengths and deficiencies as learners and to rely on themselves. What began as an academic support system converted to a personal support system as the students became acclimated to the challenges of college work. Eventually, they graduated and entered their careers with well-earned confidence in their abilities to self-evaluate and continue to grow professionally.

Elite Groups and "Required Course Apathy"

On many campuses, there are one or two programs that are more selective and therefore accrue a lofty status. For example, premedical students, engineering students, honors students, or athletes may come to consider themselves as entitled to special privileges based on their high status in the campus pecking order. Regardless of the particular elite program, however, the behavior of this group of students is the same. It often takes the form of a condescending attitude toward students and professors in their required general education courses, a contemptuous disregard for the standards of other programs, or bullying tactics towards those who treat them like everyone else on campus.

We call one of the most common syndromes associated with those who perceive themselves as members of an elite program "required course apathy." Now, instead of one or two individuals using their body language to indicate that they don't value the course, the professor is faced with groups of students who resist instruction. Professor ___ describes these students' behavior as defiant. He suggests frank discussion of the pervasive attitude and requests to the students to "at least give the topic a fair chance." For other students, required course apathy stems not from a sense of superiority, but its opposite. For example, students may resent having to study chemistry as a prerequisite to a program in the health professions because they have not succeeded in chemistry previously. They begin to think of themselves as victims unable to learn the subject, and they see the professor's demands as unrealistic and impossible because they don't believe in their ability to learn. Often these students fail to see, or are not presented, the whole picture—they need to know why they are studying a particular topic and to see the relationship of the material or assignments to their goals. It is the responsibility of the professor to spell that out in order to prevent this situation. Here the excellent teacher must delve deep into his or her instructional toolkit to discover what will motivate these students. Professor ___ reports that she surveys this kind of class to find out what *does* interest them, and uses those interests as guides to her selection of examples. She says that the key is to discover what is meaningful to the students, and to use that to break down the elitist or defensive attitudes they bring to the course. When she became disturbed with the apathy of her ethics students, she decided to incorporate community service as a course requirement. Soon, she reported, the students' experiences in the community made them much more sensitive to issues of social justice, for instance.

Professor ___ describes another variation on this theme. She teaches a class of 10 first-year honors students in an interdisciplinary culture course. The students are selected for the honors program on the basis of their academic records, their leadership, and their interest in the program. However, she reports that she has encountered several classes that were dead in terms of discussion and intellectual curiosity. The group dynamic appeared to prohibit their eager contribution to class discussion, and instead, she had to pull their responses from them. Professor ___ thought that an 8 A.M. time slot might be in part responsible for the problem, so she had the course time changed the next year, but with no better luck. A third course went better when she made students responsible for leading discussion and after she incorporated field trips, films, and guest speakers to break up the heavy reading, though again with little grade improvement. She had begun to believe that the elite status of some of the groups was either intimidating to the first-year students, whose fear of failure in front of their peers prevented them from contributing in class, or that the students really wanted the scholarship but not the education. In exasperation, she spoke with a professor who taught the same groups at the next level and who reported the same difficulty. Together they decided that the selection process for the honors program was not identifying the qualities in students that they sought to nurture: curiosity and independence. A year later, during a program evaluation, they were able to make their criticisms known. This anecdote illustrates that not all problems with groups of students are instructional problems—sometimes they are institutional problems that require policy changes.

Groups with Populations from Diverse Cultures

At a border college where large numbers of foreign students were enrolled, the smaller population of U.S. students was intimidated. The foreign students were older and many already held college degrees and had work experience. Even in an introductory course, they created a very competitive environment that was frightening for the first-year, traditional students. This resulted in a culture clash of groups within the class. With obvious intolerance, the students who were older and had experience viewed U.S. students as under prepared. Reciprocally, the younger U.S. students viewed the foreigners as obnoxious and pushy. The professor, seeing the situation for what it was, focused on the material in the course as the common denominator. The students were randomly placed in groups for collaborative projects and presentations for which a group grade was

given. It was to the advantage of both groups to learn to work together.

The Academically Weak Class

Occasionally, our participants reported problems with a small class
with no stars; the question is how to enforce standards when all students in a group are low performers. Dr. ___'s solution was to establish expectations clearly and early, to enforce the standards where
possible by using external comparisons, and to explain to students
that they are being evaluated against standards necessary to enter
into advanced courses, graduate study, or careers.

Dr. ___ also reported having difficulty with an academically
weak class, one that required many students with low ability to
read questions or to articulate organized answers. He believed that
the language problems he diagnosed betrayed a weak background
in thinking about the subject matter of the course, and hypothesized
that this was the result of too much reliance on rote learning tested
by short-answer exams in precollege experiences. His solution was
to provide critical comments in marking the exams, to discuss his
expectations in a review session, and subsequently to reassign the
essays as credit-bearing homework assignments.

Bimodal Abilities:
A Class of "Stars" and "Pluggers"

A perennial problem for all college professors is managing the
learning in classes with widely differing abilities: the classic problem of heterogeneous groups—how to challenge the average and
the "star" group of students while also addressing the needs of basic learners. Dr. ___, an English professor, was confronted with this
dilemma in her introductory American literature survey course.
She began teaching the course in the usual manner, first giving a
broad overview of the scope of the course and then proceeding historically from the colonial period. Students kept reaction journals in
which they responded to the readings, participated in close readings and discussions, and took notes on her introductory lectures.
However, the first test results showed a bimodal curve: student
scores clustered into a "very good" group and a "very poor" group,
though there were no Fs. On the second test, the split was even

more dramatic, with 58% scoring below C. Many of those who were doing poorly were English majors whom she knew as borderline students from previous courses. They had succeeded in prior courses, she believed, because they were adequate interpreters of literature, but their writing skills and their ability to learn factual information such as historical contexts, biographical material, and literary terms were undeveloped. She knew that many professors would simply accept the failure rate as a natural weeding out of students with little aptitude for the subject, yet she was unwilling to do this. How would she assist this group of "pluggers," students who worked hard for every C grade, to learn this new type of content without dumbing down the course?

Dr. ___ had just attended a workshop on collaborative learning when the problem became acute. She decided to try a radically different approach by organizing students into groups of three based on their scores on different sections of the tests. Each group consisted of a student who had done well on the short-answer material, a student who had done well on the essay, and a student who had done poorly (usually in both areas). These learning teams were responsible for generating three questions each on the readings, which they wrote on 3 × 5 filecards with the answers on the back. She eliminated her short lecture each class and substituted small-group sessions where the learning teams discussed and evaluated the questions they had created and then presented the best questions to the whole class. The class continued to keep their reaction journals, which she used as a check on their individual preparation and learning. Soon even the quietest, most clueless students were actively engaged in the discussions. The "stars" often became the leaders of their teams, and some new "stars" also emerged when the class was organized in this manner. Someone suggested that one student should be responsible for collecting the filecards and typing them up for study sheets. In every class thereafter, someone new volunteered to make copies and distribute the questions (and answers) at the next meeting. Later in the semester, when she had invited a guest speaker to this decentralized classroom, he watched in dismay as the class took charge of the discussion he was about to lead. He remarked to her later, "I could never relinquish that much control!"

At the students' request, Dr. ___ decided to weight the third and final tests more heavily than the early tests, but she made one-third of the tests cumulative, basing most of her questions on those the students had generated. The results of her experiment were conclusive: Final grades showed that only 18% scored below average, and no one failed. Students had learned how to ask interesting questions about literature, a skill that she saw as primary; the real boon, she reported, was the spirit of community and excitement that emanated from the class. A neighboring professor commented on the animated discussions that continued as the class filed out.

Large Class Management

A large class, which we define as 60 to 600 students, is not by definition a "problem." However, the anonymity that such classes allow has the effect of making some students think that they can break social rules without being held responsible. According to one of our research subjects, "Large classes can swallow students up, and they displace their anger onto the professor by declaring war by objecting to the assignments or the professor's pedagogy." The professor who teaches such a large class must overcome the impersonality of the environment in myriad ways if he or she strives to be an excellent teacher. Furthermore, research by McKeachie (1994) suggests that class size has little impact on students' lower order learning, but it does affect the learning of higher order thinking skills such as evaluation, synthesis, integration, and application. The distinguished professors we interviewed told us that they sometimes had difficulty finding the amount of control that would create an easygoing, friendly atmosphere but prevent disruptions.

The special challenges of teaching a large course are many: (a) How do you make learning active? (b) How do you manage disruptive behavior? (c) How do you deal with diversity? (d) How do you assess learning without using short-answer exams? (e) How do you adapt your teaching style to the large auditorium? and (f) How do you enjoy teaching such classes? (Weimer, 1995).

As for active learning, questioning requires more thought in the large class, where certain individuals might be prone to answer more readily and others are reticent due to stage fright. One distinguished professor solves this by creating a question box for students, and "primes the pump" by putting the first question in himself and preparing an answer. Another has microphones set up at the sides of the auditorium to make it easier for them to be heard in the large room. Another holds question and answer sessions online after each lecture. Yet another professor uses "A. L."—active learning, one-minute questions or summaries at the conclusion of class, to evaluate whether students are getting the main points of the lectures.

You may recall the active learning routines we observed in the large introductory calculus classes of Professor G: She called on various people and saw that they were having difficulty with a particular type of problem. In response to her question, "Who has no clue?" several students immediately raised their hands and were asked to take their places at one of two overhead projectors. As they reached certain points in the equation, Professor G. asked the class if they agreed with the direction the problem was going. She encouraged students to help one another by spotting one whose answer was correct, and asking her to go to the front of the room and help. While pairs of students worked at the overheads, she moved through the rows checking work. When a student responded or asked a question, she went up the rows directly to him or her and had a conversation.

One traditional way of personalizing the environment is to learn students' names, but this is really not feasible in very large classes. Instead, distinguished professors asked students to state their names before they responded or asked a question. If small group work is part of the course, students can introduce each other and exchange names and phone numbers. In such a way, smaller communities of learners begin to take shape within the large classroom. Other techniques we observed were conferences with individual students before and after class.

When large classes get a bit rambunctious or clusters of students exhibit behaviors that interfere with the smooth flow of the class, such as talking and moving around, one professor uses "decontamination through humor." She stops the class and indicates what behavior she needs to see: "I need to be sure that everyone in the room can hear my pearls of wisdom. I don't want to invoke Dr. ___'s curse, 'Someday, may *you* have students *just like you!*'"

Other problems of large group management such as tardiness were handled in a variety of ways by the professors we observed. One professor of biology advised doing something important in the first 10 minutes of each class, while another used an activity to get students' attention and launch the class. Professor ___ flicked the lights to signal students that class was about to begin.

The problem of assessing students' work in very large classes without resorting exclusively to short-answer tests was addressed by one professor. He suggested assigning one short paper per class per student, with due dates distributed randomly by the students' social security number. Another gave an essay question on each of his four tests, but each time a different quarter of the class received the essay test. Eventually, of course, all students would have to answer an essay question. Another professor suggested having students evaluate each others' writing in upper-level courses, where student and faculty ratings are highly correlated.

Competitive Clusters and Cheating

One of the most serious academic problems an instructor can confront is how to deal with individuals or groups of students who have violated their trust by cheating. We have chosen to group these problems together because of their common causes: students' lack of confidence in themselves as learners, and their notion that the system is unfair, and therefore justifies their academic dishonesty. Two of the most common forms of cheating in which individuals engage are plagiarism and destruction of resource materials; groups, however, are more likely to engage in stealing tests, representing other students' work as their own, or sharing answers on tests.

Dr. ___ describes how she deals with cases of suspected plagiarism. First, she advises, at the beginning of each course instructors should state their policies (and/or those of the department or college) on plagiarism and define the term for students. Every syllabus should include a statement referring to the policy in the college catalog. The policy statement should also include the consequences for the infringement (e.g., failure on the paper, or failure in the course). The statement could also require students who submit suspicious papers to bring in their sources or receive a failing grade, thus placing the burden of proof on the student. Next, professors should build time for submission of rough drafts of major papers into their course schedule. Although the professor does not have to read or grade them, they provide a record of the students' planning and revising that is invaluable as a tool for assessing the final product. If time does not allow for this, the instructor can do two things: (a) inform students that he or she knows that plagiarism may become a problem, and that it is up to them to report students who are using former students' responses or "canned" papers they purchase from research paper firms, and (b) scrutinize paper submissions for discrepancies between students' previously submitted writing and the paper in question.

If, after all this, the professor believes that a fraudulent paper has been submitted, an interview with the alleged plagiarist should be scheduled, preferably with a witness present. During the interview, the professor can request substantiation of questionable sources, ask the student to explain segments that seem to be beyond the student's usual level, and ask for definitions of words and terms which the professor believes are not the student's own. Professor ___ offers this advice:

> It has been my experience that many students will cave in under this pressure and admit their transgression. For them there is hope, because the violation of trust has been acknowledged. Other students—though unable to satisfactorily explain terms or deliver source material, will continue to insist on their innocence. They may claim that they were never taught how to properly attribute sources, and thus try to point the finger of blame at the professor or his/her colleagues. They may even try to turn the tables and accuse the professor of scapegoating them. These are the students whom you must "nail to the wall." It is worth the trouble, in my estimation, of ordering the sources in dispute and checking the citations, or speaking to colleagues who may have taught the same student. If plagiarism is proved, or if a pattern of suspected plagiarism is discerned, then the professor is morally obligated to report it to a higher authority. If the higher authority (usually the administration) fails to act upon the information, at least the professor has maintained his/her integrity, and the student has learned that the system is not a total sieve. Cheating by plagiarism is as much an affront to the relationship between the professor and student as infidelity is to a marriage. Moreover, to ignore it because it is simpler to do so is an act of cowardice on the part of the professor. In my opinion, it is absolutely necessary for the senior professor, who is protected by tenure, to stymie such attempts by students to defy the system and to support junior colleagues as they thrash with this problem.

Other instances of academic dishonesty in which groups of students band together in cooperative attempts to improve their academic status were also reported. The students work out elaborate and discreet systems of sharing information or occasionally make very blatant demands for information from one another. Professors with a tremendous sense of trust in their relationships with their classes are often devastated when they learn (usually from other students) that their trust has been violated by cheating. While administering exams, they may become engrossed in their own reading or leave the exam room when they should be proctoring. They believe that reminding the students of the honor code should be enough to ensure academic integrity. Once the suspected cheating has been brought to their attention, the burden of proof becomes their responsibility. Confrontation usually results in denial and the problem remains unresolved. After being awakened to cheating going on in his class, one professor incorporated a plea for cooperation from any student who observed cheating. Now before each exam he brings up the topic of cheating and suggests that those who tolerate it are hurting their own grades.

Another increasing and related problem is one of defacing or stealing materials that are meant as references for all. Library staff report that students remove microfilm and fiche and either steal or refile it so that others will not have access to it. Reference manuals are reshelved among obscure books, or they are thrown out of the library window and into the bushes to be retrieved later. Entire articles are reportedly sliced from journals, either because students do not want to bother copying or because they want to be the sole possessor of the information.

One librarian conferred with a member of a department when pages were torn from a journal that was used in a particular course. The professor had given an assignment relating to this particular journal but had already returned the papers. He recalled them and tracked down the individual who had used that particular article. The student claimed the incident to be circumstantial, and again the burden of proof remained in the hands of the professor. What do these tales teach us? As opposed to the negative approach of expecting the worst, we should attempt to protect the integrity of the examination environment or the treatment of the reference materials.

In Chapter 9, "A Problem-Solving Theory of Teaching," we will show how distinguished teaching professors direct their "radar" toward everything in the instructional environment, including themselves. Then in Chapter 10, "Application of the Problem-Solving Theory: Distinguished Professors Advise," we will present the suggestions of these teaching scholars to inexperienced professors, TAs, and junior faculty who are encountering certain instructional problems for the first time.

9

A *Problem-Solving*
Theory of Teaching

We have said that teaching excellence involves character, knowledge, actions, and outcomes. In previous chapters we presented case study narratives of observations and interviews with award-winning professors, and we analyzed the professorial character from the perspective of a set of acquired behaviors. These behaviors, which comprise emotional intelligence, are mapped on to genetic personality dispositions. Then we investigated the professors' beliefs, knowledge of pedagogy, planning, and methods. Finally we showed how the distinguished college teachers applied what they knew to solve instructional problems with individual students and groups.

Thus far we have clarified two elements in our theory of teaching excellence: the character of the professors (who they are) and knowledge (what they know and believe). What we have not yet done, and what we set as one of our chief purposes in writing this book, was to articulate a theory to explain our research findings about what excellent professors do in the classroom that distinguishes them from those who perform competently. Ultimately, theories have useful predictive features, applications, and implications. These will be the focus of Chapters 10 and 11. In this chapter, we will draw upon our observations, interviews, and experience to support the problem-solving model within our theory of excellent teaching.

The "Aha!" Experience:
Mucking Around in the Data

Theories take the form of statements of truths about something. They are developed by gathering facts, making hypotheses, experimenting, and drawing conclusions. Most of us are trained in the scientific method of inquiry, which consists of these orderly and logical steps. However, without creative intuition, researchers who employed only the scientific method would never make a serious discovery. In this section we will describe our own "Aha!" experience—the intuitive discovery of our hypothesis that the actions of excellent teachers are indeed what Robert Gagné called the highest order of cognition, problem solving (1975), and what Gardner described as intelligence (1993, p. 7).

At the beginning of our research, our goal was to discover markers of excellence among professors who had won recognition for their distinguished teaching. Our problem was that there was a lot of data, but the system to organize and explain it seemed inadequate. Nevertheless, we immersed ourselves in the research, having a hunch as to what we would find regarding the importance of problem solving, but also hoping—even expecting—to have that moment of intuition that would enable us to tie everything together.

Early on in our examination of the data, we each began to glimpse the theory we were seeking. Baiocco's education was in problem-solving theory of composing processes and the arts, whereas DeWaters had a more scientific background and had developed expertise in behavior analysis and the preparation of teachers. Like the serendipitous combination of chocolate and peanut butter that inspired Reese's Peanut Butter Cups, these two ways of looking at the essence of excellent teaching suddenly merged into the model we are proposing. Baiocco approached the investigation of excellence in teaching from a cognitive perspective, looking at the way teachers *think*, whereas DeWaters, coming from a behaviorist angle, focused on what teachers *do*. Both of us agreed upon the term of "radar" to describe the intuitive aspect demonstrated by all of the distinguished professors we observed. We saw this monitoring ability as a kind of "radar" which is always turned on, responding to cues in the instructional environment. We believed instinctively that our theory was both accurate and powerful. Our experiences told us that teachers at every level—from pre-kinder-garten to graduate school—planned, acted, and evaluated routinely and frequently and that they drew upon their experiences to guide their decision making. As we observed similarities between our theory and our data, our hunch that the process of excellent teaching is a form of problem solving was further confirmed. Thus, in a sense, the manner in which we developed the answer to our research question, "What is distinguished teaching?" exemplifies the very thing we are trying to explain—the high level cognitive skills of problem solving. As we continued our research, we expanded and refined our original hypothesis into a set of postulates about excellent teaching which derived from our observations and experience as well as from previous theoretical models of problem solving and communication.

The Eclectic Field of Problem Solving

Currently, the field of problem solving is vast and eclectic. However, a more unified theory of problem solving is emerging as the result of interdisciplinary conferences and collaboration between experts in intersecting fields such as mathematics, philosophy, cognitive psychology, education, creative studies, artificial intelligence, and psycholinguistics.

Focusing on the literature on teaching as problem solving, Schön (1983) viewed "professional action" as involving the problem-solving processes of framing or naming the problem, taking action, and responding to the consequences of the actions. Sherman et al. (1987) looked at the cognitive components in terms of strategies for attacking a teaching problem and called for a theory of teaching excellence. Ramsden (1992) supported the notion that teaching is a problem-solving activity and pointed toward a reconceptualization of teaching centering around student learning problems. Menges and Rando (1996) produced a problem-solving model of the process of seeking and using feedback to improve teaching and learning that includes four phases of a cycle: (1) seeing and gathering, (2) interpreting and valuing, (3) planning and building, and (4) doing and checking. They also presented a taxonomy of instructional problems (p. 241).

As in our initial analogy of the blind man and the elephant (p. 94), researchers in problem solving all touch on different aspects of how the mind works. Most of the research supports the concept that problems have certain characteristics: givens, goals, and obstacles. Researchers further agree that problem solving is a complex set of processes that are recursive and, unlike machines, human beings are capable of going outside the problem to find novel solutions.

Teaching as Cognitive Processing

When it comes to theory development, we believe in the law of parsimony: Simple and elegant is preferable to complex and flashy. We set as our goal the development of a theory that, though comprehensive enough to explain our findings, would also be simple enough to be user-friendly. After considering many existing theories of problem solving as potential models, we eliminated (a) those that used unfamiliar terminology, (b) those that used empirical data derived from observations remote from educational settings, and (c) those that seemed unnecessarily complex. Particularly appealing in one model, a cognitive process theory of writing (Hayes & Flower, 1980; Flower & Hayes, 1981), was the reference to "flexibility and creativity," both being characteristics of the distinguished professors we studied. Although Flower and Hayes investigated the impact of flexibility and creativity in writing processes, we examined how these characteristics were demonstrated in the teaching processes.

Our theory suggests that teaching revolves around the ability (partially innate, partially learned) of some people to identify, analyze, and solve all types of problems. We believe that the brain functions like an airport terminal, with many activities occurring simultaneously while the main business of the terminal is directed and monitored from the control tower. Through a radar-like system that scans and interprets the learning environment, distinguished teachers make instructional decisions that guide students toward the overall goal of becoming independent learners. Sherman et al. (1987) described this "radar" as *metacognition*.

Standing in front of a class, the teacher sends and receives signals. All prior experience is called upon to interpret these signals as a professor makes judgments as to what the return signal will be. The ever-changing environment (including students, the physical space, and so on) demands flexibility and creativity in order that the professor meet the challenges of a diverse population. This dynamic system is not fixed or linear. Like a radar scope, the teacher is tracking multiple, and sometimes contradictory, signals. Some signals appear in isolation and others in a squadron, and some move at different speeds, appearing in differing intensities and directions. In what appears to be a chaotic environment, there are many opportunities for misreading these signals. For example, one day as Professor N. was leading a class discussion, students began firing questions at him from all directions. In a moment of insight, he described how he could see the questions (representing the students' varying levels of comprehension) stacked like aircraft in a holding pattern, one above the other in developmental order. His "radar" told him that reorganization of the questions was essential to the students' comprehension. Although others may have misinterpreted the questions as being random, Professor N. was able to make sense of them. In the remainder of this chapter we will expand on a concept of teaching as detecting, interpreting, and reacting to signals from students. We will frame this discussion by analyzing excellent instruction in terms of problem-solving theory.

Three Components to the Process

Problem-solving theorists disagree about how to classify the major problem-solving processes. For our purposes, we have chosen to describe three processes—(a) assessment and identification, (b) planning and implementation and (c) evaluation—while acknowledging that these categories are artificial, since inherent in the notion of process is the concept of something ongoing and continuous.

Problem Identification and Assessment

During the first process, problem identification and assessment, problem solvers detect something in the environment that needs to be changed in order for them to reach a goal. In the instructional environment, this might be a student's negative attitude or a textbook which is unnecessarily complex. Typically, problem solvers will try to get a handle on the problem by attempting to find and examine causes for the problem and then divide the problem into parts, a process that problem-solving theorists call *problem analysis.*

Planning and Implementation

The next process in the problem-solving model is planning and implementing the solution. For example, an excellent teacher's plan to find a new textbook might begin with ordering examination copies from publishers. During this process the teacher might seek recommendations from colleagues and show prospective texts to selected students. These are examples of how problem solvers use divergent thinking and then convergent thinking, as they assess the merits of a particular solution. In problem-solving lingo, these activities would be called *strategies* or *subgoals.*

Somewhere during this search for solutions, the problem solver—here, our instructor in search of a better textbook—will probably decide to "give it a rest" and leave the problem for a time. This deliberate postponement of decision making is what problem-solving researchers call *incubation.*

Creative studies research shows that such time off-task is often essential to the choice of a good solution. This allows our professor the time to reconsider course objectives or even go outside the traditional avenues to find a good textbook. During this downtime, one professor we know, for example, discovered on-line information sources, downloaded them, and had them compiled into a class reader. Another could decide to write his own textbook. The moment when the choice of a new textbook is made thus can be rather routine or can involve inspiration, that intuitive leap we described earlier.

Once a likely solution is found, problem solvers begin to act. One professor might decide to adopt a new text the next time the course is offered. Another might begin to collect readings or play with the notion of writing his own text. To be sure, when they all begin using a new text, they are likely to be tentative, conducting a classroom test of how successfully the new text meets their instructional goals of clarity and emphasis.

Evaluation

The final problem-solving process, evaluation, is very like the assessment feature in the initial process of problem identification.

Throughout the course when our instructor tests the utility of her new text, she will seek to evaluate whether the solution, the chosen textbook, is effective. Thus we see that teaching well requires an experimental frame of mind.

Throughout the test run with the new textbook, an excellent teacher will be monitoring whether students are learning better. The new text has been the "intervention" in a classroom experiment. If the class learns no better than it did previously, the professor may decide to revert to a former textbook, or, since real life classrooms are not laboratories, he may conclude that other variables influenced the outcome of his experiment and decide to give the text a longer trial period.

This ability to step back and take a global view of the instructional environment in total, including one's own teaching role, is a kind of metacognitive assessment that our case study professors reported during our interviews with them. They told us that they were always asking themselves, "How's this going?" and "Is this working?" If the answer was "Not well," then they shifted gears.

But rather than do as so many faculty do and blame the students for the learning problems, they first held themselves responsible for making improvements. They asked themselves, "What am I doing that should change?" Wise professors also understand that teaching experiments often fail, but they are willing to take calculated risks in hopes that better learning will result. When an instructional experiment flops, they are able to be philosophical and to learn from their mistakes.

Here is where the optimism that we wrote of as a key characteristic of outstanding teachers is crucial. Rather than becoming depressed by poor outcomes, distinguished teachers are spurred to keep trying. Problem-solving theorists would say that they have overcome "set rigidity," that is, they have not become fixated on the problem to the extent that they cannot see alternative solutions.

The Theory in Action

Now let us see the theory in action by taking a look at how these problem-solving processes are reflected in two problem scenarios. In Chapters 7 and 8 we provided a catalog of instructional problems and illustrated how award-winning professors addressed individual learning problems and problems with groups of students. The Problem-Solving Matrix (Table 9-1) is a useful framework for organizing our analyses, though we do not claim that it is comprehensive.

The problem-solving analyses in this chapter will highlight instructional problems related to content material and instructional environments.

Scenario One: An Environmental Problem

Let's put Professor H.'s teaching under our microscope. An experienced professor of biology who has taught a course in gross anatomy for several years, he is becoming increasingly dissatisfied with his initial solution to a logistical problem. Professor H.'s laboratories do not have the television equipment he needs to enable groups of students to view close-ups of dissections. Initially, he decided to have students stand on lab stools in the back rows so they could see the procedure, but this solution proved unsatisfactory. His colleague in physics suggests that he look for interactive computer software to simulate the dissections; finding none, they decide to create one themselves—a daunting task, but one that absorbs them over a period of years.

During the first years of teaching the course, Dr. H. also has observed how students respond to their first encounters with cadavers and decides, after consulting his colleague in religious studies,

TABLE 9-1 Instructional Problem-Solving Matrix

	Identification & Assessment	Planning & Implementation	Evaluation
Individual Problems			
Group Problems			
Content Problems			
Environment Problems			
Instructor Problems			

that he would like to promote a respectful and appreciative attitude among his students toward the bodies. He gets the idea to initiate a new routine: the "blessing" of the bodies at the beginning of each semester. What we have witnessed here is the manner in which Professor H. continues to refine and improve the way in which he teaches a single course.

Scenario Two: A Content Problem

In another illustration, Dr. E., an English professor, has successfully used students' reading response journals as a springboard to writing in her communications course for first-year students. She notices that students usually choose topics related directly to their own experience (personal narratives) or else write about the short stories or news articles they are reading for class discussion. She believes that the notion of community might be an excellent way to move her traditional 18-year-old students away from their egocentric stage of development toward the social involvement of a young adult. Drawing on what she knows about the novice writer, she designs an assignment that will force the students to focus on the outside worlds of the campus and the larger community.

She also wants to help students overcome their initial shyness and begin to make acquaintances in the classroom community, so she decides to pair up residents and commuters and ask them to collaborate on an observation of a campus site and report to the class for a prospective paper. The students eagerly choose sites. Curious to see how the experiment is going, Dr. E. directs each pair to report to the class during the next meeting and to turn in a jointly authored informal report. She hopes that the experience of co-authoring will be new for the students and will give them a taste of real world writing.

All but two students complete the assignment—an excellent success rate—and several pairs also report having benefited from collaborating in their writing. This leads Dr. E. to the question of how she will award grades to co-authored papers. Perhaps this seems contrary to what we have found about excellent teachers with respect to clarity. One would think that grading policy should be decided upon before the assignment is given. In this case, because this assignment is an experiment, she decides to negotiate the grading policies with the students. The real test of the assignment's success, she believes, will be whether any students choose to develop the assignment into a quality paper and submit it for a grade.

When the students' folders are submitted, 25% of the students have written about their venture into their new campus community, with the average grade of B on the six papers. Dr. E. assesses her new assignment as meeting her goals, but still needing refinement (an illustration of monitoring).

In both of these scenarios, we have observed how excellent teachers use a set of processes to meet instructional goals. The first scenario demonstrated the development and improvement of an existing course by the professor's creation of new strategies to improve the class setting. The second narrative described how a professor created a new assignment within an old course plan.

As we have said in other chapters, outstanding college teachers are excellent planners. When they sense problems or opportunities for learning, they are experts at setting objectives, inventing new solutions, creating new plans, employing new methods, evaluating the results, and making refinements.

Phase One: Problem Identification and Assessment

Now let's examine the two scenarios in terms of the professors' problem identification and assessment.

Scenario One, Phase One: Dr. H. identified the instructional problem as an environmental interference. Students could not see the dissections.

Scenario Two, Phase One: Dr. E. was unhappy with the fact that students usually limited their choices for writing to personal narratives.

Dr. H.'s problem analysis most likely began with a sense of a logistical problem. There were simply too many students and too few cadavers to enable students to view the dissections clearly. The givens of his problem were the number of cadavers (they are very expensive) and the numbers of students in his lab sections. One solution—television equipment—was not available to him due to its expense. Yet Professor H. knew that the value of the lab experience was in the tactile and visual learning—the psychomotor dimension—that occurred during the dissections. How would he solve this logistical problem?

Dr. E.'s problem analysis most likely began with her awareness of the limitations of the personal narratives that students usually submitted as their first papers in this first-year English course. She could assign topics as many of her peers did, but she had a higher objective of making students responsible for their writing topics to assure that they were both interested and committed to their writing. Her decision to provide the community writing stimulus came out of the reading she had been doing in higher education, as well as the value she placed on collaboration.

Phase Two: Planning and Implementation

Scenario One, Phase Two: Professor H. considers the alternatives and decides to allow students to stand on stools to observe dissections.

Scenario Two, Phase Two: Dr. E. designs a community writing assignment and pairs students to visit campus sites.

In this phase of planning and implementation, Dr. H. and Dr. E.'s actions are deceptively simple. Because excellent teachers are efficient, they manage more than one goal simultaneously. This concept of multiple goal processing explains how excellent teachers can successfully conduct groups and individuals simultaneously. For example, Dr. H. was in the process of solving one instructional problem—the logistics of viewing dissections—at the same time as he was becoming aware of another problem—an irreverent attitude by students towards the cadavers.

Dr. E.'s community assignment incorporated several layers of goals and objectives, although she only articulated the superficial goal of extending their concept of community (a cognitive objective). For example, pairing residence students and commuters was a strategy designed to build friendships among first-year students (an affective objective), and the site observations were an extension of that. However, she never informed students of her overriding goal, to move students away from an egocentric writing style to an expository one, believing that goal was too abstract for them to understand until the later developmental stages of writing.

In general, we have found that teachers frequently have far-reaching goals that go beyond the immediate objectives. Gradually, as the criteria for success are met, the students gain insight and are ready to understand more sophisticated goals. Thus, teachers frequently must present what are interpreted as stringent guidelines for the students to follow in attempt to guide them toward an understanding of the larger picture. For example, professors find themselves repeating certain foundation information again and again in order to form the basis for a conceptual framework.

Phase Three: Evaluation

Now consider how these two professors approached the evaluation phase of problem solving.

Scenario One, Phase Three: Dr. H. is concerned that the "solution" he first arrives at is dangerous. He talks to a colleague, who suggests that they develop an interactive computer simulation of dissections, an anatomy almanac that students can preview prior to the dissection.

Scenario Two, Phase Three: Dr. E. assesses the assignment as successful because students eagerly present reports in class (affective objective) and an increased percentage of the class submits papers developed from the observation, rather than solely from their personal experience (cognitive objective).

In both of these scenarios, we see that the professor evaluated the effects of the strategy (solution) they had developed. Dr. H. was dissatisfied with the only solution he and his class could find at the time, and thus he began to search for a long-term solution. Meanwhile, he lived uncomfortably with the temporary solution. Dr. E. decided that the community assignment has been modestly successful and was worthy of continuing, but she would refine it further the next time. Thus we see that the problem-solving processes have come full circle: They move from assessment to assessment, and then the cycle begins again.

Teaching and Learning as Discourse

We soon discovered a significant shortcoming of Flower and Hayes' (1981) composing process theory as a model for explaining teaching behavior: Its scope is too narrow. It was developed to explain one kind of communication problem—writing. We have said that instruction is not a single act of communication but an ongoing discourse in which teachers and students use a variety of language options, not simply writing. In fact, learning and instruction mostly involve spoken communication and nonverbal communication, with writing reserved for the more formal aspects of the teacher–student relationship.

To fill this gap in the cognitive process model of writing, we have incorporated into our theoretical framework some additional concepts derived from a psycholinguistic theory of discourse (Clark & Clark, 1977; MacWhinney, 1983), because they allow us to explain the more complex and ongoing natures of the communications between students and teachers.

During a semester, students in effect carry on a conversation with the professor as they interpret what linguists call "points," and generate responses in the form of papers, contributions to class discussions, and answers on tests. Teaching and learning are cooperative acts, just as our distinguished teachers so eloquently described them as a "shared responsibility" in their philosophies of teaching in Chapter 6.

In order to begin the instructional discourse, the professor must establish the students' baseline level of comprehension. The emphasis our participants placed on preliminary status assessment, identifying the entering knowledge and skills of students, shows that they are aware of how crucial that preassessment is to successful instruction. And, because students' responses are almost always presented in some linguistic form for evaluation—either speech or writing—the outstanding teacher is also remarkably sensitive to the fact that knowledge of prerequisite terms and behaviors are essential to the understanding of certain concepts and skills. Consequently, they continually seek to give students the language and terminology they will need to learn a particular subject.

This analysis of the social contexts for discourse are salient if we apply them to instructional failures as well as successes. Within the instructional dialogue that occurs between teachers and students, outstanding teachers know that there are many opportunities for communication errors: Sometimes students incorrectly anticipate what is expected in the course; sometimes teachers' intentions are misunderstood; and other times, conventions of academe—such as the time allotted for a student to learn a particular skill or concept—interfere with instruction.

An important fact to remember is that people only solve the problems that they find. Professors who fail to recognize anything more than superficial problems in their classes, who think that because they are lecturing, students are learning, will never become excellent teachers unless they are taught to see differently.

In our study, we found that one of the ways in which distinguished teachers differed from other teachers was their ability to identify a vast array of learning problems. Like the musician who has learned to hear the subtleties of sound, or the artist who can distinguish between a hundred shades of green, the excellent teacher is expert at finding and analyzing a wider variety of instructional problems, perhaps even a different kind of problem. Our data clearly showed that novice teachers identified a more basic level of problems than did our excellent, experienced teachers. For example, novices were concerned about lecturing in an interesting way or about selecting course readings, often viewing elements in the instructional environment as the problem, unlike our expert teachers, who more often focused their attention instead on the behaviors of individuals and groups—including themselves—as the problem.

Our findings suggest that there may be a hierarchy of instructional problems, and that faculty see the classroom environment differently depending on their level of experience. Beginning teachers' instructional problem solving may be hampered by their inability to accurately locate the learning problems. Their need to survive in the academy dictates that they focus on aspects of the instructional environment that have become second nature to experienced professors, who are intimately familiar with their fields, instructional materials, presentation techniques, and the evaluation process.

Putting the Theory to Use

In this chapter, we traced the genealogy of our problem-solving theory of teaching from cognitive science, education research, and discourse theory, and we suggested that the distinguished professors we observed appeared to posses a superior ability to scan and interpret the learning environment. From our case study analysis, we presented and illustrated three problem-solving processes: (a) assessment and identification, (b) planning and implementation, and

(c) evaluation. Then, in our "Problem-Solving Matrix" (See Table 9-1), we showed how these processes might be applied across the domain of instructional problems, which we viewed as having five strands: individual learning problems, problems of aggregates of students, content problems, instructional environment problems, and instructor problems. We also suggested that the distinguished teaching professors we observed understood the cooperative nature of learning and made fine distinctions about students' learning problems.

In the next chapter, we will show how our problem-solving approach might be used to assist new professors with their teaching. We will discuss the lack of preparation of graduate students for college teaching, contrast the concerns of teaching assistants and experienced faculty, and finally present an array of solutions to common problems proposed by new professors.

10

Application of the Problem-Solving Theory

Distinguished Teachers Advise

A novice member of a sailboat racing crew was at her assigned spot on the rail of the boat during a race. The weather changed quickly and the rest of the crew began barking orders for her to follow. The skipper yelled, "Get ready for a jibe set." Attempting to comply, she moved to the foredeck and reached for one line. "Don't touch that," yelled the skipper. Touching another, she received another negative response, "No! Don't do that!" Finally she screamed back toward the helm, "Don't tell me what *not* to do! Tell me what *to* do!" As with this scenario, the assumption that novices will pick up the lingo and know what to do is a common assumption among academics. According to Sykes (1988), "Only in higher education is it generally assumed that teachers need no preparation, no supervision, no introduction to teaching" (pp. 41–42).

Like the inexperienced sailor in our analogy, teaching assistants and junior faculty are often launched without the skills to sail. But because they share the new consumer mentality we described in Chapter 2, they are no longer willing to accept the status quo, and are demanding appropriate development opportunities. We believe that news reports of a revolt by graduate students in a labor dispute with Yale University in 1995–1996 and passionate discussions in on-line national teaching assistant forums are symbolic of the disturbing conditions faced by graduate teaching assistants on campuses nationwide.

In Chapter 9, we described a problem-solving theory of teaching excellence and illustrated how distinguished college teachers use a set of cognitive skills to identify instructional problems, create and implement plans, and evaluate the results. We have also asserted in Chapter 3 that some of these skills are teachable. Why then do we think that these skills will be absorbed through osmosis by apprentices in academe? Would we send a crew of inexperienced sailors to sea expecting that they would navigate treacherous waters and reach their destination unscathed? And how would *you* like to be a passenger on the boat that was crewed by individuals who had no experience sailing but were put to sea regardless?

We believe it is essential that beginning teachers be assisted in learning how to "sail" better by defining and solving the instructional problems that confront them. In this chapter we will describe the current status of training programs for graduate teaching assistants, compare their views of instructional problems with those of distinguished teachers, show how experienced teachers would advise new faculty to address these instructional problems, and argue for a developmental approach to faculty preparation for teaching. We further believe that the development of teaching expertise can be accelerated through interventions such as those we will propose in Chapter 11.

Apprenticeship or Serfdom? The Lack of Preparation for Teaching in Higher Education

In fall 1995, news reports exposed the crisis in the lack of preparation of teaching assistants for their role as teachers. They described union votes, marches, censure motions, disciplinary hearings, arrests, and lockouts at Yale College. According to news reports circulated on-line, the dean of Yale College made dismissive comments about "getting down to business" (A. Rosati, on-line communication, December, 1995). Although these statements may have been intended to be his cogent and succinct response to a volatile issue, they could also be interpreted as lacking in sensitivity to the urgency of the students' problems.

Indeed, reports of the job action of the Yale graduate students who were fired for withholding grades in December 1995, and the subsequent decision of the National Labor Relations Board to view Yale TAs as legal employees and to charge Yale with violating federal labor law, suggest that the revolution we called for in Chapter 3 may already have begun. In a press release of the Federation of University Employees at Yale, Yale history professor David Montgomery wrote,

> We are witnessing labor history in the making. Universities across the country have come to rely more and more on both teaching assistants and adjunct professors as part-time workers carrying out more and more of the teaching responsibilities. This decision puts the protection of the law securely behind their efforts to improve their conditions, and that should improve the security of everyone in the academy. (AAUP On-Line Bulletin Board, November 21, 1996)

We view this struggle for legal recognition by graduate students as a symptom of a larger problem. Low wages, poor benefits, and lack of opportunity for collective bargaining reflect a pervasive attitude in academe that graduate students and untenured faculty are but "the serfs in his or her lordship's realm" (Solomon & Solomon, 1993, p. 53). Although teaching assistants are "the mortar of the system [who are paid].... wages that most businesses would be embarrassed to pay their parking lot attendants, [they] are given almost complete responsibility for the education of freshmen and sophomores at many large universities" (Sykes, 1988, p. 41). Monaghan said that "only half of all academic departments provide training to teaching assistants, and few follow up to improve their teaching skills" (Seldin, 1990, p. 210). Additionally, Nyquist, Abbott, & Wulff (1989) suggested that graduate schools place most of their attention on research and provide TAs only limited preparation for their teaching responsibilities. They further presented five specific reasons why TAs will need better preparation:

1. They will need to deal with the information explosion.
2. They will need to deal with diversity of the student body.

3. They must become familiar with the advances in cognitive psychology and learning theory.
4. They will need to deal with the balance between publication and teaching demands.
5. They will need to address the demand for better undergraduate education. (pp. 9–10)

A 1992 report in the *Chronicle of Higher Education* describes Syracuse University's efforts to establish a comprehensive program to prepare "a new generation of faculty members" (Mooney, p. A17) for their teaching role as described in *University Teaching: A Guide for Graduate Students* (Lambert, Tice, & Featherstone, 1996). The *Chronicle* hints at the movement away from "hit-and-run" orientations for TAs toward a more long-term approach to training (p. A18). Interestingly, the initial funding for the Syracuse project began with a now-defunct grant from the Sears & Roebuck Foundation in 1989 (Mooney, 1992, p. A15). The 1990 Carnegie Report, "Scholarship Reconsidered: Priorities of the Professoriate" (Boyer, 1990) was itself the culminating report in a series of Carnegie Foundation reports calling for improved undergraduate instruction. Although the initiatives of large projects exemplified by those at Syracuse, Memphis State, and the University of Washington may have led to significant improvements on those campuses, we suspect that the preparation of teaching assistants on many campuses nationwide has not dramatically changed.

We view this poor preparation of teaching assistants as an aspect of the larger problem of academics' universal lack of respect for their teaching role. This attitude begins in graduate school and continues through their professional lives, reflected in the "periodic offerings of in-service training that is peripheral to the instructional process" (Baiocco & DeWaters, 1995, p. 39) rather than a sustained professional development effort. Against the backdrop of the conditions described by Yale students, the academy's antiquated and negligent system of preparing graduate TAs adequately for their teaching responsibilities looks more than foolish, it looks cruel.

In the summer of 1995, we tapped into the teaching assistant forum of the electronic bulletin board of the American Association of University Professors (AAUP) and "overheard" a passionate dialogue. Teaching assistants expressed outrage and disappointment at their universities' inadequate resources, space, and training for their teaching role. Numerous messages highlighted the need for reform. Rather than listen to random comments, we initiated a brief on-line survey questioning TAs on their preparation for teaching college classes. We first distributed our survey via email to 225 teaching assistants who subscribe to the on-line TA listserve. This database was later expanded when the information exchange coordinator of a TA on-line bulletin board sponsored by the National Association of Graduate and Professional Students (NAGPS) picked up the survey and posted it to graduate student leaders across the nation. In a short period of time, 59 survey responses were received from TAs at 38 colleges and universities to questions about the amount of training they received for college teaching prior to their teaching assignments and the amount of supervision and feedback provided during their teaching.

Although our sample data were not gathered scientifically, we suspect they are suggestive of systemic problems in the preparation of TAs. Analysis of the data revealed a shocking lack of consistent support for these inexperienced teachers and an underlying expectation that graduate students will develop their teaching skills with minimal guidance. The data revealed that 17.5% had received no training and 28% had received between one and six hours of orientation or training before being assigned to teach, manage, and evaluate students. Twenty-eight percent of the teacher training was provided by TAs themselves, and more than half reported that they received no formal observation or supervision during their teaching assignments. Many reported that supervision was not mandatory and that observation often had to be requested. Of those who received supervision, 45.2% reported only one or two evaluative observations ranging over a semester, a year, or the entire two- to three-year assistantship. Half of the TAs reported that the exclusive means of feedback received about their teaching was from student evaluations; 9.8% reported receiving *no* feedback about their teaching.

These findings suggest a failure to train graduate students for teaching, which has profound effects. First, it undermines the education of undergraduate students by virtue of the underpreparedness of their instructors, the graduate students. Next, it makes the first teaching assignment a study in frustration with a trial and error pedagogy. And finally, it begins the cycle of devaluation of the teaching role by those who are just entering the professoriate. Listen to a sample of the on-line comments made by TAs:

- "Most TAs are scared to death because they have to teach classes knowing that their skills are not necessarily up to par. One of my 'rabbis' told me not to be too concerned about this because 'you will know more than they do anyway.'"

- "Most of what I've learned about teaching courses comes from being a student."
- "I think most TAs here are very discouraged with teaching after their first semester. I have heard many of them say that if they [had] read their student evaluations before they left home for break, they would not have come back."
- "When I think back on my first year of teaching, I do feel sorry for my first class, to an extent. About the most I can say for it is that I did the best I could with the resources and time I had."
- "[The training] had almost no relevance for the science TAs, who teach only in the laboratory. Since [at this university] there are about four times as many science-oriented TAs as those in other fields, I thought this was rather shortsighted.... The 'solution' is to show the students videotapes of a professor giving the prelab lecture, and let the TAs stick to babysitting."

Other graduate students who apparently had several years of teaching experience noted that the isolation of TAs leaves them without anyone to help them gain a perspective on the normal development of teaching competence.

Not all teaching assistants are provided so little support or are under so much stress. Yet many graduate students endure the hardships because they see them as rites of passage. For example, one graduate student expressed his love for teaching and his belief that "university instructors have the best positions in the world, and it bugs [him] to watch people [other TAs on-line] bite the hand that feeds them." However, this student's self-image as apprentice scholar, not indentured servant, led him and his peers to protest their inadequate office space. He wrote, "I think [the issue is] the university's responsibility to provide us with a space that would allow us to accomplish the mission that the university had set out for us—to provide for our students the best education possible." Arguing on-line for a balanced position on the conditions of teaching assistants today, he then responded to a teaching assistantship director by attacking her tacit support for the traditional method of initiating graduate students into academic culture: "It seems to me that your essential argument [about teaching conditions for TAs] is that if it was good enough for you, it's good enough for [us]."

Teaching assistants are telling us their tales, and we need to begin to listen. The notion that what they are experiencing is a rite of passage is nonsense. Those of us who have our own children attending college right now can be easily drawn into the consumer mentality as we read the concerns of TAs and the conditions under which they teach our children. Given the consistent report of lack of preparation for teaching, it would stand to reason that if TAs were asked, "Would you want your children to be one of your students?" they would more than likely respond, "No!"

Furthermore, as in the medieval apprenticeship system, TAs (with minimal preparation for teaching) must complete another test of suitability for the profession upon completion of the doctorate: the first faculty appointment. Often they become the "migrant workers of academe," passing several years as literal journeymen by accepting temporary positions or part-time posts at a number of colleges. If they do land permanent, tenure-line positions, like medieval apprentices they will have seven years to prove that they can perform as teachers, scholars, and members of their profession. Ironically, those responsible for educating these educators of the twenty-first century are often continuing the outmoded laissez-faire practices of the past. Shame on faculty and administrators for their tolerance of this short-sighted system. Shame on this system that exploits graduate students who aspire to careers in academe but woefully underprepares them for college teaching.

The Contrasting Concerns of New and Experienced Faculty

After our first round of investigation into the issues of preparation for teaching in higher education, we questioned, "Just how deep does this current of dissatisfaction on the part of both students and the TAs who are assigned to teach them run?" We designed another informal survey for teaching assistants and posted it on the national on-line bulletin boards, asking TAs to respond to two questions: (1) "What have been the most challenging problems you have encountered as a teacher?" and (2) "Have you ever had difficulty with a particular group of students?"

In analyzing TA responses to the question about specific instructional problems they had encountered, we found a profound difference in the levels of problems that were identified, in contrast to the responses of our distinguished teachers. Rather than focusing on the learners, the TAs appeared instead to be absorbed with the content they were responsible for conveying, the environmental obstacles and resources, and how they were being perceived. Teaching assistants reported that they were staying one step ahead of the new classes they were teaching and spending enormous amounts of time reviewing content, gathering materials, and figuring out how to manage their students. They were surrounded by experienced faculty who assumed that they understood the language and routines of academe. They knew that they were in a position of tentative authority and appeared to be guided by the overwhelming influence of student satisfaction. Like the new sailing crew members in the introduction to this chapter, novice instructors must assemble a base of fundamental skills in order to begin their development toward the excellence achieved by our distinguished professors, those who are able to read the winds and skillfully guide their crews toward their destinations.

Responses from teaching assistants about their specific instructional problems with individual students as well as groups of students revealed a set of recurring themes. Although the themes are also encountered by experienced professors, they differ in that the problems are fundamental. Whereas new teachers may define content problems very generally, for example, "how to make a lecture interesting," Professor G. states the same problem in more detail: "making Aristotle interesting to a generation nourished on cretinesque TV, to which the government has apparently decided to relinquish the responsibility for educating its youth." This shows his analysis of the causes of the problem as the larger environmental influences that affect student learning. We believe that distinguished teaching professors see the complexity of the problem, comparing and contrasting the existing problem with their experiential base and values. For example, the experienced professors we studied discussed content problems in terms of preserving standards (which are firmly established in their minds) and "resisting the impulse to 'dumb down' courses in an era of declining student quality" (Professor D.), or "refusing to alienate the better students.... If anything, I have found that raising the difficulty level in any class tends to increase dialogue and debate, whereas 'dumbing down' for the sake of general accessibility stifles discussion" (Professor W.).

As for problems with classroom management, inexperienced teachers voiced concerns about "really quiet students and very dominant students in discussion groups," while experienced teachers defined the problem differently. They viewed the problem in a larger framework—"allowing free speech in a class, but maintaining boundaries for behavioral expectations and respect for others' viewpoints." One professor explained, "Many faculty never consider that students need to learn the rules of discussion because many come from homogeneous environments where an 'Archie Bunker mentality' rules," and "One must be able to articulate both sides by role-playing, acting as devil's advocate, and thereby setting the rules for civilized debate, as well as making students aware of the sensitivities of others in their classroom." What they were saying was that the instructional goal extends far beyond that particular class or even that course: how to discuss *any* issue in a democratic society.

We believe it is essential that beginning teachers be assisted in learning how to better define the instructional problems confronting them. We further believe that we can accelerate the development of teaching expertise through the interventions which we will discuss in Chapter 11. Some of the suggestions that follow in this chapter are similar to those found in Joseph Lowman's *Mastering the Techniques of Teaching* (1995).

Expert Advice for Typical Teaching Difficulties

To discover how distinguished teachers would address the problems identified by novices, we sent another survey—a set of problem scenarios described by the teaching assistants—to the distinguished teachers. The following advice resulted from that survey.

Underprepared Students

Problem: "What am I supposed to do with students who are unprepared—clueless—and yet have taken (and passed) the prerequisite courses?"

Response (Professor D.): "Welcome to the wonderful world of education. There are several things you could do—and I have tried them all with greater or lesser success:

- Quizzing every class and making the score a part of the final grade, even if it be no more than 10%, is often worth the time spent. Over time, as more and more students come prepared, the remainder of the class time is better spent as preparedness goes up. Also, you could contract that when any week's quizzes have a class average of 70% or better they will cease or become less frequent.
- Use examinations to emphasize the readings, thus communicating their importance.
- Make sure your classes don't re-hash the assignment for class. (Why should I be prepared if you're going to tell me the same stuff I should have read?)
- The clueless student will always be with us; often they are having trouble with telling the truth. I would discover who taught the prerequisite and inform that colleague that his or her students are saying they never covered this. Chances are the students will have that professor again and will be caught between "a rock and the hard place." A professor who is at fault may tighten up his or her course and the problem may improve over time. You can always offer quick review sessions for the clueless, but make sure they are outside of class and at less-than-convenient times. It is amazing how the need to avoid a 7:30 a.m. review class sparks a student's powers of recollection."

Response (Professor R.): "Admittedly I see many poor writers in my literature and rhetoric classes. Generally I invite them in for a conference, urge them to rewrite their papers, coach them, then grade them according to their improvement. Teaching writing is a form of one-on-one coaching."

Response (Professor H.): "Unless they have already proven otherwise, students deserve at least one effort on the instructor's part to determine whether their lack of preparedness is attributable to poor academic skills, or to poor attitude toward learning (lack of motivation). The fact that a student has passed a prerequisite course does not necessarily guarantee that the student automatically has the appropriate study skills to cope with a related, more advanced course. Students with poor preparation may only need a bit of encouragement and guidance to improve their situation. Specifically, a comment such as "check out such-and-such from last semester's text (or notes)" may be all that's necessary to put the student on the right track. If the student did not retain the textbook/notes from the prerequisite course, the library may be a useful resource for the supporting material,...or perhaps the student needs a tutor.

If the student has an attitude problem ('Why do I have to learn this?' 'This is too boring,' etc.) the instructor may point out to the student that there are always certain academic requirements necessary for her or his major that may not be intrinsically interesting, nor obviously relevant, but that are fundamental elements in a hierarchy of knowledge leading to the more career related courses. For example, some understanding of glucose metabolism must first be mastered before a full understanding of the clinical aspects of sugar diabetes can be achieved. If the student still proves refractory after this approach, perhaps some reminder of the student's responsibility for his or her own academic success (the need for an investment of study effort to match the monetary investment in one's education) may be in order. It should soon become obvious to the instructor whether or not compliance is forthcoming, and, if not, the student, as a mature adult, must be willing to accept the possible consequences."

Assessment Techniques

Problem: "I'm having difficulty finding a fair way to grade or compare different types of output—objective and subjective. What do I do with those who get the right answers to objective questions versus those who demonstrate that they can think beyond the boundaries of the problem as I have given it, who can work creatively with insight, who have a knack for finding patterns in the data?"

Response (Professor D.): "Another perennial problem. I believe the answer here is to decide in advance the importance level of both types of knowledge. Arrange (and be honest with the students about it) the course examinations to reflect that division. Those who are creative will become more disciplined to also learn the objective stuff and the others will begin to try for greater creativity. But remember, all of this (as is true with many of my responses) has to be told to the students at Day One and in the syllabus! Once they know you are honest with them and mean what you say and write, they respond much better. As one student who did poorly on the first exam once told me, 'I'll do better next time because I'll read the book.' Me: 'Didn't I tell you that you had to read the book on your own and it would be worth one-third of the exam?' Student: 'Yes, but I've heard that all throughout high school, and you're the first person who meant it.'"

Response (Professor R.): "Actually, [as an English professor] I stress neither 'correct' answers nor strict grading. Instead I stress inquisitiveness and reward creative thinking. I teach students not to worship knowledge, but to challenge it. Einstein had it right: 'Imagination is more important than knowledge.'

"If testing implies 'right' answers, then I do not test my students. Accordingly, I use exams and, more importantly, papers as occasions for critical and creative thinking and for clear and direct writing. The 'right' answer suggests to students that they come up with someone else's preconceived answer. I prefer that my students pose their own questions on the subject, think creatively, then clearly and logically defend their own answers."

Response (Professor H.): "Areas that require a great deal of factual learning lend themselves particularly well to objective testing, especially multiple choice testing. However, a common pitfall in multiple choice questioning may be the accurate interpretation of semantic nuances which distinguish available choices. My preference is to: (a) invite students to ask for interpretations of apparently ambiguous choices during the examination; (often I will be able to rephrase something in such a way as to clarify my intention or, at the very least, point out that the student needs to read more carefully!), or (b) after the examination is returned, entertain arguments about ambiguous wording and, if justified, award additional credit where a logical alternative interpretation of the question is valid. I doubt that many instructors are capable of absolutely clear and unequivocal use of language 100% of the time.

"Other areas of a course's subject matter may be more of a conceptual than purely factual nature, and these lend themselves more appropriately to essay-type exams, or perhaps term paper assignments in which the student has more individual freedom of expression in developing an answer. The instructor needs to weigh the relative merits of keeping focused on the problem presented versus 'think(ing) beyond the boundaries of the problem' in terms of her or his goals for the exam or for the course."

Cheating

Problem: "How do I handle the administration not backing me up on actions taken for plagiarism, cheating, and disruptive behavior while at the same time nagging me to grade harder and demand more?"

Response (Professor D.): "State your policy on plagiarism in the syllabus. State the penalties and follow them. If the administration fails to back you up, challenge that administrator with an appeal to his or her superior and keep challenging. How can you fear retaliation from them when you are upholding honesty? Naturally, do all of this in writing and demand their responses in writing. Future employers will be more impressed by your position than the lack of a warm endorsement from the administrators."

Response (Professor R.): "First of all, I am convinced that cheating, plagiarism, and poor behavior in general are the students' response to a professor's rigid and impersonal attitude toward grades, lectures, and students. If a professor conveys to his or her students that they really matter, then student cheating, plagiarism, and poor behavior will be minimal. At least that's been true in my case.

"When these problems arise, I discuss them with my classes. If they cheat or plagiarize, I tell them they compromise their most important possession: their self-respect! Rather than have them give up their self-respect by cheating, I offer to give them any extra points or a better grade if it means that much to them.

"Don't worry about the administration's support. Worry about the real message that you're sending your students in the forms of your tests, grades, and lectures. Run an attitude check on yourself. Perhaps your 500 question, true-false exam needs some adjusting."

Response (Professor H.): "If a particular institution does not have clear policies regarding plagiarism, cheating, and disruptive behavior, the instructor should undertake to articulate his or her policy on these matters (including consequences for transgressions) in the course outline distributed to students at the beginning of the semester. An equally clear statement about mark sources [grades] and their relative contributions to the course grade should also be presented. The instructor may share these statements with the supervising professor (if any) or with the administration, prior to issuance to a class, to identify any problems administrators may

have. If concerns are raised, a solution to these needs to be negoti-
ated before any classroom incidents provoke confrontations."

Poor Attitudes

Problem: "I don't know what to do about adult students who choose
whining and complaining over hard work and challenge. They are
bold about wanting to know what information and skills will be
tested and what things they can ignore, what readings they should
forego, and so on. Consequently, if they were not tested or questioned about some aspect of the readings or lectures, they would
complain as a group."

Response (Professor D.): "Try to explain to them that testing is like a
sampling. All things are important but the sample cannot be ex-
haustive. I would even try on the 'consequent-complaining' a statement like, 'I expect some complaints from immature students, but
people who have been in the real work environment should know
that this is exactly how life is.'"

Response (Professor R.): "I minimize complaints and problems by
using Student Advisory Committees (SAC) (i.e., Quality Circles) to
provide me with continual feedback throughout the term. Students
can complain directly to me or to representatives on the SAC. Whatever. I listen to what my students tell me. I stay flexible. Students
justifiably complain about busy work and pettiness. I do too!"

Response (Professor H.): "Again, a clear statement regarding what is
required to earn a particular grade for the course will eliminate a
good deal of whining and complaining. It may be appropriate to
give the class some indication of skills and information that are considered of premier importance for testing, particularly if the course
is comprehensive in content; this can be done without necessarily
excluding all other information as testable material. For example, a
test should largely examine the material given emphasis in classes,
with perhaps a small sampling of questions on ancillary issues (possibly offered as a bonus question). The instructor may wish to develop outlines of lecture material to distribute to the class that
identify material to be emphasized for the class; this technique has
the added benefit of documenting the situation should a group
complaint arise."

Personal Attacks

Problem: "I have had students accuse me of being a racist."

Response (Professor R.): "A few years ago, I made a derogatory comment about an overweight person. One of my students was offended. I apologized on the spot and thanked the student for bringing it to my attention. Subsequently, I tell students on Day One that if something is bothering them to let me know immediately. If a student accuses me of being racist or sexist or whatever, I want to know about it immediately. I want to learn the basis of the charge. And if I am wrong, I want to apologize straightaway. However, if the allegation in my view is unfounded, I will ask my Chair to meet with my student and me to get it out in the open. I'm not going to hide behind my status and position as a professor to silence the student."

Response (Professor H.): "Clear articulation of how a grade will be determined and careful documentation of the student's performance must be maintained. If this occurs, then the instructor should be able to refute the accusation with evidence of evenhanded assessment of everyone in the class. If the accusation is made because of some misunderstood communication in class, or because of some interpersonal conflict, perhaps a meeting with the accuser in the presence of a mutually agreed upon third party (as mediator) may be warranted. The instructor should resort to the latter device only after making his or her own effort to identify and resolve the student's reason for the accusation."

Lack of Credibility

Problem: "I have problems with students not taking me seriously and feeling that they can verbally abuse or physically intimidate me."

Response (Professor D.): "Again, this is a Day One situation. You have to exude that you are in charge and are the authority. If you try to pose as some friend of the students and just the good guy or gal, the students will walk all over you. Beyond that I would want to know specifically what type of abuse or intimidation the person is talking about to respond more pointedly."

Response (Professor H.): "The instructor should articulate clear rules of classroom decorum and comport herself or himself with appropriate dignity and respect for students. This will generally earn, in return, the respect of the class for the instructor. If there still are some troublemakers, they should be dismissed from class until they are prepared to discontinue the intimidation. If they fail to leave when dismissed, the class should be dismissed. This may recruit peer pressure from the class for the offender to shape up. If this becomes necessary a second time, the offending student's behavior should be reported to a supervising professor (if any) or perhaps a senior colleague or administrator."

Student Irresponsibility

Problem: "Students never seem to come to me before an exam, but then want me to hold their hand when they are desperate for a passing grade."

Response (Professor D.): "Again, this is a problem best dealt with on the first day. Remind them that if they have not come in for any help before the final, they should not approach with hat in hand after the exam. If they do come for hand holding, greet them with a warm, cordial smile and friendly greeting akin to, 'Well, well, you finally found my office.'"

Response (Professor H.): "Students should be encouraged early in the semester to seek help (consult with the instructor or find a tutor) as soon as test results show them to be in academic difficulty. Students who 'know the material, but can't seem to do well on the exam' should be reminded of their responsibilities toward examinations: (a) to prepare for the exam with appropriate quantity and quality of study effort; show them it is often not enough to simply memorize information, but that sufficient understanding must be achieved to apply the information in contexts beyond those presented in class, (b) to confront their examination anxiety: this often stems from a distorted sense of the importance of a given exam ('If I fail this, it's the end of the world!').

"Encourage students to see each exam as a step in a process of communication with the instructor. Students need to complete a study effort which they feel enables their best effort on the exam; if they make a study plan (timetable) and check off the steps of its implementation, they will focus their attention on how much they have accomplished in preparation, rather than—the more usual focus— worrying about the material they have yet to cover. They need to cultivate attitudes that focus on positives instead of negatives; they also need to exercise some discipline, during the exam, to linger only short periods on difficult questions before moving on to others. Tell them it is better to return to the problem questions toward the end of the exam when the anxiety they produce will not interfere with performance on other questions. I have found that if students have consulted with me early in the semester, they are frequently able to make improvements (in their study efforts) that pay off; alternatively, the student who fails to seek help when it has been offered generally will feel much less inclined to wheedle for credit after the exam."

Grade-Grubbing

Problem: "There are large numbers of students who beg for points or ask for grade changes."

Response (Professor D.): "And thus it will always be. The firmer you are in saying no, the more your reputation spreads, and the numbers of mendicants will cease."

Response (Professor R.): "I issue specific printed instructions (i.e., 'Guidelines for Succeeding in My Course') on the first day of class. I advise students to seek help often and early. Therefore, they know the rules. I am eager and available to help them throughout the term. They realize that at the end of the term, it's too late to obtain help. The agreement is clear."

Other Problems Cited by TAs

In addition to the selected TA problems addressed by the distinguished teaching professors here, the teaching assistants also identified a widespread litany of concerns related to training, content or subject matter, classroom management and organization, the learning environment, and their specific job description.

Training

TAs report:

- No training or preparation for meeting a class, designing a syllabus, teaching the material, or organizing the grading

Content or Subject Matter

TAs say that they need to know:

- How to select a good textbook
- The best method of teaching a particular skill or subject
- How to make lectures more interesting
- How to stay one step ahead of the students while still learning the subject themselves
- How to gauge (condense or expand) the material for the allotted class time
- How to select and highlight the most important material

TAs have problems:

- Preserving standards and resisting the impulse to dumb down courses
- Bridging the gap between "the rhetoric and the reality"— between the world of the university and the real world"

Classroom Management/Organization

TAs report that:

- Large numbers of students beg for points or ask for grade changes.
- Students choose to skip optional discussion sections.
- Students leave science labs early, then request review sessions before the lab practicals.
- Students resent TA demands to use standard English.
- TAs have difficulty getting cooperation from their classes.
- There is inadequate equipment.
- They don't know what to do about student absenteeism.
- They don't know how specific to be on tests.

Learning Environment

TAs encounter:

- Desks nailed to the floor: immobile furnishings in classes that require mobility
- Inadequate textbooks
- Unavailable texts
- Students who don't buy the required materials
- The Internet host not working 100% (in a course about using the World Wide Web)

Job Description

TAs report that they:

- Don't have a clear understanding of their job responsibilities
- Have problems with other TAs not showing up to proctor or grade exams
- Are asked to prepare demonstrations with little warning from the professor
- Have poor office space

We believe that these problems are important and are best addressed through better preparation of TAs and ongoing support for their professional growth as they move into their first professional positions. The following chapter will suggest ways in which this book may be used as part of a futuristic faculty development initiative to assist faculty at all stages of their teaching careers.

11

Futuristic Faculty Development

Toward a Comprehensive Program

"I merely utter the warning that education is a difficult
problem, to be solved by no one simple formula."
A. N. WHITEHEAD

We have promised to outline a better system for preparing and developing excellent teachers. We have also suggested that this futuristic faculty development could be more economical, and should be ongoing and individualized. While the age-old tradition of Socratic mentoring is the basis for our proposal, what *is* new is our problem-solving approach to the development of teaching effectiveness and our system which creates an on-line community of teacher–scholars. We believe that this merger between the old and the new will retain the integrity and the tradition of mentoring while enriching and expanding its accessibility through the power of technology.

Our proposed system is derived from our research on faculty development, teaching excellence, and problem solving. Our model, Figure 11-1, "A Collegiate Development Network: Template for Teaching Development Initiatives," may be used by faculty on campuses with a faculty development center as well as by faculty whose colleges and universities provide little more than travel reimbursement as a form of development. This chapter will identify

A Collegiate Development Network
Template for Teaching Development Initiatives

Institutional
Development Plan

Scholarship of Teaching
Student Variables
Technology

Departmental
Development Plan

Policies & Standards
Career Stage Mentoring
Discipline-specific
Mentoring

Individual
Development Plan

Instructional Problem Solving

**FIGURE 11-1   A Collegiate Development Network: Template
for Teaching Development Initiatives**

© Jamie DeWaters & Sharon Baiocco

the specific needs of cohorts of faculty for development of teaching, as well as sketch out some applications of our theory of teaching excellence. We believe this model may be immediately useful for administrators and faculty charged with training graduate teaching assistants, hiring new faculty, and developing junior and senior professors in their teaching role, as well as with identifying distinguished teachers.

In Chapter 10 we presented the ways in which teaching assistants and teacher–scholars differ and demonstrated how outstanding teachers would address problems confronting new professors. In this chapter we will show how our theory and research findings point to the futuristic faculty development model we proposed initially.

Accepting Responsibility: Seeing Differently

To improve upon traditional faculty development and to be taken seriously, we will need to establish a teaching effectiveness initiative which addresses the individualized needs of faculty and a delivery system that is organized and comprehensive. We will also need to overcome a formidable barrier to participation in teaching development activities, the "low perceived need to improve teaching among faculty (i.e., high sense of self-competence in teaching)" (Ward, 1995, p. 30). A study by Blackburn et al. (1980) of nearly 2,000 faculty at 24 institutions revealed that 90% considered their teaching performance to range from "above average" to "superior" (Ward, 1995, p. 38). Only with objective criteria can faculty, most of whom have this self-image, improve, for as Angelo writes,

> Most faculty think they are doing a better job teaching than they probably are—a factor that reduces their felt need for assistance. ...Faculty tend to overestimate their teaching effectiveness not because of immodesty, but for lack of specific, accurate information on how well (or how poorly) their students are learning. They also lack a comparative perspective, since faculty rarely observe their colleagues' teaching. (1994, p. 5)

Therefore, this initiative should begin by making faculty aware of the stages of teaching development, where they are on the teaching continuum, and what they might do to improve. To be successful promoters of a teaching development initiative, we must acknowledge the ego involvement of most faculty in their teaching and promote self-awareness, reflection, and a willingness to experiment with teaching and learning. One means of doing this is by shifting the focus from teaching to solving learning problems, which is intrinsically rewarding; that is, successful problem-solving is pleasurable for professors because the goal of improved student learning can be reached.

Other incentives to improve will come from a variety of sources—from top-down initiatives supported by administrations or professional organizations, from a personal desire to improve, or from a bottom-up student demand for quality. Credentialing or certifying those who participate in teaching development is another incentive supported by the literature (Smith & Walvoord, 1993). This might provide documentation of a professor's interest in improving teaching and lead to promotion in rank or merit awards. As our 1994 survey of faculty development incentives revealed, faculty are most highly motivated when development programs offer them opportunities for professional growth or when they believe that programs will help them win renewal, promotion, and tenure (De-Waters & Baiocco, 1994).

But incentives alone will not be sufficient to achieve the changes we envision. This is an issue of responsibility. If college and university administrations are being pushed by politicians and the public to adopt a corporate mentality to improve productivity, then like corporations, higher education must commit institutional resources to develop workers. Faculty need to take responsibility, too. Rather than being passive receivers of mandates, we need to take action.

This is also a question of accountability. Recently at an English department leadership consortium, Baiocco raised the issue of whose responsibility it was to integrate information technology into the teaching of research processes, which are typically introduced in first-year English courses. She heard the well-worn battle cry, "Not my job! Let the library or computer technology people take care of that." And DeWaters hears her prospective students parroting the same mentality regarding classroom management. When asked to consider how they would respond, as teachers, to a student's misbehavior, they say, "I'd throw the student out of class and send her to the principal. I'm here to teach, not to discipline." Where does this "pass the buck" attitude originate? One of the answers is that we have been trained in an elitist, departmentalized manner and may therefore be inclined to believe that our discipline, and only our discipline, is important. In the Carnegie Foundation Survey of Attitudes and Characteristics of Faculty Members, for example, 77% of faculty in the United States agreed that "my affiliation with my academic discipline is very important," in contrast to 36% who agreed that "my affiliation with my institution is very important." (*CHE Almanac,* 1995, p. 33). During curriculum or program meetings this attitude leads to devisive turf wars when we should instead be united in broadening our visions.

We must join together to preserve the integrity of education through effective faculty development. We must return to the spirit of a "community of scholars," a partnership between administrators and faculty nationwide who are committed to excellence in teaching and learning. We need to take a more global view of faculty development by starting from the beginning—with the preparation of teaching assistants.

We have identified the problems of TAs, and based on their own needs assessment, we know that they are eager for development. In fact, they are forming advocacy websites to help train themselves as TAs (A. Rosati, on-line communication, February 7, 1997). Knowing what they need, we can begin to address those issues at the departmental level. They are telling us that they would most benefit from individualized direction. However, this cannot be mere reliance on a one-on-one system of mentorship; there must be a pervasive sense that this training is essential to the well-being of the entire academic community. Even though this sounds very lofty, it is, in fact, idealism and optimism that distinguish those faculty who model excellence. We need to exploit these values and translate them into initiatives for developing and enriching both new and experienced faculty.

We know that, as a group, academics have been trained to take long, tedious hours to examine problems and review data in order to arrive at conclusions. Risk-taking is almost anathema to an academic: We've been taught to build upon a traditional knowledge base rather than to respond creatively and quickly. Presently, we are being asked to change at a furious pace, and one which makes us understandably resistant and very uncomfortable. If the same old shopworn approaches to faculty development continue in the current climate of crisis, we doubt that the goal of increasing faculty productivity by improving quality can be accomplished. But this is not what we have in mind. Instead, our futuristic approach will exploit the power of technology while infusing it with what we have learned about excellent teaching based on this investigation.

Change is necessary because a college teaching career can no longer be a comfortable slot where a professor has only to keep current in his discipline. For example, a disturbing yet expansive trend in universities is the money-saving tactic of expecting graduate assistants and new faculty from all disciplines to teach first-year writing, in addition to teaching their specific content areas. Not only are they expected to teach their subjects with little or no teacher training, they are also being assigned to teach composition with no background in composition studies. This is one example of an economic trend that will be chosen for us if we do not become proactive.

Although faculty accuse administrators of making changes like this based on flashy trends, "quick sells," and oversimplified analyses, administrators point the finger back to faculty's automatic skepticism. The faculty often view such educational innovations as new ways of shuffling the deck or as cost-cutting measures which will hurt students. Although there is the perception that they are re-

jecting change, as we have said, it is more likely that they are looking for "intellectually credible" options (Angelo, 1994, p. 5).

Even though none would dispute that we are all responsible for
teaching writing, the proposal from administration to shift the primary responsibility for teaching writing from English faculty to all
disciplines is not intellectually credible because it is based on an
outmoded view of composition instruction. This curricular change
is a reasonable goal only if accompanied by a serious and ongoing
effort to develop faculty expertise in this new role of teaching composition. Other examples of trends that have been proposed for faculty development, but whose outcomes are as yet uncertain, are
writing across the curriculum, portfolio evaluation, cooperative/
collaborative teaching, theme-based curricula, leadership development, distance learning, and service learning.

Conditions mandate that we improve the quality of faculty development, that we do it economically, and that we do it *differently*. Proposals to reduce sabbaticals and increase class sizes and teaching
loads, as leaders in state governments have recently suggested, are
misguided because they assume that educational quality is not affected by these changes. In fact, instead of continuing to reinvent the
wheel, we need to raise the awareness of the scholarship of teaching,
including the stages of teaching development, student learning, and
Chickering and Gamson's (1991) best practices. By focusing on developing faculty, we provide quality assurance, and, we would be foolish to think that we can do this at no expense. What we must strive
for is efficiency—getting the most for our money. In order to do this,
we need to *see* differently. Our roles as college professors have expanded, and even if the term productivity offends us, we can no
longer ignore the demand that we perform better as teachers.

On Human Development and Teaching

Any approach to teaching development, we believe, ought to incorporate mention of adult development, socialization theory, and cognitive development. Recently, studies have suggested that faculty
"change as they progress through the faculty ranks and as their careers gradually place different demands on them" (Baldwin, 1990,
p. 20). For example, the university fosters a delay in human development by extending the apprenticeship well into what Gail Sheehy
(1995) called "prolonged adolescence."

Sprague & Nyquist (1989) suggest three phases in the development of the TA role. We see these as part of a larger model, and we believe that the rate of progression from senior learners, to colleagues in training, to junior colleagues takes much longer than they report. In our view, graduate teaching assistants and junior faculty alike are novices, first-time skiers on the bunny hill of academe, often focusing on control and fundamentals. We believe that graduate teaching assistants and junior faculty, who fall into the first age cohort, will predictably be acting out this stage in their adulthood as they begin their careers in academe. Using the adult development model, we find individuals just entering the professoriate while in their "first adulthood" during their early thirties. Sheehy wrote that "it is natural to become preoccupied at this stage [age] with crafting a 'false self,' a public self that will showcase our skills and talents, and, we hope, win us approval and success" (1995, p. 52). Furthermore, because their university training has prepared them with content knowledge, it is natural that the new faculty exploit that strength as they make the transition to academe.

Coming from a cognitive perspective focusing on "knowledge growth in teaching," Shulman wrote about the need for novices to transform the content knowledge, acquired through their doctoral studies, into pedagogical content knowledge, "the ways in representing and formulating the subject matter to make it comprehensible to others" (1986, p. 9). Teaching assistants and junior faculty are often concerned with inventing a language that they feel will convey the content, establishing their role as authorities in the profession, and managing classes. At this point on the continuum of teaching development, *they* are the center of the instructional setting, and their actions reflect this stage of thinking about teaching. According to Ramsden, they often believe that what they are doing when they lecture or transmit the information *is* teaching. They expect that students will learn automatically, and that failure to learn is the students' problem (1992). During this time, their overriding task is to move from a "weak sense of professional identity" to a strong one (Nyquist, Abbott, & Wulff, 1989).

Like intermediate skiers, professors further along in their development attempt a higher slope, test their skills, try new trails, and become aware of the need to coordinate their moves with others on the slopes. That is, they begin to view themselves as part of an instructional environment; as their confidence increases, they "begin to adapt teaching methods to their own personal styles and to figure out unique solutions to novel problems" (Sprague & Nyquist, 1989, p. 44). We hypothesize that this may be the end point for some faculty in terms of their development.

Crawley reported that tenured faculty members who are age 50 or older constitute approximately half of the full-time faculty at colleges and universities across the United States (1995, p. 65). In addition, the abolition of a mandatory retirement age underscores the need for attention to the professional growth of senior faculty. Fortunately, life cycle theorists and those who study career stages support the notion that senior faculty vitality can be restored (Kalivoda, Sorrell, & Simpson, 1994). In our experience, we have seen senior faculty thrive when they have been given an opportunity for a new professional direction, just as we have seen others burn out due to boredom or inability to adapt to changes.

A wisely designed faculty development initiative should take into account the life stages and career experiences of the persons involved and create appropriate goals and benchmarks from which to assess their development. The natural process for people in their forties and fifties, Sheehy reported, is to experience a "second adulthood," (1995, p. 53). We believe this midlife assessment (euphemistically known as a crisis) can be capitalized on as an opportunity for professional growth.

Midcareer issues include unmet expectations for the "perfect" professorship, disappointment about administrative decisions or turnovers, inadequate salary, and boredom (Wheeler & Wheeler, 1994). Development initiatives at this stage should avoid any suggestion of remediation, which is inherently insulting to a senior professor. The focus is more aptly placed on acknowledging and validating their experiences while tapping their interests and wisdom. It is essential to assist these senior faculty to find balance in their lives between the professional realities of their career stage and new opportunities.

Senior faculty might be expected to have reached a stage in their teaching development where they hold sophisticated concepts of teaching and learning, mastery of what Shulman (1986) called "pedagogical content knowledge." We acknowledge that not every professor will attain this mastery level, nor that they will, simply by virtue of their experience, become distinguished teachers. Although we agree that the stages mentioned in the literature are developmental (Ronkowski, 1993; Sherman et al., 1987), we challenge the notion that teaching excellence "can be recognized as a stage of professional growth" (Sherman et al., 1987). Instead, as we have said, we view excellent teaching as the confluence of multiple dimensions—character, content knowledge, scholarship of teaching, and problem-solving skills. Those who are recognized as distinguished teachers are unique in that they are exceptionally hard-working and gifted in many dimensions.

Hiring: The Search for Teaching Potential

Given our awareness of the developmental aspects of the careers of university professors, it would only make good sense to put that knowledge to work for us as we assess individual faculty potential for teaching development. As Genghis Khan reminds us, "Regret is the fruit of pity" (cited in Jarvis, 1991, p. 2). This aphorism underscores the importance of careful attention to selecting new faculty, ideally on the basis of their teaching potential as well as their scholarly potential. If we define excellent teaching as encompassing character, knowledge, and skill, then it is incumbent upon us to investigate each of these areas during the hiring process.

Trait theory, which suggests that individual character traits coalesce at around age 30, could be used by search committees to formulate evaluative selection criteria. Trait theory could also be used to recognize candidates in that age cohort's level of human development. Gail Sheehy predicted that many people at age 30 move from what she calls the "tryout twenties" (prolonged adolescence) to the "turbulent thirties" (with the age 35 "inventory" as its centerpiece). With the academic job market so tight, we might expect to find young academics who do not land a position within a year or so after completing the doctorate experiencing a "Catch 30," feeling that the first directions they chose in graduate school and the professoriate have not met their expectations (1995, pp. 40–41). If they are married, they may face the new stress of many two-career couples—finding acceptable positions in the same location—or they may have to uproot young families. "The thirties," Sheehy notes, "always present the maximum role demands" (p. 42). Furthermore, Sheehy called those in their late 20s today the "endangered" generation, because they do not feel safe about sex, money, relationships, marriage, street violence, or job security (p. 44).

Sheehy's observation that those in their 30s must cope with "the ever present worry…that [they] are being educated for jobs that may no longer exist" (1995, p. 47) could not be more applicable to those seeking positions in higher education. Although older generations might view graduate students who hang onto their teaching assistant positions and procrastinate about completing their doctorates as "delaying the inevitable," Sheehy's research suggested to us that there are good reasons for their hesitancy to begin their "first adulthoods." For them, the thirties become "a serious dress rehearsal for how [they] will perform if, and when, [they] are given the leadership roles" (p. 53).

Search committees are charged with screening candidates based on their carefully crafted documents, self-selected references, and interviews. Because candidates have been schooled in tailoring their dossiers to make themselves attractive to each institution, the distinctions among applicants become minute. This is especially true in the category of teaching, where candidates invariably obtain excellent recommendations (Lewis, 1996). Consequently, search committees must develop ways of assessing teaching potential which will give them clues about the applicants' promise of becoming effective teachers.

What they should be looking for is evidence of the characteristics of excellence we identified in our research: enthusiasm, sociability/friendliness, organization, conscientiousness, optimism, flexibility, and love of subject. In addition, search committees could focus their interviews on questions about candidates' philosophies of teaching. For example, they might use the "Assessment of Teaching Potential" tool shown in Box 11-1.

To investigate their approach to the inevitable problems encountered in college classrooms, we might query candidates about how they would respond to typical problems confronting teaching assistants. (See Box 11-2.)

Preparation for College Teaching: A Needs Assessment for New Faculty

We have said that those responsible for supporting the professional growth of faculty should have different expectations for teaching development at different points in a faculty's career. Once a department has chosen someone who shows promise to become an excellent

---

BOX 11-1   Assessment of Teaching Potential

What are your beliefs about teaching?

What are your approaches to teaching (your discipline)?

How would you perceive your role as teacher (e.g., coach, mid-wife, et cetera)?

Describe a successful assignment you have designed.

How would you measure the success of that assignment?

© DeWaters & Baiocco (1996)

teacher, his or her professional development should not be left to chance. In general, new and junior faculty need help with their teaching skills and scholarly writing (Kaviloda, Sorrell, & Simpson, 1994). After reviewing the literature about stages of teaching development and responses of graduate teaching assistants to our on-line survey, we identified the following basic orientation needs of graduate assistants and new faculty. They need to be:

- Acquainted with the specific rules or regulations of the campus
- Given an office that is in proximity to faculty who will mentor them in the day to day operation of the semester
- Informed about their role in faculty meetings, department meetings, on committees, and so forth
- Given some options about standards for student attendance, grading, department policies in general
- Given information about how they will be evaluated and by whom, as well as given an evaluation schedule that eventually leads to tenure
- Given an idea about how to go about solving a problem within the department hierarchy
- Informed about how to ask for help
- Encouraged to approach teaching with humility—to let go of what was "done to them" in the name of teaching and to seek out new teaching skills

BOX 11-2 Problem-Solving Interview

How would you handle the problems described below:

Problem: Underprepared students

"What would you do with students who are underprepared and yet have taken (and passed) the prerequisite courses?"

Response:

Problem: Assessment

"How would you go about finding a fair way to grade or compare different types of output—objective and subjective?"

Response:

Problem: Cheating

"What are your thoughts on handling plagiarism, cheating and disruptive behavior?"

Response:

Problem: Poor Attitudes

"What would you do about adult students who whine and complain about their outside commitments and your work load?"

Response:

Problem: Personal attacks

"What would you do if a student accused you of being a racist?"

Response:

Problem: Credibility

"What would you do if you had problems with students not taking you seriously and used verbally abusive language or physical intimidation?"

Response:

Problem: Grade-grubbing

"What would your response be to students who may beg for points or ask for grade changes?"

Response:

© DeWaters & Baiocco (1997)

We based this needs assessment on the theory that a continuum of development exists. Appointment to a faculty position does not mean that there is an automatic transition from one stage of teaching development to the next. Because graduate students must develop an independent spirit in order to survive the ABD ("all but dissertation") stage, they often enter their first positions with an understandable amount of pride. Wearing their medals proudly for having had the persistence and thick skins to make their doctoral committees happy, they often approach their first real appointment in the same way that a junior high student struts through the halls on his first day of high school (only to be put in his place by the seniors). And why would we expect it to be otherwise? Why do we expect new faculty to welcome our mentoring after we have forced them to learn to teach by adopting a do-it-yourself bravado with no Bob Vila around to "show them how in the privacy of their own classroom?"

New faculty cannot be allowed to hold onto defensive attitudes. A poor job market for new professors should make them eager to embrace and even demand a development program. According to Menand,

> The typical person who receives a Ph.D. in English spends eight years in graduate school, accumulates $10,000 worth of debt and is unable to find a job. Since 1989, the number of advertised job openings for people with Ph.D.'s in English has dropped by nearly 50 percent, and many of the positions that are advertised are withdrawn later after schools revise their budgets. The placement rate for new Ph.D.'s in English is about 45 percent. But the number of doctorates awarded in English goes up almost every year. (1996, p. 78)

Junior faculty should also welcome teaching development, as we have stated, because "many first- and second-year graduate students now teach college classes without training or supervision.... Doctoral programs could even require one more course in pedagogy than most professors have ever had in their lives" (Menand, 1996, p. 81). The point is that simply having the doctorate in hand will not get new graduates a job. In the tenure chase, junior faculty today need every advantage they can get to enhance the likelihood of their finding and maintaining a secure position.

Evaluating Faculty: Warning Signs

An effective program of development for new and old must begin with an honest look at the chronic concerns that surface from colleagues, administrators, and students. Only when we articulate the problems they reveal can we plan for change. These warnings, also noted by Lowman (1995) as "sources of dissatisfaction" signal potential trouble for faculty:

- Comments or behaviors which suggest that the students are stupid and which disclose a contempt for students' ability to learn.
- Cutting or biting responses to student challenges. Again, this is a defensive attitude which suggests an unkind, authoritarian stance.
- Use of language (jargon or obfuscation) that excludes, rather than includes, students. This suggests that the professors need to inappropriately elevate their status or that they are inaccurately assessing their students' knowledge base.
- Lack of initiative or doing only the minimum within the classroom and the department. These behaviors suggest that faculty are investing themselves elsewhere.
- Proposals for changes, advice about new resources, ideas for improving the department, and such, when the basic job (teaching) is receiving minimal attention. These suggest difficulty in establishing priorities.
- Isolation, which demonstrates a lack of awareness of the importance of collegiality.

In addition, signals that faculty are floundering in their teaching come from student ratings as well as comments students make to other professors and department chairpersons:

- Reports that faculty appear unprepared in class
- Reports that faculty's lectures are "boring," or complaints that faculty are long-winded
- Reports that faculty appear "hurried," "unavailable," or "disorganized"

We feel compelled to offer this caveat: Before deciding that some kind of intervention is needed, an administrator should investigate carefully, because those who are characterized as unprepared may actually be adjusting their daily class plan in response to the needs of students, or those hurried or unavailable professors may be victims of schedules or other responsibilities assigned to them. On the other hand, these signals may also point to a failure to possess or develop emotional intelligences such as self-control, humility, and empathy. There is an expectation that faculty who have taught for several years will have matured emotionally as well as pedagogically. These are but a few of the signals that warrant at least an attempt to intervene. We believe that intervention may guide one professor toward more competent teaching, or, if the professor possesses character as we have described it throughout this book, it may steer him or her toward distinguished teaching.

Recognizing Distinguished Teaching

One of our earliest goals was to discover markers of excellence that would enable administrators and faculty to identify and reward distinguished teaching. We have said that teaching is developmental, but that professors do not naturally progress to a stage of excellence. Nevertheless, we believe it is possible to identify distinguished teachers, those who not only have mastered the content knowledge, scholarship of teaching, and problem-solving skills required for effective teaching, but who also possess emotional intelligences or the dimension we have defined as character.

Mastery of a professor's subject matter can be evaluated by those familiar with the discipline, by a review of a professor's scholarly writing, and by examination of his course syllabi. A professor's developmental stage with regard to the scholarship of teaching can also be assessed against Shulman's (1986) model by observing her classrooms and examining her teaching philosophy or other publications about teaching, her instructional initiatives and materials, and/or her teaching portfolio. In addition, we propose the implementation of something like "grand rounds," a method whereby an experienced professor is evaluated for the ability to diagnose and prescribe solutions to complex instructional problems, under the scrutiny of a board or academy of distinguished teaching professors.

The essential dimension of character also has some external markers: outstanding commitment of time to improving teaching, election to and responsible service in campus leadership roles, and interest and initiatives focusing on global educational issues. Over a period of time in a university setting, individuals demonstrate their integrity, their modesty, their empathy, their enthusiasm, and their skills at social analysis, all of which are key ingredients of character. We know of professors who are quite competent, but who, in our view, would not be considered "distinguished" because, for example, they cut corners, fail to keep commitments, ignore others' concerns, or are self-aggrandizing.

Finally, the testimony of past and present students, student course ratings, and their success in passing credentialing examinations and in their careers provide additional evidence of outstanding teaching, though, admittedly, these outcomes are not all easy to obtain. In our view, all of the above are markers of excellence that set distinguished teachers apart from those who are merely effective.

We believe that many more distinguished teachers exist than are selected for teaching awards. The unfortunate problems surrounding the selection processes for teaching awards that we found in our survey of AAUP presidents (Chapter 4) make it clear that this is probably not the best way to identify nor to reward excellent teaching. Instead, we think that distinguished professors could be nominated by administrators, peers, and students to serve as distinguished peer mentors, with the opportunity to receive remuneration for their role as mentors and models of excellent practices. Teaching academies such as the Lilly Teaching Fellows program (Jackson & Simpson, 1994) and other attempts to encourage excellence in teaching by the Lilly Foundation, Sears & Roebuck Foundation, the Carnegie Foundation, TIAA-CREF, and the American Association of Higher Education's Teaching Initiatives ("Peer Review of Teaching," "Teaching Portfolios," and "Cases About College Teaching and Learning") support our concept of a community of distinguished teachers sharing their expertise. (See AAHE Teaching Initiative website at www.aahe.org/teachnew.htm.)

Assessing Faculty Development Needs

As Angelo states, "Even when faculty are self-aware and motivated to improve their teaching, the generic nature of many faculty development workshops often doesn't respond to a given teacher's highly personal and specific needs. Faculty needs are often problem-centered, while faculty development programs typically are topic-centered." (1994, p. 4). The cornerstones of our concept of effective faculty development are a problem-based curriculum and individualized development plans for individuals, departments, and colleges. The goal is to encourage faculty to consider their development as ongoing. (See Fig. 11-1, "A Collegiate Development Network: Template for Teaching Development Initiatives.")

We propose the following teaching assessment inventory as an example of the needs assessment that could become the foundation for an individualized development plan. (See Box 11-3.) Through the Collegiate Development Network, similar plans for teaching devel-

---

BOX 11-3   Individual Teaching Assessment Inventory

1. How important to your self-image is your role as teacher?
2. If asked to use a metaphor for your role as teacher, what would it be? (e.g., midwife, coach, and so forth)
3. How did you learn to teach?
4. What are your most distinctive teaching methods?
5. How does your teaching differ from that of other teachers'?
6. What have been the most challenging problems you have encountered as a teacher?
7. What difficulties have you had with particular groups of students?
8. How did you handle them?
9. What difficulties have you had with individual students?
10. How did you handle them?
11. What do you *say* to students who have failed or who are having difficulty?
12. What do you *do* to assist them?
13. What are your strengths as a teacher?
14. What are the areas in which you need to improve?
15. What are you doing to improve as a teacher?
16. What do you do to make your students independent?
17. How do you convey your expectations for (a) literacy, (b) ethical behavior, (c) accuracy?
18. How do you know when your teaching is successful/unsuccessful?

© DeWaters & Baiocco (1997)

opment could be offered at the departmental and the college-wide levels.

Creating a Mentoring Community

Mentoring has been seen in many fields as a valuable method for assisting professional development over the span of a career. In academe, it has been a practice that supports the development of faculty through a primary relationship (Wunsch, 1994). Usually this has implied an expert–protégé alliance. According to the literature, mentoring claims the following virtues as a development strategy: It promotes an understanding of organizational culture, networking, and assistance in defining career aspirations (Luna & Cullen, 1995). And, although face-to-face consultation to improve teaching has had widespread popularity on college and university campuses (Crawley, 1995), according to Wunsch,

> a growing body of literature and research confirms that there are as many theories about mentoring as there are personal experiences of it. There is no universally accepted definition of mentoring and there is a good deal of "magical thinking" about what happens when mentors and mentees do come together (1994, p. 1).

Although we agree that mentoring on some campuses has not been carefully conceived, we believe that it conforms to the natural ways in which faculty seek assistance in solving instructional problems. In fact, Kalivoda, Sorrel and Simpson reported that:

> [T]he most common method of handling both teaching and research problems, at all faculty levels, was to discuss the matter with one's colleagues. Discussing teaching concerns with another person, such as a spouse, a close friend, or a mentor was listed as the second most common approach to solving teaching-related difficulties. (1994, p. 263)

Matthew Ouellett, Center for Teaching at the University of Massachusetts/Amherst, advised that a teaching center serves most effectively as consultant to discipline-based mentoring programs at the departmental level. In his experience with teaching development, mentors recommended by the department head or dean lend credibility to the mentoring concept (personal communication, March 31, 1997).

We believe that the mentoring concept has many advantages, while at the same time, as it is currently organized, some inherent difficulties may be responsible for its unimpressive record on some campuses. First, the expert–protégé model does not always fit with faculty career stages; secondly, participants may confuse coaching with judging; and last, many programs lack sufficient structure and evaluation measures (Boice, 1992).

Perhaps the reason why the age-old concept of mentoring, the expert–protégé model that functioned so well in the past, is now challenged is because it does not take into account the developmental stage of junior faculty, whereas the mentoring of teaching assistants seems to be more promising. Junior faculty have just emerged from the doctoral "meat grinder," where they have taken direction for many years. Like college freshmen when they first arrive on campus, they are likely to assert their independence from supervision. It is only natural to expect resistance at this career stage. This observation would point out to those responsible for faculty development the importance of selecting appropriate approaches to teaching development. We believe that institutional initiatives which offer development options to all faculty based on their career stage needs are most likely to be successful.

Boice pointed out that "evidently, mentoring benefits when the protégé fears no loss of face or of confidentiality from a mentor who works in the same department" (1992, p. 114). However, using mentors within a department can conflict with the protégé's major need for privacy. Why is this so? We theorize that the line between formative assessment (improving teaching) and summative assessment (evaluating teaching) becomes blurred. For instance, the departmental mentor or the teaching center coach might be asked for a recommendation for the protégé's portfolio; conversely, the protégé might fear that the mentor would be in a position to use information about his or her teaching for personnel decisions.

Any program that is based on fixing teaching is doomed to fail (M. Ouellett, personal communication, March 31, 1997). To meet the development needs of both junior and senior faculty, rather than a leader–follower model, we support the creation of a mentoring community that offers the option of complete confidentiality and whose goals should be (a) improving students' learning, and (b) developing—not evaluating—teaching.

Whatever the existing system, and whomever the mentor (whether services are provided through a central teaching center, at the department level, or through outside sources), the role is the same. The teaching mentor objectively listens to and/or observes the perceived teaching problems or concerns of the professor, identifies strengths and areas that are in need of improvement, teaches him or her to self-evaluate, and offers additional expertise through modeling. And who better to serve as models for this instructional problem solving than those who have been acknowledged as distinguished teachers?

We propose a Collegiate Development Network which links faculty members seeking assistance to mentors (such as our distinguished teachers) on campus and nationwide. (See Figure 11-1.) Our model encompasses teaching development plans at three levels: institutional, departmental, and individual. At the university level, options could include initiatives supporting common teaching development needs, such as addressing the problems of a diverse student population, and problems in effective use of technology for teaching. At the departmental level, options could include addressing problems in supervision of practicums or clinicals, academic standards, or issues specific to a discipline. (See Emery, 1995, who suggests that faculty may have different development interests based on their disciplines.) At the individual level, options could include a wide range of instructional problems. (See Figure 7-1, p. 171.)

A Problem-Based Curriculum

We have theorized that faculty undergo a normal developmental process in their teaching careers. Building on Shulman's concept of development of teaching scholarship (1986), we envision a developmental problem-based curriculum as part of our futuristic teaching development initiative. If, as we believe, there are themes which persist throughout one's career as well as a hierarchy of instructional problems which faculty encounter and address in varying ways at different stages of their careers, then a problem-based curriculum could be organized sequentially by themes or categorically by types of problems. However, we propose that faculty be offered the choice of where to begin their teaching development by being given a "menu" of options. We believe the best way to individualize development is to allow faculty to have a say in the selection of instructional problems of interest to them, rather than dictating a prescribed, sequential curriculum. For example, interested faculty members could link with an on-line mentoring community and select from a menu of offerings which focus on pedagogical problem solving or participate in on-line discussions led by faculty who have been chosen as distinguished teaching fellows, either at the campus level or the national level.

Tables 11-1 and 11-2 present a sample schema illustrating how one script for a problem-solving session for teaching development might look. The schema shows how the on-line peer mentor might guide a colleague through the problem-solving processes.

Following the advice of the on-line mentor, the professor schedules a conference with a student who refuses to participate in class, describes to the student how he perceives the behavior, and outlines the consequences for continuance of the behavior. In this case, the student refuses to accept responsibility, and instead blames the professor by suggesting that his classes are "boring" and his questions "put her on the spot." The professor has been instructed to make no judgments, but to indicate that he has heard the student's point of view.

Following this session, the professor schedules a follow-up conference with the student, follows the advice of the on-line mentor, and gives the student a time frame within which to respond.

A Proposal for a Collegiate Development Network

The teaching development initiatives we have proposed exploit the concept of a mentoring community and a problem-based curriculum of instructional problem solving. These could be delivered in a traditional manner through teaching centers or campus mentoring programs. However, we have proposed wedding these to the new medium of on-line technology via the Internet. We believe that this marriage of the old and the new has tremendous potential to improve faculty development by overcoming the drawbacks of traditional mentoring and exploiting the power of technology.

**TABLE 11-1   Sample Problem-Solving Script for Session #1:
The "Bartleby" Syndrome[1]**

Class of Problem	Identification & Assessment	Planning & Implementation	Evaluation
Individual attitude problem is described by faculty on-line.	1. Student refuses to participate or respond in class (part of grade is based upon class participation).		
	Peer mentor assists in identifying the possible causes of the behavior, encouraging the faculty to give his or her best guess as to what is going on.		
	2. Professor hypothesizes that the student is either angry, afraid of failure, or both.	Peer mentor advises: 1. Professor to invite student to meet privately, describe how the behavior is being perceived, and try to identify the reasons for the behavior.	

[1]The student profiled in this table refuses to comply with requests, much like the character Bartleby in "Bartleby, the Scrivener," a short story by Herman Melville.

The network's potential for promoting academic development is enormous. It appears to provide the format for reconceptualizing programs to promote the professional growth of the faculty because it is cost-effective and convenient, and because it affords unique

TABLE 11-2   Sample Problem-Solving Script for Session #2:
            The "Bartleby" Syndrome

Class of Problem	Identification & Assessment	Planning & Implementation	Evaluation
Professor responds to student's defensive behavior.		Peer mentor advises: 1. Professor to remain neutral in the face of accusations. 2. Professor to restate the rationale for the questioning format. 3. Professor to outline the consequences for continuance of the behavior and offers assistance.	Peer mentor advises: 1. Professor to continue to give the student the option to participate. 2. Based on criteria set, professor to grade accordingly.

opportunities for individualized assistance for faculty. The popularity of websites, bulletin boards, and lists tailored to the special interests of higher education faculty also suggests that an on-line development program could work. Early concerns that electronic communication was too dull, too passive, or too impersonal appear to be unwarranted. Indeed, our experience has been that on-line communication, with its opportunity for immediate feedback, is in some ways *more* personal than traditional, infrequent, in-service workshops. Additionally, on-line networks offer the medium for enhancing professional relationships that are not bound by the campus culture and peer review system, and therefore encourage confidential exchanges of information.

Chickering and Ehrmann (1996) showed the advantages of the use of electronic technology on student–teacher interactions by comparing on-line instructional methods against their standard "Seven

Principles for Good Practice in Undergraduate Education." We believe that the same principles apply to on-line teaching development. The proposed interactions between teaching fellows and professors interested in improving students' learning would be similarly enhanced by the speed, safety, and convenience of on-line communication; the collaborative, social, and active nature of the learning; and the efficient use of time. Additionally, the use of distinguished teachers as models for instructional problem solving "communicates high expectations,"and the problem-based curriculum we have proposed allows professors to follow their individual interests, learn at their own pace, and participate in self-evaluation and group problem solving.

An additional benefit of on-line mentoring, we believe, is the ease of evaluating the effectiveness of program offerings. Via e-mail and on-line discussion sessions and surveys, program coordinators may determine participants' reactions, assess their knowledge and skills pre- and post-session, accept self-observation reports, and monitor the overall use of the teaching development program components. Thus it meets another goal for improving staff development programs' outcome assessment (Smith & Beno, 1995).

For all these reasons, we believe that the on-line format offers an exciting option and will likely form the essential infrastructure of a futuristic teaching development scheme. Our 1994 faculty development survey found that 66% of institutions we polled had access to external computer networks (Baiocco & DeWaters, 1995), and recent surveys suggest that access has increased substantially in the last three years (Fennell, 1997, pp. 6–7). New websites and chat areas for professionals continue to proliferate; and additional electronic bulletin boards and subscription lists such as AAHESGIT, offered by Technology Projects for the American Association of Higher Education, are generated. Together they are pioneering the transformation of academic discourse.

Because on-line communication overcomes former barriers of distance, time, status, and formality, it affords us a new democratic arena for elevating the status of the scholarship of teaching. The extraordinary power and beauty of the teaching that we have described should not be wasted; it is a resource which cries out to be tapped. We know that the need and interest are there for faculty to improve their teaching, and excellent teachers have demonstrated their willingness and excitement to share their expertise. Why are we waiting?

National Survey of Faculty Development Programs

This appendix documents the questions sent to AAUP presidents at 436 colleges and universities nationwide. Results of this survey are presented in the text in Tables 3-1 and 3-2 and Figure 3-1.

National Survey:
Faculty Development Programs

1. Do you have a formal faculty development program?

Yes ___   No ___

If yes, please answer the following survey. If no, *please return the survey anyway.*

2. Is your program ongoing? (i.e., activities or moneys are provided annually)

Yes ___   No ___

3. Do you have an annual budget allotted to faculty development?

   Yes ____   No ____

4. Over the past five years, what has been the annual budget trend? (Check one.)

   ____ Increased   ____ Decreased

   ____ Stayed the same   ____ Fluctuated

5. Who decides how the moneys are dispersed? (Check one.)

   ____ Faculty   ____ Administrators   ____ Both

6. How are the moneys dispersed? (Check all that apply.)

   ____ Travel money

   ____ Research funding

   ____ Consultant-led workshops/lectures

   ____ Faculty-led workshops/lectures

   ____ Development personnel/mentors

   ____ Equipment/office space

   ____ Other _____

7. Who is offered faculty development? (Check all that apply.)

   ____ All full-time faculty   ____ Junior/new faculty only

   ____ Part-time faculty

8. Who is offered faculty development? (Check all that apply.)

   ____ Groups   ____ Individuals

9. What are the incentives for faculty to participate? (Check all that apply.)

   ____ Professional growth

   ____ Money

   ____ Release time/reduced load

   ____ Other _____

10. Is there a space (office/center) on campus designated solely for faculty development?

Yes ___   No ___

11. Is there a faculty/staff person assigned to coordinate/conduct faculty development?

Yes ___   No ___

Please describe that person.

___ Administrator   ___ Faculty member

___ Part-time   ___ Full-time

12. Please check all formal, individualized faculty development activities which your institution currently offers.

___ Travel funding

___ Teaching effectiveness mentoring

___ Undergraduate level

___ Graduate level

___ Field supervision mentoring

___ Grant-writing mentoring

___ Research and publication mentoring

___ Teacher as researcher mentoring (in classroom)

___ Using technology/developing materials

___ Student advisement assistance

13. Are your faculty able to communicate with each other on a campus computer network?

Yes ___   No ___

14. Your faculty have access to training for which of the following topics? (Check all that apply.)

___ Using computer-assisted instructional software

___ Using computers in the classroom

___ Developing computer-assisted instructional programs

___ Developing multimedia teaching aids

___ Using computer networks for research

15. Please indicate your overall level of satisfaction with your institution's faculty development program.

Very dissatisfied   1   2   3   4   5   6   7   Very satisfied

AAUP Presidents Teaching Excellence Survey, Respondents, and Results

This appendix documents the survey that was presented to 50 selected AAUP presidents. Also presented here are the list of respondents and a table showing whether their institutions had awards at the time of the survey. Additional survey results are presented in the text in Tables 4-1 and 4-2.

Identifying Distinguished Teachers

1. At your institution, what are the rewards/awards for distinguished teaching?

    a. Monetary awards:

Is it a one-time stipend?	___ Yes	___ No	$_____
Is it added to base salary?	___ Yes	___ No	$_____
What is the total teaching award budget?			$_____

b. Are there other than monetary rewards?

___ Yes   ___ No

If yes, what? _____

c. What is the total number of full-time faculty at your institution? _____

d. Have distinguished teaching awards been given regularly?

___ Yes   ___ No

e. How many distinguished teaching awards are currently given? _____

2. Is there an established process for selecting faculty for distinguished teaching awards?

___ Yes   ___ No   ___ Don't know

a. If yes, what are the criteria for selection?   _____

b. If yes, what is that selection process? _____

3. If you don't know, who on your campus would be most likely to know the process?

a. Faculty member _____

b. Administrator _____

4. To what extent are you satisfied/dissatisfied with your institution's procedure for identifying distinguished teaching?

Very Dissatisfied   1   2   3   4   5   Very Satisfied

5. In your opinion, is this process a fair process?

___ Yes   ___ No

Why or why not? _____

_____

_____

6. In your opinion, is this process a consistent process?

___ Yes   ___ No

Why or why not? _____

_____

_____

7. In your opinion, are campus politics involved in the selection process?

___ Yes   ___ No

Please explain: _____

_____

_____

8. In the space below, would you please provide the names, disciplines and either email or phone numbers of the two most recent recipients of your institutional teaching awards?

Name	Discipline	Phone/e-mail

a. _____

b. _____

9. If you are familiar with either of these award recipients, would you please describe what you think characterizes their distinguished teaching?

_____

_____

AAUP Presidents or College Respondents

Jan Andrews
Vassar College

Roger Armstrong
Russell Sage College

Herman Berkman
New York University

George Bishop
D'Youville College

Una Bray
Skidmore College

Gretchen A. Brockmeyer
Springfield College, Massachusetts

Warder Cadbury
University at Albany–SUNY

Frank Colbourn
Pace University

David Colton
University of Delaware

Joanne Desotelle
Keuka College

C. Dewsnap
Bard College

Walton Ellison
Cooper Union

Fred Exoo
St. Lawrence University

Allan Frishman
Hobart/William Smith College

Estelle Gellmann
Hofstra University

Jerry Goodisman
Syracuse University

Charles Goss
Cazenovia College

Henrik Hagerhup
*Rensellaer Polytechnical Institute
(RPI)*

Ray Henrikson
Albany Medical College

Frank Higman
Niagara University

Marvin Karp
Mercy College

Martin Kotler
Pace University/Pleasantville

Lionel Lewis
University at Buffalo–SUNY

Ronald MacDonald
Smith College, Massachusetts

Frank Musgrave
Ithaca College

Victor Oliva
Adelphi University

James Reynolds
Colgate University

Brian Shero
Medaille College

Therese Warden
Medaille College

Richard Wesp
Elmira College

Teaching Excellence Awards at Various Institutions—
Survey of AAUP Presidents (December 1995)

Institution	Type	Award 1995	Award Before
Adelphi University	I	No	Yes
Albany Medical College	–	Yes	Yes
Bard College	IIB	No	–
Cazenovia College	IIB	Yes	Yes
Colgate University	IIB	No	No
Cooper Union	IIB	No	–
D'Youville College	IIB	Yes	Yes
Elmira College	IIB	Yes	Yes
Hobart/Wm. Smith College	IIB	Yes	Yes
Hofstra University	I	Yes	Yes
Ithaca College	IIB	Yes	Yes
Keuka College	IIB	No	No
Medaille College	IIB	Yes	Yes
Mercy College	IIB	Yes	Yes
Niagara University	IIA	Yes	Yes
NYI of Technology	IIA	No	–
NY University	I	Yes	Yes
Pace U–NYC	IIA	Yes	Yes
Pace U–Pleasantville	IIA	Yes	Yes
Rensellaer Polytechnic (RPI)	I	Yes	Yes
Russell Sage College	IIA	Yes	Yes
Skidmore College	IIB	No	–
Smith College (MA)	IIA	Yes	Yes
Springfield College (MA)	IIA	Yes	Yes
St. Lawrence University	IIB	Yes	Yes
SUNY–Albany	I	Yes	Yes
SUNY–Buffalo	I	Yes	Yes
Syracuse University	I	Yes	Yes
University of Delaware	I	Yes	Yes
Vassar College	IIB	No	–
TOTAL	Yes	22	23
	No	8	2
	NA	–	5

Surveys of Faculty Teaching Award Winners

This appendix documents two surveys that were presented to the 30 award-winning faculty identified in the AAUP presidents survey. Included here is the list of responding professors.

Distinguished Teacher Survey #1

1. What are the title(s) of the award(s) for distinguished teaching you have received?

_____

_____

2. What token(s) accompanied the award(s)?

_____

_____

3. By whom were you nominated?

_____

_____

4. What would you say is the primary ingredient for which your teaching was recognized?

_____

_____

5. Please identify any elected leadership positions you have held on your campus:

_____

_____

6. Do you have a written statement of your philosophy of teaching? If so, would you be willing to provide us with a copy?

_____

7. In your opinion, do you think it is possible to be both an award-winning teacher and an award-winning scholar?

_____

_____

© DeWaters & Baiocco (1995)

Distinguished Teacher Survey #2

1. How important to your self-image is your role as teacher?

_____

_____

2. What are your most distinctive teaching methods?

_____

_____

3. Where or from whom did you learn to teach?

_____

_____

4. Do you think your teaching differs from that of other teachers? If so, how?

_____

_____

5. What have been the most challenging problems you have encountered as a teacher?

_____

_____

6. Have you ever had difficulty with a particular group of students? If so, how did you handle the problem?

_____

_____

7. What is the most challenging problem with an individual student you have encountered? How did you handle it?

_____

_____

8. Can you describe a particular assignment you give that you feel is unusual?

_____

_____

9. Do you ever change your teaching plan in the midst of implementing it? When? Why?

_____

_____

10. How do you know when your teaching is successful/ unsuccessful?

_____

_____

_____

© DeWaters & Baiocco (1995)

Responding Professors

John Aistars
Cazenovia College (studio art)

Sharon Baiocco
D'Youville College (English)

Eileen Brown
Medaille College (psychology)

Meritta B. Cullinan
Molloy College (sociology)

Jamie DeWaters
D'Youville College (education)

Adma d'Heurle
Mercy College (psychology)

Charles H. V. Ebert
University at Buffalo–SUNY
(geography)

Marilynn P. Fleckenstein
Niagara University (philosophy)

Josiah B. Gould
University at Albany–SUNY
(philosophy)

Jonathan Gil Harris
Ithaca College (English)

William T. Harris
University of Delaware (economics)

Carol L. Harrison
Medaille College (media-
communications)

D. Edward Hart
D'Youville College (biology)

Clyde Herreid
University at Buffalo–SUNY
(biology/physiology/ecology)

Sandra Hinchman
St. Lawrence University
(government)

Michael Kiskis
Elmira College (American
literature)

Janice Koch
Hofstra University (science
education)

Maureen McCann Miletta
Hofstra University (education)

Wendy Mehne
Ithaca College (music)

Kim Mooney
St. Lawrence University
(psychology)

Nishan Parlakian
John Jay College, CUNY (speech &
theater)

Donald F. Peters
Niagara University (history)

John S. Pipkin
University at Albany–SUNY
(geography & planning)

Georgia Pyrros
University of Delaware
(mathematics)

James L. Ragonnet
Springfield College, Massachusetts
(rhetoric)

William J. Rappaport
University at Buffalo–SUNY
(computer science)

Jonathan Reichert
University at Buffalo–SUNY
(physics)

Karen Schiavone
Medaille College (education)

Brian Shero
Medaille College (biology)

Harlan Wollingford
Pace University (marketing)

Tools for Developing Professionalism

This appendix contains tools used successfully by the authors to assist faculty and students in developing professionalism: the "Statement on Professional Behavior," "Field Experience Core Performance Standards," "Problem-Solving Procedure," and "Performance Report" form. The first item presented here, a sample lesson evaluation, demonstrates the level of detail that is most helpful to a student teacher and supervising faculty.

Sample Lesson Evaluation

Student _____ Date _____

School _____

Planning/Organization

Boardwork is well presented (be careful you don't jam too much on at once). Be more specific when you introduce the lesson—review what you will be doing and also what your behavioral expectations are (review the rules). Transition from lesson to next activity was smooth but *always* plan for a specific conclusion to each lesson—"Today we did…. Who can tell me one thing.…" About three-quarters of the way through the lesson, you checked the time and then had to rush—try to keep a closer eye on the clock. Lesson plan was well developed, materials were creative.

Classroom/Management
Your use of vocal modulation was quite effective—the students modified their own behavior based on your volume. Cruise around the class as you present, not just when they are working independently—the student in the last seat was eating his lunch while you were showing how to make a + sign. Increase your verbal praise for behaviors such as sitting and paying attention, both to individuals and the whole group. Be task specific in your praise also, as in "That's right, Moe, you looked in the book for your answer, and that's the right thing to do." Monitor your verbal praise—don't take their good behavior for granted!

Methods/Techniques
Use of the board, overhead, and corresponding seat work was very effective. Moving the students through stations while using the volunteer to monitor allowed you to work independently with others. Good idea! You may want to investigate a more efficient system for evaluating the work completed at the stations.

Personal
Very professional appearance. Be aware of the speech and language model you are presenting to the students—when you got comfortable during the lesson, you began dropping the endings of your words (goin', doin', thinkin') and also referring to "me and Mrs. _____" is not a good model. Consider tape recording yourself for self-evaluation of the speech model you are presenting.

© Jamie N. DeWaters (1993)

Statement on Professional Behavior

Unprofessional behavior exhibited by a student in any college class, cooperating agency and/or school setting will result in failure in the course or field experience regardless of any previous grades earned related to that course.

A display of professional behavior on the part of the student can include (but is not limited to) the following attributes.

1. Reflect punctuality as dictated by the college, teacher, school, or agency representative.
2. Be aware of confidentiality issues. The use of student or teacher's names within or outside of a facility setting is considered unethical.
3. Display moderation in dress.
4. Be aware of and demonstrate appropriate appearance and hygiene.
5. Maintain self-control. When in situations which may be uncomfortable or unfamiliar to you (i.e., seeing a handicapping condition or a teaching method that is disturbing to you), remain composed. You are a guest in any community setting. Any critical remarks or disrespectful, contrary behavior will not be tolerated.
6. Show respect for individuals when you are in an observation or participatory role.
7. Be consistent. Show commitment. Once arrangements have been made for you to either observe or participate in an educational setting, you must be consistent in your attendance.
8. Demonstrate flexibility. Participatory schools and agencies cannot always guarantee that you will be in an environment that will suit your exact needs with regards to completion of specific assignments. It is your responsibility to adjust to the situation and contact the appropriate college supervisor for suggestions.

Field Experience Core Performance Standards

The Field Experience Core Performance Standards for _____ College Division of Education are requirements that are essential to the successful completion of the field portion of the teacher training program. These standards are necessary to ensure development of individuals who are competent and sensitive to the appropriateness of behavior expected of those who work with students, parents, colleagues, and administrators.

Any student participating in a field experience must

- Possess and demonstrate the appropriate emotional health required to provide a consistent model for students
- Tolerate intellectually, emotionally, and physically taxing work loads
- Function effectively during stressful situations
- Adapt to ever-changing environments
- Display flexibility
- Maintain appropriate interactions with others
- Function even in the case of uncertainty that is inherent in field situations involving teachers, students, parents, administrators and supervisors
- Maintain an even disposition
- Maintain an openness to criticism concerning professional and personal growth from the college supervisor and teacher in an accepting and nondefensive manner
- Recognize his/her position as a student and respond appropriately to those in authority (teacher, principal, college supervisor, director of field experiences)
- Refrain from arguing about observation evaluations
- Refrain from comparing or complaining about placement site, teacher, college supervisor, and other personnel

Failure to abide by these standards may result in removal from the placement. If a student is removed from a field placement due to inappropriate behavior, the decision to consider an alternate placement will be made by the Director of Field Experiences in consultation with appropriate personnel. An alternate placement is not guaranteed.

© Jamie N. DeWaters (1993)

Problem-Solving Procedure for Student Teachers and Cooperating Teachers

Student teaching is usually a very exciting time in a student career. The individual anticipates the event with questions such as, "Where will I be placed?" "What will my teacher be like?" or "Will the students like me?" Very often a student teacher will need assistance in identifying and developing strategies to improve. Students are frequently unsure of where they fit into the existing system. They may be hesitant to "jump right in" or ask the appropriate questions. They may not envision their place in an already established relationship with the teacher, team, aide, or administrators. Ordinarily these concerns work themselves out, but in some cases the teacher may have serious reservations about the student performance.

The teacher is a model who is responsible for demonstrating professional and ethical practice to the student. Occasionally, issues of student safety, communication ability, health, stamina, personality, commitment, motivation, or initiative become overwhelming and the teacher or student feels compelled to identify a problem area. In this instance, the following procedure is recommended:

Step 1. The student or teacher is responsible for attempting to solve or at least address the problem with the involved party.

Step 2. If the situation is not resolved, then the college supervisor should be contacted.

Step 3. The college supervisor will interview each party and make arrangements for both parties to meet to discuss the problem openly.

Step 4. If appropriate, the college supervisor will confer with the Director of Field Experiences and/or an official at the participating school.

Performance Report

The purpose of the performance report is to document that the student has not met minimum expectations in a planned or unplanned activity, or in any other area related to the field experience. The teacher or college supervisor is requested to complete this form after other, less formal attempts have been made to correct the problem. The college supervisor will confer with the teacher and student to develop a plan to assist the student. All forms should be forwarded to the Director of Field Experiences.

Student _____   Date _____

Supervisor _____

Incident:
Student Reaction:

Recommendation For Improvement:

Review date _____

Student signature _____   Date_____

References

Abbott, R. D., Wulff, D. H., & Szego, C. K. (1989). Review of research on TA training. In J. D. Nyquist, R. D. Abbott, & D. H. Wulff (Eds.), *Teaching assistant training in the 1990s* (pp. 111–124). San Francisco: Jossey-Bass.

Adler, A. (1928/1968). *Understanding human nature* (8th ed.). London: George Allen & Unwin.

Aleamoni, L. M. (Ed.). (1987a). *Techniques for evaluating and improving instruction.* San Francisco: Jossey-Bass.

Aleamoni, L. M. (1987b). Typical faculty concerns about student evaluation of teaching. In L. M. Aleamoni (Ed.), *Techniques for evaluating and improving instruction* (pp. 25–32). San Francisco: Jossey-Bass.

American Psychological Association. (1994). *Publication manual of the American Psychological Association* (4th ed.). Washington, DC: Author.

Angelo, T. A. (Ed.). (1991). *Classroom research: Early lessons from success.* San Francisco: Jossey-Bass.

Angelo, T. A. (1994, June). From faculty development to academic development. *AAHE Bulletin,* 3–7.

Baiocco, S. & DeWaters, J. (1995, September/October). Futuristic faculty development. *Academe: Bulletin of the AAUP, 81*(5), 38–39.

Baldwin, R. G. (1990). Faculty career stages and implications for professional development. In J. H. Schuster, D. W. Wheeler, & Associates (Eds.), *Enhancing faculty careers: Strategies for development and renewal* (pp. 20–40). San Francisco: Jossey-Bass.

Banta, T. (1996). Using assessment to improve instruction. In R. J. Menges, M. Weimer, & Associates. (Eds.), *Teaching on solid ground: Using scholarship to improve practice* (pp. 363–382). San Francisco: Jossey-Bass.

Beidler, P. (1986). *Distinguished teachers on effective teaching.* San Francisco: Jossey-Bass.

Bender, T. B. (1994). *Don't squat with yer spurs on!* Corte Madera, CA: Portal.

Berliner, D. C., & Biddle, B. J. (1995). *The manufactured crisis: Myths, fraud, and the attack on America's public schools.* Reading, MA: Addison-Wesley.

Bernieri, F., & Rosenthal, R. (1988). Coordinated movement and rapport in teacher–student interactions. *Journal of Nonverbal Behavior, 12,* 120–138.

Bernieri, F., & Rosenthal, R. (1991). Interpersonal coordination, behavior matching, and interpersonal synchrony. In R. S. Feldman & B. Rime (Eds.), *Fundamentals of nonverbal behavior: Studies in emotion and social interaction* (pp. 401–432). Cambridge: Cambridge University Press.

Bérubé, M. (1996). Public perceptions of universities and faculties. *Academe, 82*(4), 10–17.

Blackburn, R. T., & Lawrence, J. H. (1995). *Faculty at work.* Baltimore: Johns Hopkins University Press.

Blackburn, R. T., Pellino, O. R., Boberg, A., & O'Connell, C. (1980). Are instructional improvement programs off target? *Current Issues in Higher Education, 1,* 32–48.

Boice, R. (1992). *The new faculty member: Supporting and fostering professional development.* San Francisco: Jossey-Bass.

Bok, D. (1991). *The improvement of teaching.* New York: American Council of Learned Societies.

Bower, B. (1994, March 5). Piecing together personality. *Science News,* 152–154.

Boyer, E. (1990). *Scholarship reconsidered: Priorities of the professoriate.* Princeton, NJ: The Carnegie Foundation for the Advancement of Teaching.

Brandt, R. (1988). On assessment of teaching: A conversation with Lee Shulman. *Educational Leadership 46*(3), 42–46.

Breneman, D. W. (1995, September 8). Sweeping, painful changes. *The Chronicle of Higher Education, 42,* pp. B1–B2.

Buchbinder, H., & Newson, J. (1992). The service university and market forces. *Academe 78*(4), 13–15.

Can't professors teach more? (1995, May 12). [Editorial]. *Buffalo News,* p. C2.

Cashin, W. E. (1990). Assessing teaching effectiveness. In P. Seldin & Associates, (Eds.), *How administrators can improve teaching: Moving from talk to action in higher education* (pp. 89–103). San Francisco: Jossey-Bass.

Centra, J. A. (1979). *Determining faculty effectiveness.* San Francisco: Jossey-Bass.

Chickering, A. W., & Ehrmann, S. (1996, October). Implementing the seven principles. *AAHE Bulletin, 49,* 3–6.

Chickering, A. W., & Gamson, E. (Eds.). (1991). *Applying the seven principles for good practice in undergraduate education.* San Francisco: Jossey-Bass.

Cholakian, R. (1994, September/October). The value of evaluating. *Academe,* 24–26.

The Chronicle of Higher Education. (1992, August 26). *The Chronicle of Higher Education: Almanac Issue, 39*(1).

The Chronicle of Higher Education. (1995, September 1). *The Chronicle of Higher Education: Almanac Issue, 42*(1).

The Chronicle of Higher Education. (1996, September 2). *The Chronicle of Higher Education: Almanac Issue, 43*(1).

The Chronicle of Higher Education. (1997, August 29). *The Chronicle of Higher Education: Almanac Issue, 44*(1).

Clark, H., & Clark, E. (1977). *Psychology and language: An introduction to psycholinguistics.* New York: Harcourt Brace Jovanovich.

Clausen, D. (1995, September 25). Educating elephants [Letter to the editor]. *U.S. News & World Report, 119*(12), p. 8.

Consumerism: Viewing education as product instead of process. (1995, Summer/Fall). *St. Lawrence University Magazine.* (St. Lawrence University in Canton, NY) p. 17.

Cornesky, R. (1993). *The quality professor: Implementing TQM in the classroom.* Madison, WI: Magna.

Costa, P. T., & Macrae, R. R. (1995). Solid ground in the wetlands of personality: A reply to Block. *Psychological Bulletin 117,* 216–220.

Cox, B. (1994). *Practical pointers for university teachers.* London: Kogan Page.

Cox, M. D., & Richlin, L. (1993). Emerging trends in college teaching for the 21st century. *Journal on Excellence in College Teaching, 4,* 1–7.

Crawley, A. L. (1995). Faculty development programs at research universities: Implications for senior faculty renewal. *To Improve the Academy, 14,* 65–87.

Cronin, T. E. (1992). On celebrating college teaching. *Journal on Excellence in College Teaching, 3,* 149–168.

Cross, K. P. (1976). *Accent on learning.* San Francisco: Jossey-Bass.

Csikszentmihalyi, M. (1991). *Flow: The psychology of optimal experience.* New York: Harper Perennial.

Davison, W. P., Boylan, J., & Yu, F. T. C. (1976). *Mass media: Systems & effects.* New York: Holt, Rinehart and Winston.

Decyk, B. N. (1996). Leonardo's workshop: The fine art of teaching philosophy. *AAPT (American Association of Philosophy Teachers) News, 19*(3), 1, 3–10.

Descartes, R. (1960). Discourse on method. In J. Bronowski & B. Mazlish (Eds.), *The Western intellectual tradition: From Leonardo to Hegel* (pp. 220–221). New York: Harper & Row.

DeWaters, J. & Baiocco, S. (1994). [Survey of faculty development programs]. Unpublished raw data.

Drummond, T. (1996, December 3). *A brief summary of the best practices in college teaching.* [On-Line]. Available World Wide Web: http://nsccux.sccd.ctc.edu.

Eble, K. E., & McKeachie, W. J. (1985). *Improving undergraduate education through faculty development: An analysis of effective programs and practices.* San Francisco: Jossey-Bass.

Ekman, P. & O'Sullivan, M. (1991). Facial expression: Methods, means, and moves. In R. S. Feldman & B. Rime (Eds.), *Fundamentals of nonverbal behavior: Studies in emotion and social interaction* (pp. 163–199). Cambridge: Cambridge University Press.

Emery, L. J. (1995). Teaching improvement: Disciplinary differences in faculty opinions. *To Improve the Academy, 14,* 91–103.

Eurich, N. P. (1985). *Corporate classrooms: The learning business.* Princeton, NJ: The Carnegie Foundation for the Advancement of Teaching.

Fairweather, J. S. (1993a, July/August). Faculty rewards reconsidered: The nature of tradeoffs. *Change, 44–47.*

Fairweather, J. S. (1993b, Fall). Academic values and faculty rewards. *The Review of Higher Education, 17*(1), 43–68.

Feldman, K. (1987). Research productivity and scholarly accomplishment of college teachers as related to their instructional effectiveness: A review and exploration. *Research in Higher Education, 26,* 227–298.

Feldman, K. A. (1996). Identifying exemplary teaching: Using data from course and teacher evaluations. In M. D. Svinicki, & R. J. Menges (Eds.), *Honoring exemplary teaching.* (pp. 41–56). San Francisco: Jossey-Bass.

Fennell, M. (1997, February/March). Presidents survey 1996–1997. *The Independent,* 6–7.

Flower, L. S., & Hayes, J. R. (1981). A cognitive process theory of writing. *College Composition and Communication, 32,* 365–387.

Fuhrmann, B., & Grasha, A. (1983). *A practical handbook for college teachers.* Boston: Little, Brown.

Gagné, R. M. (1975). Human problem solving: Internal and external events. In B. Kleinmuntz (Ed.), *Problem solving: Research, method and theory* (pp. 127–148). Huntington, NY: Robert E. Krieger.

Gardner, H. (1983). *Frames of mind.* New York: Basic Books.

Gardner, H. (1993). *Multiple intelligences: The theory in practice.* New York: Basic.

Gatto, J. T. (1992). *Dumbing us down.* Gabriola Island, BC: New Society.

Gibbs, G. (1995). Promoting excellent teaching is harder than you'd think: A note from an outside observer of the roles and rewards initiative. *Change, 27*(3), 16–20.

Gifford, B. R. (1992, Fall/Winter). Where is the knowledge? Knowledge management, research and pedagogy in the electronic age. *Education Libraries, 16,* 14–22.

Gil, D. H. (1987). Instructional evaluation as a feedback process. In L. M. Aleamoni (Ed.), *Techniques for evaluating and improving instruction* (pp. 57–64). San Francisco: Jossey-Bass.

Goleman, D. (1995). *Emotional intelligence: Why it can matter more than IQ.* New York: Bantam.

Gurnett, K. (1995, August 13). Libraries break tradition to attract patrons. *Buffalo News,* p. A11.

Hammons, J. O., & Shook, J. R. (1994). The course syllabus reexamined. *Journal of Staff, Program, and Organizational Development, 12*(1), 5–17.

Hatton, E. (1989). Levi-Strauss's bricolage and theorizing teachers' work. *Anthropology and Education Quarterly, 20,* 74–96.

Hayes, J. R., & Flower, L. S. (1980). Identifying the organization of writing processes. In L. W. Gregg and E. R. Steinberg (Eds.), *Cognitive processes in writing* (pp. 3–30). Hillsdale, NJ: Lawrence Erlbaum.

Highet, G. (1959). *The art of teaching.* New York: Vintage.

Horwitz, T. (1994, February 15). Class struggle: Young professors find life in academia isn't what it used to be. *The Wall Street Journal,* pp. A1, 6–7.

Huber, R. (1992). *How professors play the cat guarding the cream.* Fairfax, VA: George Mason University Press.

Hughes, R. (1993). *Culture of complaint.* New York: Warner.

Jackson, W. K., & Simpson, R. D. (1994). Mentoring new faculty for teaching and research. In M. A. Wunsch (Ed.), *Mentoring revisited: Making an impact on individuals and institutions* (pp. 65–72). San Francisco: Jossey-Bass.

Jarvis, D. K. (1991). *Junior faculty development: A handbook.* New York: MLA.

John, O. P. (1990). The "Big Five" factor taxonomy: Dimensions of personality in the natural language and in questionnaires. In L. A. Pervin (Ed.), *Handbook of personality: Theory and research* (pp. 66–100). New York: Guilford.

Johnstone, B. (1995, Spring). *OAP 515: Contemporary criticisms of higher education syllabus*. Unpublished manuscript, University at Buffalo, Buffalo, NY.

Kalivoda, P., Sorrell, G. R., & Simpson, R. D. (1994). Nurturing faculty vitality by matching institutional interventions with career-stage needs. *Innovative Higher Education, 18*(4), 255–272.

Kanter, S. L., Gamson, Z. F., & London, H. B. (1997). *Revitalizing general education in a time of scarcity*. Boston: Allyn & Bacon.

Kelley, R. & Caplan, J. (1993, July/August). How Bell Labs creates star performers. *Harvard Business Review, 71,* 128–139.

Kurtines, W., & Gerwitz, J. (Eds.). (1984). *Moral behavior and development: Advances in theory, research, and applications*. New York: John Wiley.

Lambert, L., Tice, S., & Featherstone, P. (1996). *University teaching: A guide for graduate students*. Syracuse, NY: Syracuse University Press.

The Landscape. (1995). *Change, 27*(4), 41–44.

Leap, T. L., & Crino, M. D. (1993). *Personal/human resource management* (2nd ed.). New York: Macmillan.

Leatherman, C. (1990, December 5). Definition of faculty scholarship must be expanded to include teaching, Carnegie Foundation says. *The Chronicle of Higher Education, 31*(14), pp. 1, 16–17.

Lewis, L. S. (1996). *Marginal worth*. New Brunswick, NJ: Transaction.

Lowman, J. (1995). *Mastering the techniques of teaching*. (2nd ed.). San Francisco: Jossey-Bass.

Lowman, J. (1996). Characteristics of exemplary teachers. In M. D. Svinicki & R. J. Menges (Eds.), *Honoring exemplary teaching* (pp. 33–40). San Francisco: Jossey-Bass.

Lucas, C. (1994). *American higher education*. New York: St. Martin's.

Luna, G. & Cullen, D. L. (1995). *Empowering the faculty: Mentoring redirected and renewed*. (ASHE-ERIC Higher Education Report No. 3). Washington, DC: The George Washington University.

MacWhinney, B. (1983). Motives for sharing points. (National Science Foundation Linguistics Program Grant #BN57905755). Pittsburgh: Carnegie Mellon University.

Maslow, A. (1968). *Towards a psychology of being*. 2nd ed. New York: Van Nostrand.

Massey, W. F. & Wilger, A. K. (1995, July/August). Improving productivity: What faculty think about it—and its effect on quality. *Change, 27*(4), 11–20.

Maxwell, M. (1979). *Improving student learning skills*. San Francisco: Jossey-Bass.

McCabe, R. H., & Jenrette, M. S. (1990). Leadership in action: A campuswide effort to strengthen teaching. In P. Seldin & Associates (Eds.), *How administrators can improve teaching: Moving from talk to action in higher education* (pp. 181–198). San Francisco: Jossey-Bass.

McDaniel, T. R. (1994). College classrooms of the future. *College Teaching, 42*(1), 27–31.

McKeachie, W. J. (1994). *Teaching tips: Strategies, research, and theory for college and university teachers* (9th ed.). Lexington, MA: D. C. Heath.

McPherson, M. S., & Schapiro, M. O. (1995, July/August). Future needs for post-secondary education. *Change, 27*(4), 26–32.

Menand, L. (1996, September 22). How to make a Ph.D. matter. *New York Times Magazine, 6*, 78–81.

Menges, R. J. (1990). Using evaluative information to improve instruction. In P. Seldin, & Associates (Eds.), *How administrators can improve teaching: Moving from talk to action in higher education* (pp. 104–121). San Francisco: Jossey-Bass,.

Menges, R. J. (1996). Awards to individuals. In M. D. Svinicki & R. J. Menges (1996). *Honoring exemplary teaching* (pp. 3–9). San Francisco: Jossey-Bass.

Menges, R. J., & Rando, W. C. (1996). Feedback for enhanced teaching and learning. In R. J. Menges, M. Weimer, & Associates (Eds.). *Teaching on solid ground: Using scholarship to improve practice.* (pp. 233–255). San Francisco: Jossey-Bass.

Menges R. J. & Svinicki, M. (1991). *College teaching: From theory to practice.* San Francisco: Jossey-Bass.

Menges, R. J., Weimer, M., & Associates. (1996). *Teaching on solid ground: Using scholarship to improve practice.* San Francisco: Jossey-Bass.

Miller, E. (1995). *Rewarding faculty for teaching excellence/effectiveness: A survey of currently available awards including faculty comments and desires in regard to the process of rewards.* Unpublished doctoral dissertation, Texas A & M University, College Station.

Miller, R. (1974). *Evaluating Faculty Performance.* San Francisco: Jossey-Bass.

Mooney, C. J. (1990, December 5). Critics say faculty-reward system discounts the importance of service. *The Chronicle of Higher Education, 37*(14), p. 16.

Mooney, C. J. (1991, May 22). A long-time critic crusades to expose the flaws of the faculty-reward system. *The Chronicle of Higher Education, 37*(36), pp. A13, A17.

Mooney, C. J. (1992). Syracuse seeks a balance between teaching and research. *The Chronicle of Higher Education, 38*(29), pp. A1, A14–16.

Morgan, M. M., Phelps, P. H., & Pritchard, J. E. (1995). Credibility: The crux of faculty development. *To Improve the Academy, 14*, 57–63.

Nyquist, J., Abbott, R., & Wulff, D. (1989). (Eds), *Teaching assistant training in the 1990s.* San Francisco: Jossey-Bass.

Nyquist, J., & Wulff, D. (1996). *Working effectively with graduate assistants.* Thousand Oaks, CA: Sage.

Palmer, P. (1990, January/February). Good teaching. *Change,* 11–16.

Parade. (1989, March 19), p. 17.

Pascarella, E. T., & Terenzini, P. T. (1991). *How college affects students.* San Francisco: Jossey-Bass.

Paul, A. M. (1996, October) Putting teaching to the test. *Yale, 60*(1), 52–57.

Perley, J. (1995, September 30). Higher education: Winds of change. Paper presented at Western New York AAUP Meeting. Niagara University, Sanborn, NY.

Pervin, L. A. (1984). *Personality: Theory and research* (4th ed.). New York: John Wiley.

Petrie, H. (1995, Fall). The state of the GSE. *Graduate School of Education Newsletter,* State University of New York at Buffalo in Buffalo, NY, p. 1.

Plotnik, R. (1996). *Introduction to psychology* (4th ed.). Pacific Grove, CA: Brooks/ Cole.

Popcorn, F. (1991). *The Popcorn report.* New York: Doubleday.

Pratt, L. R. (1994, September/October). A new face for the profession. *Academe, 80*(5), 38, 41.

Qualters, D. (1995). A quantum leap in faculty development: Beyond reflective practice. *To Improve the Academy, 14,* 43–54.

Quinn, J. W. (1994, January). *Teaching award recipients' perceptions of teaching award programs.* Paper presented at the Second AAHE Forum on Faculty Roles and Rewards, New Orleans, LA.

Ramsden, P. (1992). *Learning to teach in higher education.* London: Rutledge.

Rice, R. E. (1991). The new American scholar: Scholarship and the purposes of the university. *Metropolitan universities: An international forum, 1*(4), 7–18.

Roberts, H., & Associates (1994). *Teaching from a multicultural perspective.* Thousand Oaks, CA: Sage.

Ronkowski, S. A. (1993). Scholarly teaching: Developmental stages of pedagogical scholarship. In R. E. Rice & L. Richlin (Eds.), *Preparing faculty for the new conceptions of scholarship* (pp. 79–90). San Francisco: Jossey-Bass.

Sacks, P. (1996). *Generation X goes to college.* Chicago: Open Court.

Salovey, P. & Mayer, J. D. (1990). Emotional intelligence. *Imagination, Cognition, and Personality, 9,* pp. 185–211.

Sanoff, A. P. (1995, September 18). The consulting game. *U.S. News & World Report: America's Best Colleges 1996 Annual Guide,* pp. 119–122.

Scheier, M. F. & Carver, C. S. (1993). On the power of positive thinking: The benefits of being optimistic. *Current Directions in Psychological Science, 2*(1), 26–30.

Schön, D. (1983). *The reflective practitioner,* New York: Basic Books.

Schön, D. (1987). *Educating the reflective practitioner: Toward a new design for teaching and learning in the professions.* San Francisco: Jossey-Bass.

Schwartz, C. (1992). Is good teaching rewarded at Berkeley? *College Teaching, 40*(1), 33–36.

Seldin, P., & Associates. (1990). *How administrators can improve teaching.* San Francisco: Jossey-Bass.

Seligman, M. (1991). *Learned optimism.* New York: Knopf.

Shaughnessy, M. P. (1977). *Errors and expectations: A guide for the teacher of basic writing.* New York: Oxford University Press.

Sheehy, G. (1995). *New passages: Mapping your life across time.* New York: Random House.

Sherer, Pamela. (1995, September). *Information and technology tools & resources on campus: Engaging faculty in active learning programs.* Paper presented at the Lilly Conference on College and University Teaching–New England, University of New Hampshire, Durham, NH.

Sheridan, H. (1990). Icabod Crane dies hard: Renewing professional commitments to teaching. In P. Seldin & Associates (eds.), *How administrators can improve teaching* (pp. 165–180). San Francisco: Jossey-Bass.

Sherman, T. M., Armistead, L. P., Fowler, F., Barksdale, M. A., & Reif, G. (1987). The quest for excellence in university teaching. *Journal of Higher Education, 58,* 66–84.

Shulman, L. S. (1986). Knowledge growth in teaching. *Educational Researcher, 15*(2), 4–14.

Shulman, L. S. (1988, November). A union of insufficiencies: Strategies for teacher assessment in a period of educational reform. *Educational Leadership, 46*(3), 36–41.

Slack, J. (1994, November/December). The university's technology policy. *Academe, 80*(6), 37–41.

Smith, C., & Beno, B. (1995). Evaluating staff development programs. *Journal of Staff, Program, and Organizational Development, 12*(3), 173–182.

Smith, H. & Walvoord, B. (1993). Certifying teaching excellence an alternative paradigm to the teaching award. *AAHE Bulletin, 46*(2) 3–5, 12.

Snyder, C. R., Harris, C., Anderson, J. R., Holleran, S. A., Irving, L. M., Sigmon, S. T., Yoshinobu, L., Gibb, J., Langelle, C., & Harney, P. (1991). The will and the ways: Development and validation of an individual–differences measure of hope. *Journal of Personality and Social Psychology, 60*(4), 570–585.

Soderberg, L. O. (1985). Dominance of research and publication: An unrelenting tyranny. *College Teaching, 33* (4), 168–172.

Solomon, R., & Solomon, J. (1993). *Up the university: Recreating higher education in America.* Reading, MA: Addison-Wesley.

Sorcinelli, M. D., & Davis, B. G. (1996). Honoring exemplary teaching in research universities. In M. D. Svinicki & R. J. Menges (Eds.), *Honoring exemplary teaching* (pp. 71–76). San Francisco: Jossey-Bass.

Sparks, D. (1992). Merging content knowledge and pedagogy: An interview with Lee Shulman. *Journal of Staff Development, 13*(1), 14–17.

Sprague, J., & Nyquist, J. (1989). TA supervision. In J. Nyquist, R. Abbott, & D. Wulff (Eds.), *Teaching assistant training in the 1990s* (pp. 37–52). San Francisco: Jossey-Bass.

Sternberg, R. J. (1985). *Beyond IQ: A triarchic theory of human intelligence.* Cambridge: Cambridge University Press.

Streisand, B. (1995, September 18). Real-world troubles. *U.S. News & World Report,* pp. 125–126, 128.

SUNY Distinguished Teaching Professorships Policies and Procedures 1995–96 Series, pp. 1–4.

Svinicki, M. D. & Menges, R. J. (1996). *Honoring exemplary teaching.* San Francisco: Jossey-Bass.

Sykes, Charles J. (1988). *Profscam.* Washington, DC: Regnery Gateway.

Tooley, J. (1995, September 25). A heavy loan burden. *U.S. News & World Report,* p. 84.

Tuckman, H. (1979). The academic reward structure in higher education. In D. Lewis & W. Becker, Jr. (Eds.), *Academic rewards in higher education* (pp. 165–190). Cambridge, MA: Ballinger.

Upcraft, M. L. (1996). Teaching and today's college students. In R. J. Menges, M. Weimer, and Associates (Eds.), *Teaching on solid ground: Using scholarship to improve practice,* (pp. 21–41). San Francisco: Jossey-Bass.

Ward, B. (1995). Improving teaching across the academy: Gleanings from research. *To Improve the Academy, 14,* 27–40.

Weimer, M. (1993). *Improving your classroom teaching.* Newbury Park, CA: Sage.

Weimer, M. (1995, September). *The challenges of teaching the big class.* Paper presented at the Lilly Conference on College and University Teaching–New England, University of New Hampshire, Durham, NH.

Wheeler, D. W., & Wheeler, B. J. (1994). Mentoring faculty for midcareer issues. In M. A. Wunsch (Ed.), *Mentoring revisited: Making an impact on individuals and institutions.* (pp. 91–100). San Francisco: Jossey-Bass.

Wheelwright, P. (1951). *Aristotle.* New York: Odyssey.

Whitman, N., & Weiss, E. (1982). *Faculty evaluation: The use of explicit criteria for promotion, retention, and tenure.* (ASHE-ERIC Higher Education Report No. 2). Washington, DC: American Association for Higher Education.

Wiesenfeld, K. (1996, June 17). Making the grade. *Newsweek,* p. 16.

Wiggins, J. S. (1996). *The five-factor model of personality: Theoretical perspectives.* New York: Guilford.

Wilshire, B. (1995). Re-imagining the university and the planet. *Change, 27*(4), 52–54.

Witchel, R. I. (1991). The impact of dysfunctional families on college students' development. In R. I. Witchel (Ed.), *Dealing with students from dysfunctional families* (pp. 5–18). San Francisco: Jossey-Bass.

Wuncsh, M. A. (1994). (Ed.). *Mentoring revisited: Making an impact on individuals and institutions.* San Francisco: Jossey-Bass.

Index